Praise for *The Psychic Ar*

"This is a handbook for unlocking your genius....Ma
to be one of the rare luminaries who will come to de
of modern occultism."
—BENEBELL WEN, author of *Holistic Tarot*

"Whether you're a beginner or an experienced reader, Mat offers easy-to-follow steps to supercharge your tarot readings and boost your psychic abilities."
—MARY K. GREER, author of *Tarot for Your Self*

"This comprehensive manual contains practical exercises designed to help tarot readers develop their psychic skills....An instant classic."
—THERESA REED, author of *The Cards You're Dealt*

"A 365-degree view of the practice of tarot reading, *The Psychic Art of Tarot* has something for readers of every level."
—T. SUSAN CHANG, author of *The Living Tarot*

"Auryn has written a thoroughly fascinating tarot book, and we're all lucky enough to live in the right timeline to read it."
—MELISSA CYNOVA, author of *Kitchen Table Tarot*

"This book fills a long-needed gap in the divination space....The author leads you into a world where using your innate intuition allows the full richness of tarot to emerge."
—NANCY HENDRICKSON, author of *Ancestral Tarot*

"Auryn is one of the brightest stars in today's gloriously lively occult firmament....His knack for breaking things down into easily assimilated pieces sets this book apart."
—THALASSA THERESE, divinitrix, creatrix, and producer of the San Francisco Bay Area Tarot Symposium

"A brilliant guidebook brimming with exercises and techniques to awaken your intuition. Get ready to activate your highest psychic potential."
—ELLIOT ADAM, bestselling author of *Fearless Tarot*

"Another valuable, thoughtful, and insightful creation....Mat expertly leads you to create your prolific practice step by step."
—JEN SANKEY, author of *Enchanted Forest Felines Tarot*

"If you have ever doubted your psychic abilities, this book will at first give you a gentle nudge, then an exciting push, until you dive deep into your own inner workings and discover your potential."
—SIDDHARTH RAMAKRISHNAN, PhD, author of *The Neuroscience of Tarot*

"Auryn provides original spreads, exercises, techniques, practices, and meditations to help you develop your insight and your facility with the tarot."
—**SKYE ALEXANDER,** author of *The Modern Witchcraft Book of Tarot*

"Written in an intimate one-on-one narrative style, this book seamlessly weaves together historical references and personal anecdotes."
—**CIRO MARCHETTI,** creator of the *Gilded Tarot Royale*

"Auryn expands the world of the tarot from the mundane earthly sphere to the endless possibilities open and ready to be received in connecting to the spirit world."
—**AILYNN HALVORSON,** author of *The Tarot Apothecary*

"If you only read one of Mat's books, let this be the one...His exercises take you deep into a joining of your natural gifts with those you develop through practice."
—**MELANIE BARNUM,** author of *Real Life Intuition*

"This book gives all tarot enthusiasts a deeper, more profound connection with the tarot. Mat Auryn guides the reader through insightful and essential foundations for psychic work."
—**ETHONY DAWN,** author of *Tarot Grimoire*

"Mat Auryn has seamlessly woven together two often misunderstood as mutually exclusive topics: tarot and psychic abilities."
—**CHRIS ONAREO,** host of the IGTV shows *Show Us Your Deck!* and *We're Booked!*

"A generous, thorough, and welcoming guide to using tarot and other divination tools to activate, explore, and more fully understand psychic abilities."
—**MEG JONES WALL,** author of *Finding the Fool*

"I have been reading tarot professionally for over twenty-five years, so when I tell you that *The Psychic Art of Tarot* is the book we have all been waiting for, that means a lot!"
—**DEBORAH BLAKE,** creator of *The Everyday Witch's Tarot*

"Auryn leads readers seeking to enhance their tarot practice beyond basic card meanings....This book aims to supercharge your divination practice."
—**JAYMI ELFORD,** author of *Tarot Inspired Life*

"This is easily the best book about tarot I've ever read, and I believe it can help anyone give an empowering tarot reading with more intuition, psychic abilities, and confidence."
—ASTREA TAYLOR, author of *Inspiring Creativity Through Magick*

"Auryn has penned yet another masterpiece. His latest work distinguishes itself with its inventive approach and refreshing ideas....His thorough research and unique viewpoint are commendable."
—MICHELLE WELCH, author of *Spirits Unveiled*

"Mat continues to prove himself a fountain of knowledge....His love of exploration creates the unique insights of *The Psychic Art of Tarot*....Reading tarot is truly an art but explaining and teaching it even more so. Today, Mat gives us a master class."
—ARTHUR WANG, artist and creator of the *TrueBlack Tarot*

"This wonderful book is a must have for anyone truly wishing to deepen their tarot knowledge....Do yourself a favor and add *The Psychic Art of Tarot* to your spiritual library."
—LILITH DORSEY, author of *Tarot Every Witch Way*

"Auryn's innovative approach to tarot will show you how to open your psychic senses in ways you never thought possible....*The Psychic Art of Tarot* is front and center in my own tarot library."
—MADAME PAMITA, author of *The Book of Candle Magic*

"Auryn has delivered yet another classic for the modern Witch's canon. This clean, clear, and detailed book provides not just tools and techniques for the tarot practitioner, but its own spiritual path. Above all, Mat offers a kind tone as he breaks down potentially confusing concepts into lovely practices."
—COURTNEY WEBER, author of *Tarot for One*

"Auryn shines as a beacon of insight and inspiration....What really sets *The Psychic Art of Tarot* apart is its integrative approach of blending psychic development and energy work techniques with foundational tarot practices."
—ALYSA BARTHA, author of *Essential Tarot Mastery*

"In a world of books claiming to give the reader a new outlook in reading the tarot, *The Psychic Art of Tarot* actually offers a different approach to gaining more intuitive readings by adding psychic development to traditional interpretations."
—JEAN-LOUIS DE BIASI, author of *The Divine Arcana of the Aurum Solis*

"Mat Auryn once again takes his top-notch expertise and disseminates it into something informative and usable. This book is rich in tarot and occult history and theory but brings it into today with exercises anyone can do."
—CASSANDRA SNOW, author of *Queering the Tarot*

"*The Psychic Art of Tarot* is among the best teachings on tarot I've read....10/10 recommend for both new readers who want a great foundation and for more experienced folks."
—SARA L. MASTROS, author of *The Sorcery of Solomon* and *The Orphic Hymn Grimoire*

"A brilliant and highly accessible work empowering readers to accept and leverage their inherent psychic nature through the lens of the cards. It's a highly unique offering, as there is nothing out there that so comprehensively intertwines tarot divination with the psychic arts."
—MARIA MINNIS, author of *Tarot for the Hard Work*

"An essential cartomancy guide exploring tarot philosophy, divinity, energetic alignment, psychic exercises, and immersive meditations all meant to empower your natural intuitive gifts."
—SASHA GRAHAM, author of *The Magic of Tarot*

"*The Psychic Art of Tarot* unpacks essential tarot topics that are left unexplored in other tarot books....It includes a wealth of theoretical and practical knowledge and a treasure trove of valuable exercises and techniques."
—CHARLIE CLAIRE BURGESS, author of *Radical Tarot*

"Mat Auryn is by far the best author writing today at helping magical people become more psychic...The practical exercises Mat has created for his tarot book are true genius."
—CAROLINE KENNER, cofounder of the Fool's Dog tarot app company and cocreator of *Boadicea's Tarot of Earthly Delights*

"Mat marshals the wisdom of our natural instincts and unique life experiences in service to tarot reading...*The Psychic Art of Tarot* raises the bar and redefines the tarot guidebook."
—RICHARD KACZYNSKI, author of *Perdurabo*

"I am grateful for Mr. Auryn's well written book in overcoming the stigma of becoming a psychic tarot reader."
—NANCY ANTENUCCI, author of *Psychic Tarot*

The Psychic Art of Tarot

About the Author

©Shane Ernest, Rare Photography

Mat Auryn is an influential author and teacher in the fields of occultism and witchcraft, with an audience that extends beyond the United States to an international level. His deep knowledge and experience comes from years of dedicated study, practice, and training in a variety of occult traditions and esoteric orders, often under the guidance of prominent knowledgeable mentors. His award-winning books *Psychic Witch* and *Mastering Magick* offer practical insight and practices for those interested in psychic and magickal practices. The books draw from a range of traditions such as astrology, Hermeticism, Wicca, Traditional Witchcraft, New Thought, Thelema, parapsychology, Jungian analytical psychology, Neoplatonism, and alchemy, making them versatile yet accessible guides for the spiritual seeker. His books have won multiple awards and been translated into more than thirteen languages, widening their impact.

Beyond writing, Mat worked for many years as a professional psychic and tarot reader in Salem, Massachusetts, as well as his own private practice. He also contributes to both specialized and mainstream publications, including a regular column in *Witches & Pagans* magazine. His work has been featured in *Cosmo*, *Newsweek*, *The Boston Globe*, *Oprah Daily*, and others, and is also on display at the Buckland Museum of Witchcraft. Mat was the first recipient of "The Most Supportive Witch" award by *Witch Way Magazine*. He is also the co-host of *THE CIRCLE IS podCAST* with actress and author Rachel True. Mat is on the faculty of the Omega Institute for Holistic Studies in Rhinebeck, New York, where he teaches and leads retreats on psychic ability and magick. Now residing in California's Bay Area, Mat is the co-owner of Datura Trading Co. and Modern Witch University. He shares his knowledge and insights through writing, workshops, interviews, social media, and lectures, consistently emphasizing the importance of personal growth and positive change through psychic and magickal empowerment. You can learn more about him and his work at Auryn.net.

MAT AURYN

Author of *Psychic Witch*

THE PSYCHIC ART OF

Foreword by Rachel True

Opening Your Inner Eye for More Insightful Readings

WOODBURY, MINNESOTA

FIRST EDITION
First Printing, 2024

Book design by Rebecca Zins

Cover design by Kevin R. Brown

Cover Illustration by Arthur Wang

Interior illustrations by Llewellyn Art Department

Figure on page 223 by Tim Foley

Tarot Original 1909 Deck © 2021 with art created by Pamela Colman Smith and Arthur Edward Waite. Used with permission of LoScarabeo.

Tarot of Marseille. C. Burdel Schaffhouse, 1751. Used with permission of LoScarabeo.

Pamela Colman Smith photo on page 171 from *The Craftsman*, Vol. XXIII, No. 1, October 1912.

Llewellyn Publications is a registered trademark of Llewellyn Worldwide Ltd.

Library of Congress Cataloging-in-Publication Data

Names: Auryn, Mat, author. | True, Rachel, writer of foreword.
Title: The psychic art of tarot : opening your inner eye for more insightful readings / Mat Auryn ; foreword by Rachel True.
Description: First edition. | Woodbury, Minnesota : Llewellyn Publications, [2024] | Includes bibliographical references and index. | Summary: "Drawing on decades of experience as a professional reader, bestselling author Mat Auryn presents a comprehensive guide to unlocking your psychic potential and shows you how to unite traditional tarot techniques and your own intuition, which will enhance your readings with astounding levels of accuracy and insight. With 78 exercises, meditations, and rituals accessible for practitioners of every experience level, *The Psychic Art of Tarot* provides step-by-step instructions for understanding your unique psychic style and mastering an array of skills including mediumship, soul alignment, auras, energy work, scrying, and more"—Provided by publisher.
Identifiers: LCCN 2024017140 (print) | LCCN 2024017141 (ebook) | ISBN 9780738768342 (paperback) | ISBN 9780738768410 (ebook)
Subjects: LCSH: Tarot. | Psychic ability.
Classification: LCC BF1879.T2 A945 2024 (print) | LCC BF1879.T2 (ebook) | DDC 133.3/2424—dc23/eng/20240603
LC record available at https://lccn.loc.gov/2024017140
LC ebook record available at https://lccn.loc.gov/2024017141

Llewellyn Publications
A Division of Llewellyn Worldwide Ltd.
2143 Wooddale Drive
Woodbury, MN 55125-2989
www.llewellyn.com

PRINTED IN THE UNITED STATES OF AMERICA

Other Books by Mat Auryn

Psychic Witch: A Metaphysical Guide to Meditation, Magick, and Manifestation (Llewellyn)

Mastering Magick: A Course in Spellcasting for the Psychic Witch (Llewellyn)

Pisces Witch: Swimming in the Starry Seas with Ivo Dominguez, Jr. (Llewellyn)

Ephemere Tarot: The Guidebook with Arthur Wang (TrueBlack Tarot)

Forewords and Prefaces by Mat Auryn

Of Blood and Bones: Working with Shadow Magick and the Dark Moon by Kate Freuler (Llewellyn)

Seasons of Moon and Flame: The Wild Dreamer's Epic Journey of Becoming by Danielle Dulsky (New World Library)

Queering Your Craft: Witchcraft from the Margins by Cassandra Snow (Weiser)

Mountain Conjure and Southern Root Work by Orion Foxwood (Weiser)

Pure Magic: A Complete Course in Spellcasting by Judika Illes (Weiser)

Consorting with Spirits: Your Guide to Working with Invisible Allies by Jason Miller (Weiser)

Men and the Goddess: An Anthology Revisited by Erick Dupree (self-published)

Scott Cunningham: The Path Taken: Honoring the Life and Legacy of a Wiccan Trailblazer by Christine Cunningham Ashworth (Weiser)

Magical Tarot: Your Essential Guide to Reading the Cards by Madame Pamita (Weiser)

In Memory of Rachel Pollack

(1945–2023)

"If you wish to develop your psychic, or more intuitive, side in readings, just try it out. When you read for people, let your mind stay open for flashes or images, and more—be willing to express them…It's important not to fall into the trap of accuracy. Tarot is not a trick or a stage performance, and if you worry about making mistakes, you won't dare to say anything."

—Rachel Pollack,
Rachel Pollack's Tarot Wisdom: Spiritual Teachings and Deeper Meanings

Dedication

My incredible partners, Chas, Devin, and Storm: Your support in writing and revising this book, coupled with proofreading and insightful feedback, has been indispensable in shaping its final form. Beyond the book, I'm grateful to share my life with such remarkable individuals.

Aeptha: Our paths crossing feels less like chance and more like a pivotal moment in a chain of life-altering synchronicities. Your unique contributions to the world are invaluable, and it's been an honor and privilege to get to know you.

Chris LeVasseur: Working at Enchanted during Salem's intense October season served as the launchpad for my career in full-time tarot reading as well as honed my psychic abilities to become the reader I am today. Thank you for the opportunity and for letting me crash at your place every October so I wouldn't have to fight traffic getting in every day.

Chris Onareo: To the guy my husband jokingly refers to as my "tarot boyfriend." Your early beta reading of this manuscript was incredibly valuable, and your friendship means even more to me.

Danielle Dionne: You were the first to see teaching potential in me, and your friendship turned my skepticism about mediumship on its head, igniting my own practice. From tarot to mediumship and even writing, you've been a true friend and a living example who has made me push my own boundaries.

Elysia Gallo: Thanks for always putting in the hard work and helping me turn my scattered thoughts and messy drafts into something that is actually coherent to other people. Working with and getting to know you has been one of the best parts of being with Llewellyn.

James Anderson Foster: Thank you for the continued support and for bringing my books to life in audiobook form. Narration is an artform, and there's no one else I would rather have to be the voice of my work.

Judika Illes: Your counsel has been a sanctuary for my authenticity, invigorating my spirit during extremely challenging times. Balancing both authorship and editorial roles, you are unrivaled in your dedication to occult writing, and I cherish our invaluable friendship.

J. R. Mascaro: It's so rare to know someone whose personal gnosis and spiritual experiences mirror my own, and it's an added bonus that you're a great guy all around. You've been extremely validating for my own experiences with the serpents, and I have no doubt the future holds great things for you.

Mary K. Greer: Before we even met, your books served as my unofficial mentorship, shaping my voice and style in tarot readings. Your humility despite your success, the insightful tarot discussions we've shared, and the atmosphere you create at events have had a lasting impact on me, and your work has undeniably impacted the field of modern tarot for the better.

Madame Pamita: You're my favorite purple-haired person, equally as magickally talented as you are a good person. Being your friend makes my life better in so many ways, and I'm so glad I decided to stop at your booth to check out your candles all those years back.

Michelle Welch: Your genuine kindness has been a touchstone for me, and your invitation to speak at the NWTS and TIDE tarot events introduced me to an amazing community of like-minded tarot folks. Your and Roger's work serves as the heartbeat of the in-person tarot community, and for that we're all grateful.

Rachel True: Having you, someone I admired through iconic roles in *The Craft* and *Half and Half*, write my foreword and transition into a real-life supporter has been surreal. Your off-screen authenticity and wit—and particularly the impactful tarot reading you gave me—confirm that you're the real deal in every way.

Robbi Packard: Your shop, The Robin's Nest, gave me my first teaching gig and showed me the art of blending business with authentic community building. Thank you, Robbi, for your steadfast support and for making the Nest a spiritual home where I first spread my wings; you've impacted not just my life but countless others.

Theresa Reed: Getting to know you has been a real treat, and your dedication to writing and teaching has been an endless source of inspiration. Thank you for your friendship and for holding space for me when I need to vent.

Consecration

This book is consecrated in the name of the falcon-winged angel set over the tarot, messenger of the divine and guide of the seeker, he who guards and reveals the arcana and whose every feather is a card from the tarot.

This book is consecrated in the name of she who governs luck, fate, chance, and destiny, she who holds the cornucopia of abundance and spins the Wheel of Fortune, she who reminds us that life is a journey with many twists and turns, and how we respond to fate is up to us.

This book is consecrated in the name of the ibis-headed divine scribe and master of wisdom, he who is the keeper of the sacred knowledge, the inventor of writing, and the patron of all scribes, scholars, and magicians: he whom the tarot mysteries are named after.

O
THE FOOL.

Other Acknowledgments

Abbathoniah, Adam Sartwell, Aden Ardennes, Aidan Wachter, Aileen Halvorson, Ali Dossary, Alison Chicosky, Aly Kravetz AKA the BronxWitch, Alysa Bartha, Amy Blackthorn, Anaar Niino, Andy Kiess, Anne Niven, Ari Mankey, Arin Murphy-Hiscock, Arthur Wang, Astrea Taylor, Becky Zins, Benebell Wen, Ben Stimpson, Bill Krause, Bobbi Sobel, Brett Bevell, Brett Hollyhead, Caroline Kenner, Cassandra Snow, Charles Harrington, Charlie Claire Burgess, Chelsea Wolfe, Chris Allaun, Chris Orapello, Christine Ashworth, Christopher Penczak, Ciro Marchetti, Coby Michael, Courtney Weber, Dana Newkirk, Danielle Dulsky, David Salisbury, Dawn Hunt, Deborah Blake, Denis of Foolish Fish, Derrick Land, Diotima Mantineia, Damien Echols, Dodie Graham McKay, Durgadas Allon Duriel, Elliot Adam, Elizabeth Autumnalis, Enfys J. Book, Erick DuPree, Erika Robinson, Ethony Dawn, Gabriela Herstik, Grey Townsend, Greg Newkirk, Gwendolyn Reece, Gwion Raven, Hannah Cartwright, Heron Michelle, Hilary Whitmore, Holly Vanderhaar, Hugo Largaespada, Ivo Dominguez, Jr., Jack Grayle, Jacki Smith, Jake Richards, Jamie Sawyer, Jason Mankey, Jason Miller, Jay Sankey, Jaymi Elford, Jean-Louise De Biasi, Jeff Cullen, Jennifer Teixeira, Jen Sankey, Jesse Hathaway, Jim Dickinson, Jim Welch, John Beckett, Julia Halina Hadas, Juliet Diaz, Kanani Soleil, Karen Bruhin, Kate Freuler, Katrina Messenger, Kristine Gorman, Laurie Bizzarro, Laura Eidolon, Laura Tempest Zakroff, Leanne Marrama, Lilith Dorsey, Lisa Cook, Lonnie Scott, Marcus Wolf, Maria Minnis, Markus Ironwood, Martha Kirby Capo, Mary Gates, Matthew Venus, Mawiyah Kai EL-Jamah Bomani, Melanie Barnum, Melissa Cynova, Michelle Belanger, Meg Rosenbriar, Mhara Starling, Michael G. Smith, Mickie Mueller, Mitch Harowitz, Mitchell Harrington, Morgan Daimler, Mortellus, Moss Matthey, Najah Lightfoot, Nancy Antenucci, Nancy Hendrickson, Nathan Hall, Nathaniel Johnstone, Nicholas Pearson, Nick Dickinson, Orion Foxwood, Pam Grossman, Pamela Chen, Phoenix LeFae, Richard Davis, Richard Kaczynski, Ryan Logan, Sabina Magliocco, Sandra Mariah Wright, Sara L. Mastros, Sasha Graham, Sharon Knight, Sherry Shone, Siddharth Ramakrishnan, Silver RavenWolf, Skye Alexander, Sorita d'Este, Stephanie Buscema, Stephanie Taylor Grimassi, Steven Intermill, Steve Kenson, Sue Ustas, Susan Diamond, T. Susan Chang, T. Thorn Coyle, Tara Love-Maguire, Thalassa Therese, Thealandrah Davis, Thorn Mooney, Thumper Forge, Tim Reagan, Toni Rotonda, Vincent Higginbotham, Zola Jesus

I
THE MAGICIAN.

Contents

∞

Exercises and Techniques

∞

∞

Foreword

Tarot has been a golden filament for me, intricately threading all the various aspects of my life together. It has served as a trusty conduit for a lifetime of intuitive self-care, and it has afforded me a mode of psychic connection to the collective unconscious and far beyond. If I were to follow that golden thread back, unraveling it to the origin of my life interlaced with tarot, I would find that the initial stitch was my awakening to the language of tarot itself. This awakening occurred when I was around four years old, living in NYC's Greenwich Village. I had just left my foster care situation, where I had spent the majority of my early years, to live with my father and his new bride. My stepmother was an actress and part-time school teacher who'd taught us to read early on. This led to my fascination with the titan-sized floor-to-ceiling bookcases lining a prime swath of apartment real estate that I called the library.

One of the first books to catch my eye was Carl Jung's *Man and His Symbols*, in all its brightly colored '70s mandala cover art glory. I doubt my reading comprehension skills were up to snuff, yet I was captivated by the imagery within. A few years later, a friend of my parents gave me a tarot deck. I was immediately struck, in one of those rare high-vibration Tower card–style epiphanies, by a flood of flashing images from the Jung book I'd been fixated on. The deck's classic Rider-Waite-Smith imagery and the imagery included in Jung's book were of the same nature to my mind's eye. Even more intriguing to me, these images seemed to be written in a language I could parse. Given an apprenticeship, I knew I could find the correlation between the images and how they related to myself. Beyond that, I wondered if I could utilize these symbols to communicate with something far greater than myself.

I continued my tarot studies after I moved to California to film the romantic love interest in the Chris Rock flick *CB4*. I was in my early twenties and fortunate enough to be able to support myself through acting. Without the need for a job like the bartending gig I'd left behind in NYC, I had loads of free time. Most of this time was spent wondering if I would ever work again—a common actor's lament. I'd fallen into a habit of spacing out in front of the TV because I found focusing on the problems plaguing fictional characters easier than facing my own. Then my television broke. Being American, this felt like a personal attack. And then a quiet voice that sounded like the rustle of falling leaves advised me to skip fixing it and develop other, lesser-used muscles, mainly my intuition. I immersed myself in deep tarot studies to stave off a worry that a lack of auditions might kick off a bout of the dreaded artist's malaise. This was pre-internet, and esoteric information had to be actively sought out, mostly in alternative bookstores, the kind that were just starting to come out of hiding after the satanic panic of the '80s.

I purchased many books, including those by Mary K. Greer, Starhawk, and Rachel Pollack. I consider these women, whom I've never met, to be my teachers. I kept copious grimoires—notebooks where I charted the tarot suit patterns like they were stars in the night sky. I hand drew the cards and got to know some of the many sides of myself through the story of the major arcana. All of this began to ignite my own magic and amp up my psychic vibration in the world. Nine months later, a friend came over and began toying with the TV cord. "It's just a loose wire" they exclaimed as the tubes buzzed and suddenly sizzled back to pre-LCD life. Two weeks later, *The Craft* script showed up in my life. I absolutely think it was attracted to me because of those months. It was a delicious and evergreen gift, as well as a concrete lesson from Saturn, Jupiter, Spirit, and the universe for my diligence. It helped me understand that one *can* actually prepare for the unknown without knowing it. It also solidified tarot's applicable and practical benefits in my life. It kicked off a new quest to go beyond the easily accessible practical magic tarot offers and go deeper. It was time to dive into the abyss—to get into root and bone magic, touch the things that dwell above and below. I remain in the scholarship of tarot even as I type these words.

This grand love affair with tarot would eventually evolve into *True Heart Intuitive Tarot,* my book and deck set. While preparing for my book launch, I did a day of tarot reading in Salem, Massachusetts. This is when and where, one blustery Samhain-adjacent day, I had my first fateful encounter with the magic that is Mat Auryn. Equal parts enigmatic and charismatic, he's the kind of cultivated spirit you don't often encounter out in the wild. In person, Mat sports an extraordinarily clear and expansive energy field. I know this because I felt Mat before I ever physically saw Mat. I was cleansing my deck after several hours of back-to-back readings when I felt a psychic crackle, a rumbly summer thunder, then a quick jolt tickling the nape of my neck. I sat up straighter. Moments later, in walks the devilishly handsome, psychically shiny (and shining for miles), perfectly put-together creature that is Mat. My first thought was, "What are you doing here? *You* don't need a reading." I said the equivalent. He assured me he did indeed truly want one. I'd find out later he'd sought me out precisely because his reputation would not precede him for once. He wanted an unbiased reading. When you're as well known of a psychic witch as he is, I can see how that'd be a challenge. To say we had a lovely communion together is, in my mind, an understatement.

Now that I know Mat's station in the esoteric community, I'm appreciative he didn't see me as an interloper. That he didn't come in energetically with preconceived notions about me being just some girl from that witch movie belies his openness. He seemed to innately understand that one can be many things all at once. During Mat's reading, the cards revealed a pretty fabulous now, with tremendous success to come. A fair amount of major arcana happiness and joy abounded. I asked him if he had a major project coming up. Indeed, he did. It was his first book, *Psychic Witch*, which he had just finished writing but was waiting for it to go to print—a book that would go on to set records. Maybe he already saw this for his own future, but I appreciated his openness, bright authenticity, and inquisitive mind. He's a student of life and magic. He's got a descended-from-a-demi-god sorta vibe but couples it with a streak of humility, much like myself when I'm high vibe, I noted.

If you're familiar with Mat's past bestselling works, *Psychic Witch* and *Mastering Magick*, you know he's an astounding fount of esoteric and magical knowledge. He's a sage teacher who is equally compelling as a writer. In this latest book, *The Psychic Art of Tarot*, Mat has pulled from a lifetime of magic and psychic practice. It's clear he understands and profoundly values tarot's place in the pantheon of esoteric paraphernalia and as a convenient tool for psychic activation. Rather than some who position themselves in their ego as the gatekeeper of all things mystical, Mat is as much a keeper of the flame as he is an ardent passer of the magical torch to as many as are willing to listen. This makes him even more charming, and his wit shines. It's clear to me that for Mat, being a facilitator and advocate for others in their journey fuels and magnifies his own magic. I am forever grateful that Mat Auryn welcomes and invites all, including myself, to unlock the magic within. If you're willing to get clear with yourself—something tarot is tailor-made for—I can think of no better companion and champion than Mat.

Under the tutelage of a teacher like Mat, tarot for exploring and harnessing your inner depths for intuitive and psychic insights can be smoothly incorporated into an existing practice. Tarot has a knack for offering incisive insights fairly quickly with regular practice. Mat's approach invites us to navigate through the cards to the spaces where our most potent inner wisdom is hidden, waiting to be unlocked. The challenge of plumbing the depths of our own psyche is a recurring theme in both tarot and the Fool's Journey. Luckily, Mat knows how to lean in with insight and compassion when it comes to rooting around in the self. He urges us to bring forward our deepest magic, the kind that is unique to each person.

Whether you are looking to connect with yourself, the collective unconscious, or travel far beyond, Mat has you covered. If you are looking to step up or into your magical practice, look no further for a learned, knowledgeable, encouraging, dedicated, and compassionate guide. Like his other books, Mat's work remains layered, dense, and deeply substantive while still remaining accessible to all. To create as comprehensive a tarot compendium and guide to psychic activation as Mat has means his work is surely destined to reside among the modern classics in the field. His breadth of knowledge and his innate and learned abilities are second only to his preternatural ability to connect with and champion the awakening of magic and psychism in others. Mat does not simply write words on a page for you to ingest. He infuses his books with his energetic life force and his elemental magic. This book is a perfect example of just that.

—Rachel True

II
B
J
TORA
THE HIGH PRIESTESS

Introduction

∞

The Psychic Art of Tarot

While reading tarot at metaphysical shops, I noticed a question that was frequently asked by customers when booking at the counter: "Are the readers here psychic or do they use cards?" A lot of my fellow tarot readers get touchy when asked this question, but I personally think it's a valid one. Tarot seems to have moved away from its psychic roots these days. So, when a customer walked up to me at the shop and asked whether I used psychic skills or just interpreted the cards, I took a moment to mull it over. The young woman seemed genuinely sincere with her question. I explained that, in my experience, a tarot reading could be a blend of both psychism and card interpretation. I added that some readers, including myself, may lean more heavily on their psychic abilities, while others might focus solely on the traditional symbolism and meaning of the cards. That doesn't make one reader inherently better than the other, just that they each have different approaches. I also mentioned how tarot acted as a conduit that allowed me to more easily tap into my intuitive and psychic insights. While tarot readings and psychic readings may technically be separate practices in themselves, they can work in harmony to provide deeper levels of guidance, insight, and personal growth that are much more precise than when they aren't paired together. This woman's question not only reminded me of the importance of recognizing the interplay between psychic abilities and tarot reading, but it also made me realize how divided they seem to be these days as practices. However, bridging this connection can lead to a richer, more precise and empowering tarot reading experience.

One way to think about psychic ability is to compare it to music. Some people can learn music by ear without musical training, which means they can hear the notes of a song and then play them precisely, but this is a rare skill. In my perspective, using tarot as a divinatory tool is more like reading sheet music. Sheet music takes those musical notes and arranges them in a structure that can be understood, read, and re-created. Similarly, tarot provides a structure and format that anchors and helps make sense of psychic information that might otherwise be jumbled or unclear without that structure as a reference point. Taking this approach strengthens your psychic ability through regular use of tarot cards. It's similar to how practicing with sheet music can eventually help you learn to play the piano by ear. One of my goals with this book is to show how tarot can be used to strengthen your psychism as well as how psychism can greatly enhance your tarot readings.

The Psychic Arts

The phrase "psychic arts" stirs my imagination when it comes to discussing psychic abilities and phenomena. It suggests that we look at intuition, spirit, and psychic skills not just as a skill set but also as an expressive endeavor. Similar to how art serves as a conduit for our innermost truths and emotions, psychic abilities also offer a form of personal and shared expression. They demand consistent practice and dedication but also provide room for experimental curiosity and innovation. The comparison to music strikes a particular chord with me, emphasizing the blend of technique and creative exploration. While musicians must master techniques and scales, they must also embrace creativity and allow for the spontaneous, the improvised, if they are going to write their own songs.

In a similar manner, when honing psychic skills, we delve into specific practices and approaches. This includes learning how to manage energy effectively, sharpening our intuitive senses, and establishing meaningful contact with spiritual entities. These methods provide a foundational structure, much like the basic chords in music, but the true magick happens when we move beyond the structured learning and connect with the music itself to allow our innate creativity to flow freely in a way that is uniquely ours. It's that intuitive improvisation, the moments where we're in the zone or flow state, where we connect with our psychic abilities in unique, personal ways.

These are the moments when we truly express our psychic artistry, just as a musician might be struck with inspiration for a song they have to write or an artist has a vision of a painting that they feel overwhelmingly compelled to get out of their head and onto canvas. Just as there are no hard-and-fast rules in art—only guidelines and techniques that help us mold our creative expressions—psychism is similarly unbounded. We're not restricted by rules or limitations. The idea is to enjoy the process, take some risks, and discover what you're uniquely good at. Like the artistic process, the value often lies in the act of exploring, maybe even more than in what you ultimately find. It's really about the thrill of stumbling upon something new. It's about finding your voice within the choir of psychic phenomena and using it to create your own harmony with the tarot.

Persistence with the Psychic Arts

As exciting as learning metaphysical and spiritual exercises for psychic development can be, it's natural for some to feel a bit uncertain or hesitant initially, similar to the feeling of picking up a guitar for the first time. In many areas of life, persistence is key. Just as we wouldn't anticipate mastering a complex tune after a few guitar lessons or painting a masterpiece the first time we try to paint, proficiency in any area, including psychic development, requires time, dedication, and consistent practice. If you treat these endeavors with the same eagerness and patience you'd give to learning any new skill, I'm sure you'll notice progress.

This is because mastering psychic development parallels the process of mastering any art. An artist doesn't craft a perfect piece on their first attempt. Similarly, refining psychic abilities is an ongoing endeavor. Think of an artist sketching repeatedly before finalizing their artwork. Each sketch is a step toward their ultimate vision. Likewise, each effort in your spiritual exercises, even if it seems fruitless at first, moves you closer to harnessing your psychic prowess. Art isn't about instant perfection; it's an evolution of growth and continuous learning. Over time, consistent practice lets artists find their unique style and grasp their medium. The psychic journey mirrors this. With dedication, you'll uncover techniques that align with you, hone your intuition, and deepen your spiritual connection. Instead of getting disheartened by initial hurdles, view them as stepping stones.

Every renowned artist or musician once started as a novice. Their success and skill came from their dedication and self-belief. Your psychic exploration is similar. Stay devoted and treat it with the patience you'd give to any other art. The rewards of psychic development are well worth the dedication. I have witnessed the benefits of consistent practice in both myself and in countless others, and as such it is something I'll continuously emphasize the importance of. A single drop of water might seem like it doesn't do much at first, but if that droplet is followed by another and another, over time it can create entire caverns from its persistence.

Everyone Is Psychic

One of my firm beliefs is that every single person possesses psychic abilities. It actually saddens me when folks say they're not psychic. While it may be true that individuals are not fully utilizing their psychic potential, the potential itself still exists within them. Everyone has some level of psychic ability from birth; it's not exclusive to a chosen few. Your skills will grow with the effort you invest in them. A primary issue with people's understanding of psychism stems from how it's portrayed in shows, films, and books. Although the portrayal of psychic abilities in fiction can sometimes mirror the actual experience, especially in advanced stages, it often differs significantly, particularly in the earlier stages of development. Psychism involves perceiving subtle forces; as a result, the way we experience it also tends to be subtle. This is why practices like meditation and mindfulness nurture and enhance these abilities. They assist us in being present and attentive to the subtle sensations associated with psychic perception.

How To Use This Book

This book goes beyond the basics of tarot and is aimed at those who already have some understanding of basic card meanings. It's for readers at any skill level who want to use tarot as a tool to better access their intuition and psychic senses. The focus here is on making your readings more personally relevant, helping you apply the card meanings directly to your own life situations. It's all about leveling up your tarot readings with psychic ability. If you're tired of vague, broad tarot readings, this book's goal is to teach you how to make your readings more specific and insightful. This book is for anyone who wants to improve their tarot reading skills through psychic insight. With the knowledge and techniques in this book, you'll be able to give more empowering and accurate readings that will help you (and your querent, if you are reading for someone else) gain clarity and understanding.

In this book, we'll approach the tarot with a sense of reverence for its rich history while also advocating for a more expansive, intuitive engagement with the cards. Contrary to some contemporary views, I do not propose discarding the "little white book"—a reference to the guidebook that often accompanies tarot decks and outlines the established meanings of each card. When people say this, they mean to ignore all the traditional meanings associated with tarot over time in favor of a purely intuitive approach. These traditional interpretations have stood the test of time for good reason, and they will provide a structured framework and foundation upon which countless readers will build their understanding. While respecting and valuing this foundation, we shouldn't become tethered solely to these established meanings. At its heart tarot is a tool for introspection, growth, and transformation. It will communicate not just through fixed symbols but also through the emotions, thoughts, and insights that these symbols will evoke in the reader and querent.

There will be numerous occasions throughout this book where the insight gleaned from a card might veer away from its traditional interpretation as guided by intuition, personal experiences, and psychic insights. A well-grounded understanding of the tarot's traditional meanings will act as a sturdy base. Think of it as sculpting: first you will start with a rough block of stone, understanding its structure and form. Once you're familiar with the medium, then you can begin to chisel away, refining and adding your unique vision to the piece. By striking a balance between the established meanings and your intuitive insights, you can achieve a holistic and personalized engagement with the tarot. This book will aim to guide you on this journey, embracing both the age-old wisdom encapsulated in the tarot and the fresh, evolving insights that will arise from your unique interaction with the cards.

It's my goal to not only convey ideas and techniques but truly animate them with vivid demonstrations and personal examples. A frequent question I encounter when teaching psychic skills is about the "right" way to experience a technique. Understanding that everyone's experiences are unique, I find it valuable to share my own perceptions during these practices. By recounting moments from my tarot reading journey, I hope to ground abstract concepts with tangible examples. Throughout this book, you'll find sections labeled "What This Can Look Like." These sections move past theory to offer a window into how these principles come alive in actual tarot readings based on my years of experience. By sharing these stories, I hope to bridge the gap between abstract ideas and hands-on practice, enriching your grasp of tarot. While I've tried to separate the chapters into clear sections to the best of my ability, you'll find that the topics often bleed into each other. That's because there's a lot of intersection when it comes to meditation, intuition, psychic ability, mediumship, and so on.

While I covered the topic of awakening and developing psychic abilities thoroughly in my book *Psychic Witch: A Metaphysical Guide to Meditation, Magick, and Manifestation*, I didn't explore tarot cards or other divinatory practices in-depth. That's where this book comes in: I want to provide you with alternative approaches to foundational energy exercises that can enhance your tarot readings. Not only that, but I'll be introducing completely new techniques that will drastically improve your tarot sessions. If you're already familiar with *Psychic Witch*, you're sure to find ways in this book to combine those techniques with your tarot work, but don't sweat it if you haven't read *Psychic Witch*. This book will give you a solid foundation regardless, offering useful techniques to enhance your tarot readings. No matter what you've read before, the aim is to equip everyone with practical insights you can use.

Throughout this book, the Rider-Waite-Smith deck will serve as our primary tool, its vivid imagery guiding our journey unless otherwise specified. As the most widely used deck globally as well as the foundation for a majority of modern decks, it offers a familiar language for us to converse in. Nonetheless, the beauty of tarot lies in its adaptability. With a dash of creativity, you can apply all the exercises contained within these pages to the Thoth, Marseilles, or any other tarot or even oracle deck of your choosing.

This book is designed more as a sequential guide than a referential compendium. While it may be enticing to hop around from chapter to chapter, the exercises are primarily structured to follow a progressive order. I suggest you dive into the whole book first, then tackle the exercises afterward. As you read, you'll come across techniques that have been successful for both me and my students, but keep in mind that what clicks for one person might not for another. These techniques are more like helpful suggestions than strict rules. Feel empowered to tweak these methods to fit your own spiritual path and needs. After all, just like art, intuitive abilities flourish with a bit of personal flair. What really counts is finding approaches that resonate with you both effectively and safely since everyone's journey is unique.

Navigating the language of spirituality, metaphysics, and occultism can get confusing, especially since the same terms can have varied meanings depending on who you talk to. Two people can be using the same term but mean different things by them, causing confusion. To avoid such misunderstandings, we must establish common ground in our understanding of key terminology, especially if this is your introduction to my work. Key terms such as *three souls*, *psychic*, *intuition*, *divinity*, and others are fundamental to our discussions. Sharing the same understanding of these terms will pave the way for clear and coherent communication, allowing us to delve deeper into these subjects. Think of this common language as a compass. It will guide us through our exploration, ensuring we maintain clarity and stay on the same page. Through this shared understanding, we can navigate the concepts discussed in this book more effectively.

III

THE EMPRESS.

1
∞

Divination, Divinity, and You

On the playground as a kid, you'd often find me absorbed in fortune-telling. If you're reading this, there's a good chance we may have had similar interests and maybe we would have bonded over them and been friends. I remember plucking daisy petals, alternating between "they love you" and "they love you not," with the last petal determining someone's affection. I also frequently brought my Magic 8 Ball to school, eager to shake it and offer predictions to the other kids. Another favorite of mine was M.A.S.H., a game predicting future life scenarios based on a drawn spiral and listed options. Also around that time, I mastered the "cootie catcher," a paper-folding device resembling origami you'd manipulate on your fingers. It had color-coded flaps revealing answers similar to a Magic 8 Ball, with results such as *yes*, *no*, *maybe*, and *ask again*.

So, it's absolutely no surprise that I was naturally drawn like a moth to a flame to the tarot as a fortune-telling tool. I received my first tarot deck somewhere around the age of nine or ten. Since then, it's been pretty much a lifetime companion and my weapon of choice when it comes to psychic readings. If you felt a reaction to my mention of fortune-telling, you're not alone. The term often sparks an immediate emotional response, largely because of the stigma surrounding it. The media often paints fortune tellers in a negative light, either as naive and delusional individuals or manipulative frauds. While it's true that scam artists exist in every spiritual and professional sphere, they're an exception, not the rule. Much of the bias and stigma against fortune-telling has roots in prejudice against the Romani communities, who still face discrimination today.

You might find it startling that some outdated laws banning fortune-telling are still around, even in the United States! A recent news story highlighted the Serpent's Key, a metaphysical shop in Pennsylvania, because the police chief confronted the owner, informing them that offering tarot reading services to the public was illegal due to a law against fortune-telling.[1] This incident showcases how the label "fortune-telling" has been used to discredit and target practices linked to the occult or alternative spiritual paths. These archaic laws often serve to oppress, target, and harass, particularly when used against businesses or individuals perceived as "alternative" or "unconventional." I'm passionate about reclaiming and clearing up the confusion surrounding the phrase "fortune-telling" and all the stigma that surrounds it.

The stigma is everywhere, even in our own tarot communities. How often have you come across books or social media posts asserting that tarot isn't about predicting the future and cautioning against anyone who claims otherwise? They often argue that tarot is solely a tool for introspection and guidance. I beg to differ; it encompasses *all* of these facets. As someone who has worked as a professional psychic, medium, and tarot reader for many years, I've used tarot to guide both myself and many others in understanding potential future events and making informed decisions. I've also led many workshops teaching others how to harness their psychic abilities in tarot readings. The real caution should be against readings that present a predetermined future without choices. An adept tarot reader skillfully blends various techniques to offer readings that foster introspection, enhance self-awareness, and provide insights into potential future outcomes that are the most likely.

Exploring the origins of particular words can shed light on their essence. If you look at the word *fortune* and trace its origins, you'll find that it's based on the Latin word *fortuna,* meaning "luck" and "chance." Thus, fortune-telling essentially means you're telling the chances of future events. It's about anticipating potential outcomes based on the present energy flow rather than making fixed prophecies that can't be changed. Interestingly, For-

1 Hauser, "Pennsylvania."

tuna was also the name of the Roman goddess representing luck and chance. Tarot combines prediction with the art of divination. The term *divination* traces back to *divinare*, signifying the act of drawing insight from higher powers. So, divination not only forecasts future events but also imparts guidance and deeper insights through divine inspiration.

Defining Divinity

In this book, when terms like Spirit (with a capital S), Source, the Divine, or divinity arise, I encourage you to engage with them from a place that feels genuine to you. These terms possess a certain charm in their flexibility and expansiveness, granting each reader the opportunity to infuse them with their own personal and distinctive meaning. For some, "Spirit" might conjure images of ancestral guardians; for others, it might mirror a deep connection to nature. "Divinity" could remind one person of a sacred scripture or external beings, yet for another, it might be the overwhelming awe felt while gazing at a starry night. The notion of "Source" can be likened to the beginning of a river for some, symbolizing the origin of all things, or it could be visualized as the spark of inspiration behind a grand idea for others. To some, these terms might represent the whisper of intuition or the voice of conscience, while for others they could be seen as guiding principles akin to the North Star that sailors navigate by. These words are not here to dictate a specific doctrine or dogma but rather to provide points of reflection. They are bridges to your own experiences, beliefs, and insights. Whether you connect with them on a religious, philosophical, or psychological level, what's paramount is the personal journey of exploration and discovery they facilitate. Imagine these terms as open doors; your choice of how to step through and perceive what lies beyond is entirely up to you.

For myself, the beauty of these terms lies in their encompassing nature. This situation doesn't require a strict either/or choice. In my perspective, each interpretation and resonance is valid and true in its own right. Whether one feels a divine connection through religious texts or experiences awe in the face of nature's wonders, it all points to a greater understanding of our place in the universe. To say that it's purely spiritual or exclusively psychological is to limit the vast expanse of human experience. Our spiritual beliefs often intertwine with our psychological realities and vice versa. For instance, someone might find solace in prayer during tough times, simultaneously tapping into both spiritual faith and a psychological coping mechanism. Someone who turns to meditation for mental clarity might, over time, develop a deep sense of connectedness that feels distinctly spiritual. I believe in the coexistence of multiple truths. The divine can be a cosmic force, an inner voice, a connection to ancestors, external entities, or a feeling of oneness with the world, all at once. The Spirit might be the wind rustling through trees, the intuition guiding one's decisions, and the force binding all life together. For me, every interpretation, every personal experience, adds a layer of richness to these terms. They don't negate each other; they complement and deepen our understanding.

While I believe divinity can be found in everything, each time we broach the subject, I'm inviting you to journey beyond your immediate sense of self and personal identity. It's not about denying one's self but rather about broadening its horizons. Every mention of the divine here beckons you to connect with something more numinous, powerful, and vast. It's about touching a part of yourself or the universe that operates on a grander scale. It could be the aspect of yourself that remains untainted, raw, and pure—the most divine state of your being that isn't bound by societal constructs, fears, limitations, or concepts of your physical self, such as your higher self. The intent is to allow you to experience a realm of consciousness where your individual ego is just a drop in the vast ocean of existence. It's the realm where personal boundaries blur, and you are welcomed into a space of universal truths, boundless love, and wisdom. It's the part of you that resonates with timeless energies and sacred connections.

The Three Souls and Different Modes of Perception

In a lot of spiritual and esoteric traditions, the concept of the self is often seen as being composed of three primary facets, much like the familiar term *mind, body, and spirit*. These aspects are referred to as the middle self, lower self, and higher self, respectively. In witchcraft we often refer to these as the "three souls" to acknowledge the inherent divinity of all aspects of ourselves. The lower self connects us with our animalistic nature. As physical beings, we experience sensations and emotions within our bodies. This inner dimension of ourselves enables direct interaction with it through our senses and emotions. The middle self, in contrast, represents our intellectual side. It processes patterns and information, as well as formulates thoughts and words. This aspect grants us a sense of identity, the ability to perceive and assign meaning to our emotions experienced by the lower self. By doing so, we understand their origins and effects on our lives. Then there is the higher self, the most abstract of the three. This aspect of ourselves surpasses both time and space's limitations that bind our earthly incarnations. The higher self embodies our pure divine essence that remains unaltered throughout our lifetimes. This is the closest to the concept of "spirit" or "soul" in the mind of the average person.

Intuition and psychic abilities, while intertwined and often used interchangeably, present unique characteristics and exhibit distinct features in my personal view and how I define them. Intuition emerges from the unconscious processing of sensory details in our environment, leading to a specific insight. In contrast, psychic abilities involve utilizing the clair senses, which operate independently of tangible environmental information. Because we may not be aware of where the information is coming from, intuition often feels like a psychic experience. The subconscious processing of environmental cues can create a sense of knowing or feeling about something without a clear explanation, making the experience seem mysterious or otherworldly. Despite their differences, intuition and psychic abilities often work hand in hand. By honing intuitive skills, individuals can also improve their psychic abilities, learning to trust their inner guidance and follow their instincts. Consider intuition as the middle self interpreting messages from the lower self, which processes physical environmental information, while psychic abilities involve the middle self receiving wisdom and insight totally unrelated to information in one's environment from the higher self through the clair senses.

In my book *Psychic Witch*, I extensively explored the significance of working with the three souls within the context of psychism and magick. I explained the importance of recognizing and engaging with each of the three souls in relation to psychic abilities. Each soul acts as a distinct lens that allows us to perceive reality in unique ways, thereby expanding our understanding of the psychic realm. To clarify this idea, I used an analogy of thinking about the lower self as a magnifying glass, the higher self as a telescope, and the middle self as a pair of reading glasses. By actively engaging with each soul individually, we gain different vantage points to interpret the energetic information that comes our way. This multifaceted approach grants us access to different layers of reality, enabling us to effectively perceive, navigate, and manipulate them. Limiting ourselves to a single set of lenses, such as solely relying on reading glasses in this metaphor, means missing out on the details that exist at the microscopic and macroscopic level.

The Genius in the Psychic Arts

When someone is exceptionally brilliant in a field such as the arts, we often call them a genius. The term *genius* actually has ancient origins, tracing back to Roman and Greek beliefs about a guiding spirit, also called one's "Genius," that protected and guided individuals. This ancient concept has evolved into the modern occult notion of the Holy Guardian Angel (HGA), whose role also involves guiding a person toward their true will, which is essentially their life's divine purpose. In ancient times this Genius spirit was thought to be the source of all inspiration. Today artists often talk about feeling deeply immersed in their work, guided by something beyond themselves, in an altered state of consciousness, describing it as "the flow state" or "being in the zone."

People often debate what exactly the HGA is. Is it just another facet of our higher self or is it an entirely different being? The question is more complex than a yes-or-no answer would suggest, challenging our habit of reducing complex issues to simple terms, as our middle selves love to do. There's a lot of value in thinking of the Genius or HGA as something external to us, whether it actually is or not. Elizabeth Gilbert explores the concept of the Genius spirit and creativity in her book *Big Magic*, emphasizing the benefits of perceiving one's Genius as external, much like the HGA is often viewed. She writes:

> They called it your genius—your guardian deity, the conduit of your inspiration. Which is to say, the Romans didn't believe that an exceptionally gifted person was a genius; they believed that an exceptionally gifted person had a genius. It's a subtle but important distinction (being vs. having) and, I think, it's a wise psychological construct. The idea of an external genius helps to keep the artist's ego in check, distancing him somewhat from the burden of taking either full credit or full blame for the outcome of his work. If your work is successful, in other words, you are obliged to thank your external genius for the help, thus holding you back from total narcissism.[2]

However, in psychic work, thinking of your Genius or HGA as your higher self or an aspect of it does more than just make the process smoother. It serves as a constant reminder of your inherent divinity. This way of thinking helps make your spiritual and psychic activities feel like a natural part of who you are, not something separate or external. It helps you trust the guidance and wisdom you receive as a natural process of your spirit, all of which helps keep you aware of your own sacred essence. So when we approach the higher self, it's beneficial to see it as simultaneously part of ourselves and something external to us. It's a paradox, but this liminal approach is one that I highly recommend, as no one can say with certainty what the truth is from our limited human perspective, and I'd be cautious of anyone who claims it's solely one or the other with conviction. Whatever the answer may be, the

2 Gilbert, *Big Magic*, 67.

higher self has some sort of connection to this divine wisdom, and through working with our higher self we can tap into this channeled essence of our own Genius, whether that's in the arts or in psychism.

Evaluating Your Motives for Psychic Tarot Readings

The art of reading tarot and combining it with psychic abilities is a deeply spiritual process that connects the practitioner with higher consciousness and divine wisdom. It's a powerful process of providing insights, guidance, and illumination to both the reader and those seeking readings. However, due to their potential power and influence, it's recommended to approach these practices with well-intentioned motives and respect. Ethics are paramount in any psychic or spiritual work, including tarot reading, but ethics are also deeply personal and should be determined by the individual. Tarot and psychic abilities tap into a greater consciousness and should be treated with reverence. Reckless or ill-intentioned use can lead to misinformation during a reading and a loss of connection with these spiritual tools. The purity of intent influences the accuracy of readings and the quality of psychic perception.

Approaching tarot reading and psychic abilities with good intentions creates a safe and nurturing space for everyone involved. It encourages trust, being open, and a readiness to delve into personal growth, self-discovery, and healing. It's not solely about foreseeing the future or uncovering concealed aspects of the present; it's also about helping others and operating from a foundation of love and compassion. Positive intent also affects the energy of the reading. When the reader operates with love, compassion, and service, the reading becomes a conduit for positive energy and healing. It offers comfort, reassurance, and valuable guidance to those seeking answers. Keeping a clear, pure intent ensures the reader's spiritual health as well as the integrity of their practice. It aligns them with their higher self and the greater good, avoiding being led astray by ego-driven motives, manipulating the querent, or projecting your own issues onto them.

Making Vows to the Self

When you make vows to your inner divinity, you open yourself up to incredible spiritual growth and personal insight. Through making a sincere promise, these vows prioritize personal integrity and ethical commitments to your higher self by accessing the deepest parts of yourself. Your psychic abilities are an essential part of your higher self, acting as a bridge to divine wisdom. As you honor your vows with sincerity and integrity, you will move closer to aligning with your inner divinity and your psychic perception will sharpen, becoming more powerful and accurate. Unlike other types of resolutions that are frequently abandoned, these vows are geared more toward your personal integrity and ethical commitments. So don't be discouraged if you haven't fulfilled your New Year's resolutions yet; one of these days I'll make it to the gym just like I pledge to every New Year's Eve. Instead, these vows are more about your frame of mind and the inner place you operate from than they are about making changes to your lifestyle.

Coming to tarot reading and psychic practices with positive intentions sets the stage for a safe, nurturing experience for everyone. This positive atmosphere encourages trust, openness, and a readiness to delve into personal development, self-exploration, and healing. When you're in right relationship with your motives, tarot transcends mere card reading and becomes an act of service rooted in love and compassion. This genuine approach also impacts the reading's energy. A reading conducted from a place of compassion and altruism becomes a channel for beneficial energies and healing potential. It provides solace, affirmation, and useful advice to those in search of answers. Maintaining an unclouded, benevolent intent is key not only for the querent but also for safeguarding the reader's own spiritual well-being and ethical standards. Such an approach helps align the reader with their higher self, promoting the greater good rather than being diverted by selfish ambitions. When we read tarot for others, our focus should always be on assisting them. That may seem like a no-brainer, but it's astonishing how many people are trying to flex how great of a tarot reader they are when reading for another person. That approach serves and helps no one.

EXERCISE 1

TRIPLE SOULS PLEDGES TO SELF

I find it helpful to use the Sun card for the middle self, the Moon for the lower self, and the Star for the higher self, as these are symbolic correspondences I have in my own practice regarding these aspects of the triple souls. Making vows to each of these divine parts of myself keeps me focused and open to the psychic world. Below are three example vows for these aspects. Feel free to use these or create your own, ensuring they truly resonate with your intentions and are commitments you can genuinely uphold. Keep in mind that these vows are not obligatory but can serve as guides to stay on track and maintain our connection to the parts of us we tap into during psychic readings.

1. Place the Sun card from your tarot deck in front of you. Say to your middle self something like this: "I pledge to embody the radiant qualities of the Sun in my discourse. I will express myself lucidly and genuinely, guiding others with honesty and integrity. I will use the tarot to help others see the path forward for the highest good in their life."
2. Position the Moon card before you and direct your gaze upon it. Address your lower self in a manner such as this: "I vow to embrace and understand my emotions and subconscious with love and compassion. I promise to utilize my intuition and emotional awareness to assist others on their journey of self-discovery and healing. I will read for them as a guide, nurturing their growth with empathy and kindness."

3. Set the Star card in front of you and fix your gaze upon it. Commune with your higher self using words like this: "I commit to listen to the psychic guidance of my higher self, utilizing my psychic perception and connection to cosmic wisdom to aid others and myself. I will celebrate and nurture authenticity in myself and others, lighting the way of hope and inspiration for those whom I read for."

The Elements of Being: Energy, Essence, and Information

A concise explanation of the different modes of perception associated with the three selves is presented by Ivo Dominguez, Jr. in his books *Spirit Speak* and *Keys to Perception*. He refers to these modes of perception as "energy," "essence," and "information," which he collectively calls "the Elements of Being."[3] The middle self primarily focuses on information. It processes and categorizes reality, breaking it down into words, symbols, stories, and discrete objects. The lower self directs its attention toward the energy aspect of phenomena, both internal and external, experiencing it through emotions and sensations. The higher self's focus is on essence, which can be challenging to grasp intellectually. Essence refers to the intrinsic nature or indispensable quality of something, particularly when it comes to abstract concepts that determine its character.

When it comes to psychic tarot readings, we can draw parallels to the act of painting. The higher self plays a role in providing the essence of a reading. Think of it as the outlines, strokes, shapes, and forms in a painting that give birth to the images. It offers the primary concept, inspiration, and vision of the artwork, ensuring that the main idea, such as a painting of a child with a flower, remains distinct from other possibilities, such as that of a dolphin in the ocean. This is where an unmanifested conceptual idea transforms into a manifested painting, bringing it to life. In contrast, the lower self contributes the energy aspect of a reading, much like the addition of color, shading, and

3 Dominguez, Jr., *Keys to Perception*, 65–70.

tones in a painting. It expresses the emotions and moods that permeate the overall artwork. This energy breathes life into the reading, infusing it with depth and evoking emotional responses. The middle self, on the other hand, provides the information of a reading. It can be compared to the composition of a painting, guiding the placement of various elements within the artwork and explaining the reasoning behind those choices. The middle self offers the story and narrative that the painting seeks to convey, bringing together the elements and creating a cohesive and meaningful whole.

Now, let's apply these concepts to the context of a tarot reading. The middle self plays a role in giving the reading structure through the provision of information. It understands the positions of the cards in the spread, draws from your internal database of card meanings, and recognizes the associations linked to each card. Like a spider, it then weaves together all the threads from the three selves into a cohesive web to offer an interpretation, explanation, and understanding of what the cards are conveying.

The lower self, on the other hand, contributes intuitive information to the reading. It absorbs energy impressions about the person sitting in front of us and the cards on the table. It provides us with emotional insights and physical sensations, which add depth and color to the information we receive. This aspect enhances our understanding of the reading and provides us with greater insight into its meaning. It can also provide those internal hunches that move you to steer away from a card's list of traditional keywords to home in on one specific aspect of that card or something totally unconventional for its interpretation.

The higher self brings insights about the overarching ideas and messages conveyed in a reading, whether they directly relate to the cards or not. This is when our clair perceptions come into play, which we will delve into later on. The higher self also allows for the incorporation of mediumship, enabling us to receive and perceive additional insights within the reading that may have nothing to do with the cards laid out in front of you.

Tripart Soul	Perception	Element of Being
Higher Self	Psychism	Essence
Middle Self	Intellect	Information
Lower Self	Intuition	Energy

EXERCISE 2

TAROT CARD ANALYSIS THROUGH ENERGY, ESSENCE, AND INFORMATION

1. Start by selecting a tarot card from your deck. Focus on the card's imagery, symbols, and colors.
2. Take a moment to connect with the energy of the card. Notice any emotions, sensations, or intuitive insights that arise. Describe the energy you sense from the card, such as its vibrancy, intensity, or calming presence.
3. Now explore the essence of the tarot card. Look beyond the surface imagery and delve into the archetypal and symbolic meanings associated with the card. Research its traditional interpretations and consider the deeper overarching and archetypal themes it represents.
4. Examine the information depicted in the tarot card. Analyze the elements, characters, and scenes. Think about the details and how they add to the card's overall message. Identify any practical advice or guidance that can be gleaned from the card's imagery.
5. Now combine the insights from the energy, essence, and information interpretations. Notice how the energy you felt from the card aligns or contrasts with its archetypal essence and the information it conveys. Look for patterns or connections between the three aspects. Consider how each aspect enhances or influences the others to create a holistic understanding of the card's significance.

6. Take some time to reflect on the combined interpretation of the tarot card. How does exploring the card through these three lenses deepen your understanding of its message and relevance? Embrace any new insights or revelations that arise during this process. Consider how you can integrate these understandings into your daily life or tarot practice.

Putting It All Into Action

WHAT THIS CAN LOOK LIKE

Allow me to share an example that demonstrates these concepts in action. A few years ago, while working as a tarot reader in Salem, I had a querent who sought guidance regarding their career. As I prepared for the reading, my middle self took charge, deciding on a three-card spread. The chosen cards were the Three of Pentacles, the Queen of Swords, and the Wheel of Fortune. Drawing from my knowledge of tarot meanings, a clear message began to unfold. The middle self skillfully wove together the symbolic threads presented by the cards, emphasizing the importance of collaboration and leveraging intellectual prowess in the pursuit of professional success. It became apparent that the querent possessed the potential to create an impactful career path by combining their skills with the experience they had gained through past experiences, but that something had to be communicated clearly in their workplace. The message conveyed a powerful insight that could shift things in their favor and lead them toward fulfillment.

As the reading progressed, my lower self tuned in to the querent's emotional energy, sensing a mix of excitement and apprehension. Intuitive impressions surged within me, evoking a familiar sensation akin to when inspiration strikes and ideas flow effortlessly. This told me that the querent had an idea they wanted to pitch at their workplace. However, there was also a sense of frustration, indicating that in the past, the querent's ideas had not been heard or valued. The lower self's contribution deepened the reading, emphasizing the importance of trusting one's instincts and embracing bold choices. It was my higher self that then brought forth vivid visions offering specific guidance. In my mind's eye, I saw a wise and supportive mature man with silver hair, a mustache, and glasses. The man appeared to be smiling and nodding, signifying his approval. This indicated that the querent could freely discuss their ideas with this individual. Next, a different vision arose: a middle-aged man with red hair, clad in a finely tailored suit, clutching a clipboard, his face marked by a skeptical expression. This symbolized caution, suggesting that pitching the querent's ideas to this individual may hinder rather than support their aspirations. The higher self's visions guided the querent toward the right individuals to engage with and those to approach with caution, ensuring a fruitful and aligned career path.

I relayed this information to the querent, who confirmed that the description of the middle-aged man matched their supervisor, who never seemed to listen and was overly critical despite the querent's stellar performance. The other man described resonated with the querent's boss. As a result, the main advice was to bypass the supervisor and directly pitch their idea to the boss. This insight brought clarity to the querent's situation. Further insights emerged as my lower self homed in on the Wheel of Fortune, offering an unorthodox prediction. I explained that if the querent followed the advice, they would rise in rank, embodied by the Queen of Swords. Moreover, this transformation would likely occur within a year, as the Wheel of Fortune symbolizes the zodiac's annual cycle.

Remarkably, a year later the querent returned to inform me that the reading had proven accurate. They had successfully replaced their supervisor and experienced the career advancement predicted in the reading. This real-life scenario serves as a compelling example of how the collaboration of the three selves in a tarot reading becomes evident and weaves together to interpret the cards and provide a prediction. By recognizing and embracing the interplay of these three selves, the tarot reading offered the querent a unique understanding of their career journey that traditional tarot interpretation may not have provided on its own. It empowered them to make informed decisions, leverage their unique strengths, and seek out the right connections and guidance to navigate their path with confidence and clarity.

EXERCISE 3

TRIPLE SOUL INSIGHT SPREAD

This exercise is designed to help you tune in to your lower, middle, and higher selves using a nine-card triangle tarot spread. Each point of the triangle corresponds to one aspect of your three souls (lower, middle, higher), and each will have three associated cards. The lower self is representative of your body and emotions, the middle self embodies your mind, and the higher self symbolizes your spirit.

1. Find a quiet, comfortable space where you can focus without interruption. Take a few deep breaths, centering your mind and setting the intention for your reading.
2. Shuffle your tarot deck, keeping your intention clear in your mind to gain insight into the current state of your lower, middle, and higher selves and identify any blockages and solutions.
3. Once you feel ready, draw nine cards from your deck. Lay them out in a triangle formation. The first three cards (1, 2, 3) go to the bottom left of the triangle, the next three cards (4, 5, 6) at the top, and the final three cards (7, 8, 9) at the bottom right.
4. Interpret the cards based on their positions:

   Lower Self (Cards 1, 2, 3):

   CARD 1: This represents your lower self's current state. Reflect on how this card speaks to your current emotions and physical state.

   CARD 2: This card indicates the blockages, imbalances, or challenges that your lower self needs to address.

CARD 3: This card suggests solutions or actions that can bring balance and healing to your lower self.

Middle Self (Cards 4, 5, 6):

CARD 4: This card signifies the current state of your middle self, relating to your intellectual and cognitive states.

CARD 5: This card highlights the blockages or imbalances that might be affecting your mental well-being or thought processes.

CARD 6: This card provides potential solutions or steps to balance and optimize your mental state.

Higher Self (Cards 7, 8, 9):

CARD 7: This card represents the current state of your higher self, or your spiritual aspect.

CARD 8: This card sheds light on any spiritual blockages, imbalances, or challenges that may need attention.

CARD 9: This card offers guidance or actions to balance and nurture your spiritual self.

5. Spend some time meditating on each card, observing any thoughts or feelings that arise. You may wish to journal your insights for further reflection.

middle self

lower self *higher self*

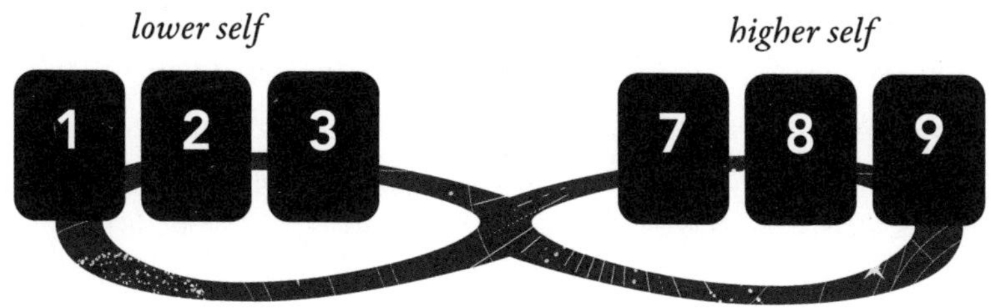

Trusting Yourself

The biggest roadblock to tapping into psychic skills often comes from self-doubt. Many people think these abilities are for "special" individuals and doubt their own potential. But in my experience, those who are highly tuned in to their psychic abilities share some traits. They have active imaginations, a sense of play, creativity, and a balanced attitude. They're serious about their abilities but also know how to have fun with them. Driving this home, Rachel Pollack brilliantly writes that "to learn to play seriously is one of the great secrets of spiritual exploration."[4] One important trait they all seem to have is the ability to ignore self-limiting thoughts, especially when using their imagination. They're not afraid to make mistakes, and that's so important for personal and psychic growth.

To gain psychic empowerment, you need to first conquer self-doubt, open yourself to imagination, and create space in your life for improvement and expansion. Allowing yourself to be comfortable with the possibility of being wrong as you develop psychic skills is also essential. Immersing yourself in the process without judgment regarding the information received often reveals surprising accuracy that previously may have been underestimated. Once a solid psychic foundation is established, then focus on honing accuracy in your psychism. This involves practicing by giving readings to oneself or to friends and family members on subjects that are not life-changing decisions. By focusing on less weighty matters, individuals can refine their skills and build confidence in their psychic abilities.

Allowance of Your Life Force

Psychism requires a state of allowance that is commonly found in creativity and playfulness. Consider those moments when you are drifting off to sleep or letting your mind wander into fantasy. There is a passive quality to this process as your brainwaves begin to shift. However, what sets psychics apart is their ability to tap into this state intentionally through focused attention.

4 Pollack, *A Walk Through the Forest of Souls*, 6.

It's a delicate balance between disciplined focus and receptive flow that occurs. Forcing the process by trying too hard or having internal resistance can hinder the natural flow. In this regard, relaxation becomes key. Relaxation positively affects both the mind and the body. It increases blood flow and alters breathing patterns. This subtle shift enhances your connection with the life force of your higher self and lower self. Breath is associated with the higher self, while blood is connected to the lower self. In other words, relaxation strengthens your bond with both the divine nature of your higher self and the physical nature of your lower self, deepening the connection to those aspects.

EXERCISE 4

CALMING RELAXATION TECHNIQUE

This technique aims to promote a sense of calm and relaxation by focusing on controlled breathing and gradually releasing muscle tension. The breathing technique incorporated in this exercise is referred to as "square breathing," which can both relax you and slightly alter your consciousness. It can be a helpful tool to quiet the mind, relieve stress, and prepare yourself for psychic exploration or any other activity requiring a relaxed state.

1. Shut your eyes and take a slow four-count breath in through your nose.
2. Feel your upper belly expand as you inhale and hold your breath to the count of four.
3. Exhale slowly through pursed lips, as if you're blowing on a dandelion to make a wish, to the count of four. Keep your inhales and exhales measured and steady to avoid feeling dizzy.
4. After exhaling, hold your lungs empty to the count of four.
5. Take another deep breath to the count of four and focus on tensing your hand into a fist.
6. Hold the tension and your breath to the count of four, then slowly release it and open your fingers while exhaling.
7. Notice the relaxation that spreads through your hand.

8. Repeat this process of tensing and releasing with your entire body, area by area.
9. After going through the various parts of your body, now tense every muscle you can at once, then consciously release the tension, paying attention to the sensation of relaxation.
10. To enhance the process, mentally affirm to yourself to relax as you release the tension throughout your body.

Altered States of Consciousness

Our brain activity consists of electrical pulses created by neurons communicating with each other. These pulses are measured in cycles per second, known as hertz, and correlate to different states of awareness. The five primary states are gamma, beta, alpha, theta, and delta, each identified by its own range of hertz cycles. Learning to shift between these states allows us to adjust our level of consciousness at will. Researcher Robert Beck found that many people displaying psychic abilities had a brainwave pattern of 7.8–8 hertz, falling within the alpha range (7.5–13 hertz). This state is often linked to activities like meditation, imagination, and daydreaming. Beck's research highlights the link between the alpha state and psychic abilities.[5]

EXERCISE 5

ENTERING THE ALPHA STATE

To enter the alpha brainwave state, there are various methods available, all following a similar pattern. These techniques typically involve focusing on a combination of colors and imagery, immersing oneself in these mental images and making them vivid within the mind's eye. Often there is a sense of ascent or descent incorporated, such as counting down or a similar process. Once you have successfully entered the alpha state, pay close attention to any thoughts or sensations that arise during this altered state of consciousness. Be receptive to the subtle impressions and insights

5 Brennan, *Light Emerging*, 17–18.

that may come to you. I also highly recommend conducting a tarot reading after entering the alpha state. You will likely notice a significant difference in the reading experience. The process becomes more fluid, with ideas and images effortlessly popping into your mind as you engage in the reading. It's as if the information flows seamlessly, creating a deeper and more intuitive connection with the cards and their meanings.

1. Perform the calming relaxation technique (exercise 4).
2. With your eyes closed, imagine yourself standing alone inside an elevator. In front of you are the elevator doors and a panel next to it displaying all the floor levels and buttons for going up and down. Press the up button and feel the elevator smoothly ascending to the next floor.
3. As the doors glide open, you find yourself in a softly illuminated room where your gaze is naturally drawn to a lamp. Approach the lamp and switch it on. Instantly the room fills with a warm red glow.
4. Return to the elevator and press the up button again. After the elevator goes up to the next floor, you step into another room that is softly illuminated. This time, find an orange lamp and illuminate the space with its gentle glow.
5. Repeat this process as you ascend through each floor, discovering lamps with yellow, green, blue, and purple lights in each room.
6. When you reach the last floor, you come across a lamp radiating a pure white light. Turning on the white light, feel its luminous energy filling the room.
7. You can now open your eyes, understanding that you've successfully entered the alpha state of consciousness. Affirm within yourself that any insights or information you receive in this state will be accurate and beneficial. You are now prepared to engage in meditative, psychic, or divinatory techniques with a heightened sense of awareness and connection.

EXERCISE 6

THE BALANCED PILLARS OF WISDOM

In this exercise, we draw on the imagery of the High Priestess in the Rider-Waite-Smith deck, where she sits between the white and black pillars J and B (for Jachin and Boaz of the legendary mystic Temple of Solomon). These pillars symbolize the duality of existence and the balance of energies within us. The High Priestess embodies wisdom, intuition, and mystery—qualities also associated with the renowned sagacity of King Solomon. Just like the High Priestess card teaches us to harmonize and integrate the contrasting energies within ourselves, nurturing self-awareness, energetic equilibrium, and alignment, this exercise helps you embrace the interplay of your conscious and subconscious aspects, acknowledging the significance of their balanced union to find greater harmony and alignment in all facets of your being.

1. Envision two pillars on each side of you: a white pillar to your left and a black pillar to your right, just like the High Priestess card.
2. Recognize that these pillars embody a balance between the contrasting energies within you. The white pillar embodies your conscious mind's logic and reason, while the black pillar embodies your subconscious mind's intuition and psychism.
3. Feel how these energies interweave and complement each other within you. Notice how your thoughts align with logic and your intuitive insights connect with wisdom.
4. Acknowledge and appreciate the harmony between these aspects of yourself. Their coexistence brings a sense of wholeness and completeness.
5. Affirm: "I embrace the balanced union of my conscious and subconscious energies of logic and intuition, reason and psychism."
6. Envision the pillars blending their energies, creating a unified and balanced energy field within you and recalibrating any imbalances.

7. Observe how these energies balance and interweave, fostering a holistic integration of your being. Embrace the symbolism of the pillars, recognizing the unity of opposites within you. Through their representation of balance, you can appreciate the significance of both logic/intuition and reason/psychism in creating a balanced state of consciousness.

IV
THE EMPEROR.

2
∞

Energetic Foundations

Psychic ability is closely tied to the practice of energy work, both for its development and actual use during readings. Energy work is all about grasping and shaping various types of energetic forces. This idea isn't just spiritual or mystical; it's actually physics. When you break down what we consider "solid" objects, you find that they're made up of rapidly moving particles of energy. These particles vibrate at distinct frequencies, making them appear solid to our senses. So, the physical world as we know it is really just diverse expressions of energy. Our senses can detect only a fraction of this energy spectrum. Take magnetic fields, radiation, and ultraviolet light, for example—these are forms of energy we can't see or feel, but their presence and effects can be scientifically verified. This speaks to the wider reality of energy forms beyond our immediate sensory perception.

The fundamental building block of all existence is energy. This concept is critical for understanding psychism. Different types of energy are constantly interacting and shaping our world, even when they escape our basic sensory perception. As psychics, we tap into energies that aren't commonly recognized in scientific understanding. I'm convinced that everyone has the innate ability to sense these subtle energies, which science has yet to fully explore. While science has done an excellent job identifying and studying various forms of energy, the psychic knows that other unique kinds of energy are out there awaiting formal acknowledgment. Their absence from scientific literature doesn't make these energies any less real or important. Acknowledging these subtle energies doesn't undermine the valuable work that science has done in demystifying our world. Both perspectives can coexist, enriching our understanding of the universe.

Energy work is performed through the power of imagination, primarily using visualization and tactile sensory imagination. Visualization involves creating an etheric thoughtform. In simple terms, a thoughtform is a mental image, idea, or construct fueled by our thoughts and feelings. It can vary in complexity or consciousness, ranging from a form in our aura that influences our feelings or thoughts to an energetic visualization to a semiconscious or fully conscious spirit that we create. The type of thoughtform we will be using the most during our energy work in this book is less of a conscious "energy robot" and more like an energetic overlay that we visualize and empower. Visualization alone is often insufficient for effective psychic work. To make the thoughtform more potent and suitable for psychic purposes, we must incorporate our willpower. Willpower represents our determination and intention to manifest something. By infusing the thoughtform with our willpower, we draw energy from the astral realm, which is the realm of willpower. This infusion of astral energy transforms the etheric thoughtform into an astral thoughtform, which possesses greater power and can be utilized in psychic activities such as psychic readings and energy manipulation. This energetic infusion grants the thoughtform the strength and effectiveness required for psychic work. By combining visualization with tactile sensory imagination, willpower, and energy, we can enhance our psychic abilities and achieve better results in psychic practices and readings.

Laying the Foundation

Throughout this chapter, I present several exercises that are integral to preparing oneself for energy work prior to conducting a reading. It doesn't matter whether you dabble in tarot card reading from time to time or are a seasoned practitioner juggling a hectic schedule of readings. It's important to regard these exercises as a fundamental aspect of your tarot reading routine. The importance of entering the alpha brainwave state from the previous chapter and performing these exercises cannot be overstated. They serve as the groundwork that ensures a clear, focused mind and a spiritually attuned heart. For those who are professional readers or frequently conduct readings, these exercises hold even greater significance. Amid a demanding day brimming with back-to-back sessions and a constant influx of querents, the potential for energy drain and emotional exhaustion is real. It's within this context that a consistent practice of energetic preparation becomes not just beneficial but essential. These exercises help maintain your energy levels, keeping your psychic faculties sharp and your mind clear throughout your sessions. By prioritizing these preparatory practices, you're safeguarding your ability to provide insightful and valuable readings, regardless of how demanding your schedule might be. Therefore, make these exercises, or an adaptation of them, a nonnegotiable part of your tarot reading routine.

By dedicating time to these exercises before you begin your day of readings, you lay a solid foundation for optimal energetic alignment and receptivity. Engaging in these exercises allows you to attune to your own energy, ensuring that you are in the best possible state to offer insightful and accurate readings. This practice creates a synergy between yourself, the cards, and the energies you work with. By approaching your readings with mindfulness and intention, you enhance your ability to tap into intuitive insights, interpret symbols, and provide meaningful guidance to those you're reading for. By making these exercises a nonnegotiable part of your routine, you cultivate a sense of energetic discipline and establish a ritual of energetic preparation. The well-being of your own energy is integral to the quality and effectiveness of your readings. Incorporating these exercises into your daily routine not only benefits you as a reader but also enhances the overall experience and satisfaction of your querent.

The Preliminary Exercises

Each time we delve into a new topic, technique, or practice, I will be assuming that these preliminary exercises have been performed. They act as the launching pad from where we delve into more complex explorations of energy work and psychism. However, you might discover different techniques that resonate better with you. This exploration and personalization isn't just welcomed, but encouraged. The key is to ensure that whichever techniques you choose, they fulfill each energetic purpose outlined in these foundational exercises. After all, it's not about adhering rigidly to a set of practices, but about fostering an energetic environment conducive to insightful, empathetic, and genuine tarot readings. I also strongly recommend re-grounding yourself at the end of any energy session.

Preliminary Exercises Refer to These Exercises Done In Order:

1. Calming Relaxation (exercise 4, page 27)
2. Entering Alpha (exercise 5, page 28)
3. Balanced Pillars (exercise 6, page 30; optional/as needed)
4. High Priestess Grounding (exercise 8, page 41)
5. Temperance Energy Flow (exercise 9, page 43)
6. Heart Centering (exercise 10, page 45)
7. Lunar Armor (exercise 11, page 48)
8. Establishing Your Energetic Space (exercise 16, page 56)
9. Energy Cleansing and Charging Your Cards (exercise 13, page 52; optional/as needed)

The Wells of Power

There are various types of subtle energy that we can engage with, and as we delve deeper into the realm of energy work, these energies can be further categorized into even subtler forms. However, before we embark on this journey, it's essential to first address your own vital energy. This refers to the energy that naturally flows within you—your personal life force, so to speak. It encompasses your energetic makeup, your aura, and your energy centers. When engaging in energy work, relying solely on your own vital energy to power your energy work isn't advisable. It's akin to the adage that you cannot pour from an empty cup. This holds particularly true when it comes to energy work and psychic practices. Utilizing your own life force in this manner will ultimately deplete you, leading to myriad issues, with fatigue and burnout being just a few of the potential consequences. Instead, we draw upon three other sources of energy, referred to as the "wells of power." These wells serve as alternate sources from which we can draw energy from to direct, move, and manipulate other forms of energy. The intention isn't to fuel our energy work directly with our own vital energy on its own. By tapping into these alternative wells, we ensure that we can sustain our energy levels and avoid the pitfalls associated with solely relying on our personal life force.

Divine Energy

Divine energy, the first well of power, embodies the sacred energy that emanates from the divine source, representing the ultimate essence of creation and spiritual realms. It encompasses higher consciousness, unconditional love, and divine wisdom. This energy is believed to originate from a higher power, whether it be deities, spirits, the universe as a conscious mind, or a supreme cosmic force. It serves as the underlying force within and between all things, often referred to as quintessence, Spirit, or ether, among other names. As such, it's also the base energy of all the other forms of energy. Within this well of power, we also find the energy of spiritual entities who can offer assistance in our endeavors, such as deities, spirit guides, archetypes, or other nonphysical allies.

Terrestrial Energy

Terrestrial energy, the second well of power, encompasses the energy flowing within the earth and permeating the natural world. It resembles the life force inherent in nature. Some individuals may express concerns about depleting or harming the earth when accessing this energy source. However, there's no need for worry because the amount of subtle energy we derive from the earth is exceptionally minuscule in comparison to its extensive energy reservoirs. The energy we tap into from the earth is about that of the microorganisms within our bodies. These organisms continually engage in various activities that often go unnoticed and seldom, if ever, have adverse effects on our well-being. Similarly, the energy we harness from the earth is incredibly modest when contrasted with its overall energy capacity. Consequently, our utilization of terrestrial energy has a nearly negligible impact and doesn't harm or deplete the earth in any significant manner.

Celestial Energy

Celestial energy includes celestial bodies like stars, planets, and galaxies. It represents the cosmic energy that fills the immense expanse of space. This celestial energy not only exists in the cosmos but also influences us through astrology and planetary effects. Astrology recognizes that the positions and movements of celestial bodies affect our lives and shape our personalities by emitting energy that varies with their positions and interactions with other celestial bodies. It has been a practice employed by magicians and occultists since ancient times to tap into these celestial energies as a source of power. By connecting with this celestial energy, we can establish a link with the cosmic forces and explore the intricate relationship between the universe and our own existence.

Grounding and Centering

Grounding and centering are essential when it comes to energy work and psychic readings. These practices provide stability and focus to our endeavors. Neglecting them can lead to unfavorable outcomes. Before engaging in any psychic or energetic work, always be mindful to ground and center. While grounding and centering are often mentioned together, it's helpful to understand their distinct functions. Grounding releases excessive energy that could overwhelm or harm us. It acts as a relief valve, allowing the expulsion of surplus energy from our bodies and energy systems, similar to how a relief valve works in a pressure system. In psychic or energy work, we often encounter potent energies, making grounding essential to prevent an unhealthy buildup of energy. Through grounding, we restore balance by shedding excess energy, enabling us to work safely and effectively with energy. It's also important to ground at the end of energy work, as it acts as a reset button for our energy system, forming an indispensable step in any energy work practice.

In her seminal book *Tarot for Your Self*, Mary K. Greer captures the essence when she remarks,

> In any psychic work, the goal is to make yourself a clear channel so that you do not hold any of the work inside your body, where it can create blockage and possibly be experienced as tension or even illness. By grounding your energy, you note but do not hold onto your experiences, allowing them to pass through you...[6]

To illustrate, think of the Tower card, which depicts a tower being struck by lightning. Grounding would be like if we placed a lightning rod on top of the tower, safely redirecting and dispersing the energy like a grounding wire so that it can safely run through the tower and into the ground, instead of destroying it.

Centering, on the other hand, brings our focus to the present moment, shielding us from distractions that arise from a multitude of tasks, responsibilities, and wandering thoughts. Prior to diving into energy work, taking a moment to center ourselves allows us to approach challenges with a composed mindset. Centering establishes a stable energetic focal point from which we can operate with clarity, stability, and balance. It allows us to take that metaphorical lightning bolt of energy we received and direct it with precision to our goal.

EXERCISE 7

WELLS OF POWER EVALUATION SPREAD

This introspective and empowering exercise is designed to explore and enhance your connection to various sources of energy. This spread delves into four main aspects: divine energy, terrestrial energy, celestial energy, and personal vital energy. Through drawing specific cards for each well of power and their respective guidance cards, this exercise offers valuable insights into one's spiritual alignment, connection with nature, cosmic influences, and personal energy levels. The spread also provides personalized advice on how to improve these connections and maintain a relationship with each energy source. By engaging with this tarot spread, you can gain a deeper understanding of the different energies available to

6 Greer, *Tarot for Your Self*, 49.

them, enabling you to enrich your spiritual practices, energy work, and overall well-being. It's helpful to use this spread semi-regularly to check in on your connection to energy sources, and it is extremely helpful when you're just feeling disconnected or blocked in your psychic practices.

1. **Divine Energy**—Draw a card to represent your current connection to the divine source and spirit realms. This card signifies how well you are attuned to the energies of higher consciousness, unconditional love, and divine wisdom.
2. **Terrestrial Energy**—Draw a card to reflect your connection to the earth and the natural world. This card indicates your ability to tap into the natural life force that exists within and around you.
3. **Celestial Energy**—Draw a card to symbolize your connection to celestial energy and how receptive you are to the cosmic energies that surround and influence you.
4. **Personal Vital Energy**—Draw a card to explore your current state of personal vital energy. This card represents the energy that naturally flows within you, your life force, and your energy centers.
5. **Improving Divine Energy**—Draw a card to receive guidance on how you can enhance your connection to the divine well of power. This card provides practices or actions that can deepen your spiritual connection and understanding.

6. **Improving Terrestrial Energy**—Draw a card to obtain guidance on how you can improve your connection to the terrestrial well of power. This card suggests ways to align with nature, ground yourself, and harmonize with the earth's energies.
7. **Improving Celestial Energy**—Draw a card to gain guidance on how you can strengthen your connection to the celestial well of power. This card suggests practices to connect with cosmic forces, align with astrological influences, and embrace universal energies.
8. **Improving Vital Energy**—Draw a card to receive guidance on how you can enhance and maintain your personal vital energy. This card provides insights into practices that can help you replenish and protect your life force.

EXERCISE 8

HIGH PRIESTESS GROUNDING

Incorporating the imagery of the High Priestess card, this grounding technique draws inspiration from her serene presence as she gracefully releases excess energy, stress, or negative emotions, much as the water flows off her robe like a water relief valve. Just as the High Priestess is firmly grounded on her throne despite all the water flowing through her, you too can find stability and grounding regardless of how much energy is flowing through you.

1. Get comfortable and sit with both of your feet resting flat on the floor. Close your eyes and take a few deep breaths to center yourself, anchoring your presence much like the High Priestess sits securely on her throne.
2. Now become keenly aware of the natural energy flowing through you. Picture this energy as a shimmering water current, much like the water that gracefully flows on the High Priestess's robe.

3. Visualize any excess energy, stress, or negative emotions within you as this shimmering water current, gracefully flowing down and out of your feet, finds its way to the earth below.
4. With each breath, permit this excess energy to flow through you, much like water cascading down a gentle waterfall, releasing and washing away any tension or burdens.
5. As the energy flows down, envision it effortlessly dissolving into the earth, being absorbed and transformed by the earth's natural healing energy, just as the High Priestess's robe gracefully meets the ground.
6. Embrace the sensation of lightness and relief as you let go of the excess energy, allowing you to remain firmly seated and composed, just like the High Priestess, who is grounded on her throne while channeling her wisdom.
7. Affirm to yourself that any surplus energy or emotional weight you cannot handle, whether your own or not, is now being released and transformed and will be for the duration of any energy exercise you engage in, leaving you with a sense of calm and inner balance and allowing you to be grounded.

8. Continue this practice for as long as you need, feeling yourself becoming more grounded and free from any unnecessary burdens, firmly anchored in the energy that flows through you.
9. When you are ready, gently bring your awareness back to the present moment, knowing that the grounding is continuously occurring even when you take your mind off of it. You can return to this practice whenever you need to release excess energy and find a sense of peaceful stability in your life, much like the High Priestess's serene and firmly seated presence on her throne.

EXERCISE 9

TEMPERANCE ENERGY FLOW

This meditation draws on the imagery of the Temperance card, utilizing the cups as symbolic vessels for the wells of power of terrestrial and celestial energies. By visualizing the flow of energy between the cups, you harmonize terrestrial and celestial energies within yourself and create a flowing circuit of energy currents to fuel your psychic ability and your energetic overlays, or thoughtforms. You can also practice this meditation whenever you seek to restore balance, integrate energies, and connect with the unity of all existence.

1. Take a brief pause to comfortably position yourself in a seated posture, ensuring your feet are either flat on the floor or that you're sitting cross-legged.
2. Shut your eyes and begin to take calm breaths, allowing your body to relax further with each gentle inhalation and exhalation.
3. Now envision the imagery of the Temperance card. In your imagination, visualize the central figure holding two cups, one in each hand. These cups are filled with flowing liquid light, representing terrestrial and celestial energies. Envision that one of each of these cups are directly above and below you.

4. Focus your attention on the cup below you, symbolizing terrestrial energy. Visualize it as a vessel filled with earth's nurturing, enlivening essence. See this cup overflowing with rich, golden energy, representing the life force that runs through the earth itself. Feel the stability and grounding energy emanating from it.
5. Next, shift your attention to the cup above you, symbolizing celestial energy. Picture it brimming with otherworldly, radiant energy, representing the cosmic forces that surround and permeate the universe. Visualize this cup overflowing with shimmering silver energy, embodying wisdom and inspiration from celestial realms.
6. Imagine a gentle flow of energy moving back and forth between the two cups like a rhythmic dance of liquid light around you.
7. As you inhale, visualize the terrestrial energy from the cup below you flowing up through your body, nourishing every cell

and fiber. Feel its grounding, stabilizing, and healing qualities as it circulates within you.

8. With each exhale, imagine the celestial energy from the cup above you cascading down like a waterfall of radiant light. Feel its uplifting, expansive, and illuminating qualities as it merges with the terrestrial energy within you.
9. Continue this visualization, inhaling the terrestrial energy and exhaling the celestial energy, allowing them to flow within you. Sense the balance and integration of these energies as they intertwine and blend, creating a symphony of vibrations.
10. On your next inhalation and exhalation, as the terrestrial and celestial energies meet within you, feel them coalesce and produce a third type of energy: divine energy.
11. As you maintain this flow, feel a deep sense of harmony and equilibrium permeating your entire being as you experience divine energy. Experience the unity of earth and cosmos within you and the interconnectedness of all things.
12. When you are ready, move directly to the next exercise or gradually bring your awareness back to the present moment, gently opening your eyes and carrying this sense of balance and connection with you throughout your day.

EXERCISE 10

HEART CENTERING

This technique allows you to connect with your heart center and cultivate a sense of presence and love in the present moment. Through consistent practice of this technique, you can enhance your capacity to stay rooted and simultaneously connect with the love and compassion that reside both within you and around you. This state of love, compassion, and empathy will enhance your readings, allowing yourself to genuinely connect with another person while having the energy from the Temperance flow centered within you for use with clearer precision.

1. Place your hands on your chest. Take a moment to breathe deeply, calmly, and maintain a steady rhythm.

2. While you breathe in and out, bring your awareness to the soft, steady beat of your heart.
3. Direct your attention and focus toward your heart center. Visualize a warm and radiant light filling your chest, representing the energy of compassion.
4. With each beat of your heart, imagine this light expanding and growing brighter, enveloping your entire being. Allow this light to fill you with a deep sense of love and compassion.
5. As you continue to breathe and feel the energy of your heart center, affirm to yourself that you are fully present in the current moment. Recognize that each beat of your heart signifies the present, anchoring you in the now.
6. Repeat an affirmation silently or aloud, such as "I am here, right now, emanating perfect love and trust."
7. As you repeat the affirmation, let the peace and love from your heart center radiate outward, filling your entire being with a deep sense of calm and warmth.
8. Take a few more moments to bask in this state of centeredness, feeling the peace and love emanating from your heart. When you are ready, gently release the affirmation and the visualization, knowing that you can return to this state of centering whenever you need to find inner peace and balance. If you're ready, you can move on to the next exercise.

Protection

Have you ever felt drained or like you've absorbed the mood of the person you read cards for? If you have, you're in good company. Many folks who are sensitive to energy experience this quite often, and it doesn't only happen during tarot readings. A perfect illustration of this is exaggerated in one of my favorite shows, *What We Do in the Shadows*. This "mockumentary" follows the daily lives and misadventures of a group of vampire roommates living in modern-day Staten Island as they struggle with mundane issues like paying rent and navigating social dynamics, all while being hilariously out of touch with the modern human world. One of the main characters is Colin Robinson, a psychic vampire who, unlike the other vampires who feed by draining their victim's blood, drains people's energy through boredom or irritation. Another example is the reoccurring character Evie Russell, who feeds on emotional energy intentionally by constantly making people sympathize with her and her stories of misfortune and victimhood, thereby rejuvenating herself at their expense. As a tarot reader, you will very likely come across both these archetypes of people regularly, though it's extremely rare that they're doing it consciously. Regardless of their motives, the impact of such draining encounters is real and worth consideration, especially since there's a higher chance of coming into contact with such people if you read for the public and are constantly interacting with their energy.

Luckily, there's a few solutions: the first is grounding; the second is energetic shielding. By using energetic shielding techniques, we can protect our own energy and prevent external energies from negatively affecting our readings or draining us. Whether it's the energy emitted by the person seeking the reading or the environment around us, you need to establish boundaries. When we shield our own energy, we create a protective barrier that filters out unwanted or disruptive energies. It's essentially setting limits on what can enter our personal space and energy field. Don't underestimate or dismiss this practice as mere paranoia. Think of it like putting on a seatbelt before driving or applying sunscreen before spending a long time at the beach. These actions aren't rooted in paranoia; they're preventive measures that enhance our safety and well-being, especially long term. The significance of energetic shielding becomes even more pronounced when we engage in direct energy work, which is a focus of this book. As readers, it's essential to proactively shield ourselves to maintain our energetic integrity. By doing so, we can create a tranquil and protected space that allows for accurate and unbiased readings unaffected by external energetic influences.

EXERCISE 11

LUNAR ARMOR

This exercise utilizes energetic shielding, inspired by the imagery of the charioteer's lunar armor from the Chariot card. The lunar armor promotes balanced receptivity and the filtering of energies, allowing helpful energies to flow while deflecting unbalanced influences. This shielding approach ensures you're in a receptive state without being overwhelmed by external energies, keeping you guarded while remaining open to psychic impressions.

1. Close your eyes and envision the lunar armor worn by the charioteer on the Chariot card forming around your body. Focus on the gentle luminescence of the lunar energy within the armor, symbolizing receptivity, filtering, and protection. Connect with the imagery of the lunar armor, recognizing its ability to allow helpful energies while deflecting unbalanced influences.
2. With each breath, visualize the lunar armor energizing, enveloping your aura in an energetic shield of radiant lunar energy. See the armor emitting a soft, silvery blue glow as it establishes a protective layer around your body. It embodies the qualities of receptivity and amplification, acting as a mirror

that effortlessly allows helpful energies to pass through while bouncing off unbalanced or discordant vibrations.

3. Take a deep breath and imagine a surge of empowering lunar energy infusing the armor, strengthening its receptivity and filtering capabilities.
4. Feel this energy fortifying the armor, effortlessly filtering and safeguarding your personal energy during tarot readings. It maintains a state of balance and receptivity, supporting your intuitive and psychic connection.
5. Release any concerns or distractions, placing trust in the lunar armor to safeguard your personal energy, enhance your tarot readings, and uphold your receptive state.

Setting Your Intentions for the Reading

Before you start a tarot reading, having well-defined intentions sets the stage for a concentrated and insightful session. Setting these intentions lets you outline what you hope to achieve, helping steer your reading in a specific direction. This focus increases the chance of gaining valuable insights. Moreover, the act of intention-setting sanctifies your reading environment. It opens the door to divine influence and fosters a link between you, the cards, and the spiritual world. As a result, the reading resonates more deeply and becomes a transformative and impactful experience.

Intention setting is an opportunity for you to call upon spiritual allies or higher powers for guidance and assistance. By stating your intentions clearly, you open yourself to receive additional wisdom and support during the reading. This collaboration between you and the divine deepens the connection and expands the insights that can be gleaned from the cards. Another important aspect of setting intentions is your ability to filter and channel energies during the reading. By setting clear intentions, you can establish boundaries and direct the flow of energy in a way that ensures only relevant and meaningful information is received. This focus allows for a more efficient and accurate reading, providing the querent with the guidance they seek.

Clear intentions promote ethical conduct and respect within the reading space. By establishing intentions that prioritize the highest good of all involved, you create a safe and supportive environment for both yourself and the querent. This ethical foundation fosters trust and integrity in the reading process. Before a reading, I specifically ask to only see what both I and the person I'm reading for truly need to know—no more and no less. This focused approach is twofold. Firstly, it ensures I receive only relevant information, filtering out unnecessary distractions. It also shows respect for the individual's privacy. This way, I don't accidentally delve into personal areas they'd prefer to keep private. In short, it's about building trust, honoring boundaries, and delivering considerate and meaningful insights.

I follow a double CHARGE acronym to remember my intention. I aim for the readings I conduct to be:

C	Clear and Concise
H	Helpful and Healing
A	Accurate and Authentic
R	Relatable and Revealing
G	Gentle and Guiding
E	Emphasized and Easy

EXERCISE 12

PRE-READING EVOCATION

Here's how the tarot evocations sound in my mind when I perform them. The following evocation is tailored for readings for others, but with slight modifications, it can also be used for self-readings.

I call upon my spirits, allies, and guides. Draw near, friends, and help with the task at hand. I ask that I receive what we need to know, no more and no less.

May the readings I receive be clear and concise so that we may fully understand the messages that are being conveyed.

May it offer help and healing, granting them the support required to navigate life's challenges and opportunities.

May the readings be accurate and authentic,
reflecting their situation with specificity.

May the information be recognized and relatable for
them so they may connect with the messages in a way
that resonates with their experiences and wisdom.

May the guidance I receive be gentle and guiding,
helping them to navigate the twists and turns
of their life with compassion and grace.

May there be emphasis on the messages where needed, and
may this reading provide them with ease and comfort.

Energetic Maintenance for Your Deck

Tarot is a tool, and like any other tool we want to ensure that it's working at optimal condition. To keep your tarot cards in optimal condition, regular energy maintenance is essential. The combination of cleansing and charging your deck ensures that your readings are precise and free from any disruptive or unwanted energy. By performing these practices regularly, you create a clear and vibrant energetic state for your cards, allowing them to deliver the most accurate and insightful messages. Cleansing is what it sounds like: the process of removing lingering energies from past readings or encounters that may interfere with your present readings. It ensures that the energy from previous readings don't influence the outcomes of subsequent ones.

There are various methods you can employ for cleansing your cards, such as using incense smoke (such as frankincense) or plant bundles (such as rosemary). Alternatively, exposing your cards to the gentle glow of moonlight or the radiance of sunlight can also cleanse their energy. Just be aware that leaving them out in sunlight too long can fade the artwork. Crystals, particularly selenite, possess powerful energy-purifying properties and can be used in this process. For example, you could use a piece of selenite on top of the deck or pass a selenite wand over each card while focusing your intent on clearing and cleansing the deck's energy. Energizing your cards is like making sure they're fully "charged," just as you'd charge a battery. Doing this strengthens your bond with the deck. When you charge your cards, you're basically tuning them to resonate with your personal energy, making the readings more tailored to you.

EXERCISE 13

ENERGY CLEANSING AND CHARGING YOUR CARDS

Here's my go-to technique for cleansing and energizing my tarot cards. All that you need is your tarot deck; you won't need any additional items. Find a spot where you won't be bothered or distracted.

1. Get comfy and sit in a chair or sit cross-legged on the floor. Start by taking some deep breaths to let go of any stress or tension. Allow your thoughts to settle down as you focus on your breath.
2. Imagine the moon, its silver light shining down upon you. Visualize the moon's energy flowing down into your body, cleansing and purifying your energy. Allow the silver light to fill you up and flow down into your hands.
3. Next, hold your deck in your hands and feel their weight and texture. Imagine the silver moonlight flowing down through your hands and into the cards, cleansing them of any psychic energy they've picked up from others or previous readings. Feel the cards becoming lighter and clearer, infused with insight and intuition.
4. As you do, declare:

   With lunar power, each card's cleansed anew
   Removing marred debris that blocks the view
   All remnants that obscure and shroud insight
   Are infused with silver glow for psychic sight.

5. Now, visualize the sun, its golden light shining down upon you. Visualize the sun's energy flowing down into your body, cleansing and charging your energy. Allow the golden light to fill you up and flow down into your hands.
6. Once again, hold your tarot cards in your hands and feel their weight and texture. Imagine the golden sunlight flowing down

through your hands and into the cards, cleansing them of any unbalanced or stagnant energy. Feel the cards becoming energized and full of power, charged with accuracy and precision.

7. As you do, declare:

With solar power, each card's cleansed anew
Removing stagnant forces that ensue
All unbalanced energies are made right
And are infused with precision's golden light.

8. Shuffle your cards four times, each time envisioning one of the four elements balancing its elemental energy in the cards. For example, during the first shuffle, imagine the energy of earth grounding and stabilizing the cards. During the second shuffle, imagine the energy of air bringing clarity and insight to the cards. During the third shuffle, imagine the energy of fire bringing passion and creativity to the cards. And during the fourth shuffle, imagine the energy of water bringing emotional depth and intuition to the cards.
9. Once you've completed your shuffles, thank the moon and the sun for their cleansing and charging energy. Thank the elements for balancing the energy in the cards.

The Energy of Your Hands

The awakening of your hand centers is important in any energy work, and your hands can be a powerful tool for tarot readings. It's with our hands that we connect and interact with the world around us. As such, they're also one of the best ways to interact with energetic realities, allowing us to direct energy as well as heighten and perceive sensitivities through clairtangency and psychometry. This heightened physical awareness may also make you more sensitive to the energy of the tarot cards, allowing you to develop a deeper connection to them and access more intuitive insights and guidance. As your hands become more in tune with energy and you hold a tarot card, you may feel a range of physical sensations. This could feel like warmth, coolness, vibrations, tingling, or pulses. These sensations can serve as signals from your intuition, indicating that the card has something to say. By paying attention to these sensations and allowing yourself to be guided by your intuition, you can unlock deeper insights in your reading, knowing that those cards where you feel this are essentially being highlighted.

EXERCISE 14

AWAKENING YOUR HAND CENTERS

This exercise is to help you awaken and sense the energy within your hands. This energy can be used for healing, psychic readings, directing energy, and many other metaphysical practices.

1. Inhale deeply. Allow your mind and body to find a peaceful and relaxed state.
2. Rub your hands together for ten seconds. This gets the blood flowing and activates the hands' nerves. Blood carries and moves energy in your body, and stimulating the nerves in your hands like this helps you focus on the sensations within your hands.
3. Focus your attention on your hands. Notice the way they feel and any sensations that arise when you bring your awareness to them.
4. Picture a sphere of pure, radiant white light before you. See this ball of light as a source of healing and energy, and reach out with your dominant hand to touch it. As you touch the ball of light, imagine that you're absorbing its energy into your hand. Feel the warmth and tingling sensation that increases in your palm and fingers.
5. Gently move your hand away from the radiant ball of light while noticing how the energy continues to reside within your hand.
6. Repeat this process with your nondominant hand, feeling the energy flow into that hand as well. This is the awakening of the energy within your hands.
7. Visualize a simple object, like a pen or a key, and imagine holding it in your dominant hand. Pay close attention to the object and see if you can sense its energy. You might feel a

tingle, warmth, or a sense of weight. Use your sense of touch to explore its shape, texture, and any other characteristics that come to you.

8. Repeat this process with different objects until you feel comfortable with your ability to sense their energy.
9. When you're ready, bring your hands together and imagine a flow of energy moving between them. Feel the connection between your hands and the energy that you have awakened within them.

EXERCISE 15

FEELING THE ENERGY TO KNOW WHEN TO STOP SHUFFLING

People who are new to tarot often ask me one of the most common questions: When should they stop shuffling the cards and start drawing them? The answer to this question is and isn't a straightforward one. Several factors can help you determine when it's the right time to conclude your card shuffling and begin drawing them. The key is to listen to your intuition and instinct. As you shuffle the deck, pay attention to any sensations or feelings that arise. You might sense a sudden increase in energy or a shift in the sensations within your hands. Trust your intuition and your body's responses to guide you in deciding when to stop shuffling and draw a card. Sometimes you just have a knowing of when it's time to stop shuffling. Here's an exercise that can help with that.

1. With a deep breath, begin to exhale slowly. Let your mind and body relax.
2. Now, grab your deck of tarot cards with your nondominant hand. This hand is your "moon hand," which is more energetically receptive, and by using it, you're opening yourself up to the cards' subtle vibrations and messages.
3. Focus your attention on the deck and sense the energy emanating from it. Do you sense a tingling feeling or perhaps a warm rush of energy? It could even be a gentle, subtle pressure. Whatever you feel, know that it's the energy of the cards calling to you.

4. Start shuffling the cards at your own pace, with deliberate and unhurried movements that feel comfortable to you. It could be a simple overhand shuffle or an elaborate one that incorporates a riffle shuffle. The aim is to establish a connection with the cards and perceive the energy that flows among them.
5. As you shuffle, be aware of the sensations in your hands. Pay attention to any shifts in energy and any changes in pressure or temperature. These are signs that you're making a connection with the cards.
6. Keep shuffling until you feel a clear signal in your hands that it's time to stop. You might feel a sudden change in the energy of the cards or your hand or it could be a sense of the cards settling naturally in your hands. Trust your intuition, and let your body guide you.
7. When you feel the signal, place the deck face down on the table and tune in to the deck's energy. Notice any sensations or messages that come to you. This will prepare you for drawing your first card and opening yourself up to tarot's guidance and wisdom.

EXERCISE 16

ESTABLISHING YOUR ENERGETIC SPACE

We can now focus on establishing our energetic presence and creating a space that resonates with our personal energy. Just like the neon signs outside psychic, tarot, or palmistry readers' studios signifying their reading space, we can visualize vibrant energetic signs of our name surrounding us. These signs that we'll be creating emit a strong energy, attracting positive vibes while warding off disruptive ones. By empowering ourselves with strength and confidence, we imprint our energetic signatures throughout the space, reinforcing our presence and ensuring a calm environment for readings or energetic work. This energy technique ensures that our energy is more potent than any spirits, unbalanced forces, or potential disturbances that may try to interfere with the reading and the reading space.

1. Close your eyes and take a few moments to clarify your intention for this exercise, creating a space of energy that is solely yours.
2. Focus on your breath. Observe the natural rhythm of your inhalation and exhalation. Notice the sensation of the breath entering and leaving your body.
3. With each inhalation, imagine drawing in fresh, revitalizing energy from the flow of terrestrial and celestial energies moving through your body. Visualize this energy as a bright, glowing light.
4. As you exhale, imagine releasing any tension, stress, or stagnant energy from your body, allowing it to disperse and dissolve into the surrounding space.
5. Direct your attention to your dominant hand and visualize it glowing with vibrant energy.
6. With each inhalation, imagine the energy flowing from your breath into your hand, filling it with power and vitality.
7. Slowly rotate your body to face one direction of the room. Use your finger to write out your name. Visualize your name written in glowing energy on the wall, like a neon sign.
8. With each breath, reinforce the energy flowing through your hand and visualize your name becoming brighter and more vibrant on the wall.
9. Take a few moments to appreciate the energy signature you've created.

10. Gradually turn to face each direction of the room, taking your time to repeat the energy-writing process for your name in each direction.
11. As you face each direction, focus on maintaining a steady flow of energy and visualize your name becoming more pronounced and vivid.
12. Once you have faced each direction and completed the energy-writing exercise, bring your attention back to your breath.
13. Take a few moments to observe any sensations or shifts in your energy field.
14. Gently open your eyes. With gratitude, acknowledge the energy within and around you.

When the Psychic Energy Is Too Much

For many years, I worked as a professional psychic tarot reader in Salem, Massachusetts, throughout the year, including October. Describing Salem as a lively and dynamic town constantly buzzing with activity and enthusiasm during this period doesn't fully capture the spirit of it. Its association with witchcraft, both historically and in modern-day occult practices, is a massive draw for people worldwide, especially during the Halloween season. Most of these people want to get a tarot reading on their visit because "when in Rome." To throw gasoline on the fire, the shop I read for was Enchanted, the home-base shop for the famous psychic witch Laurie Cabot, who conducts psychic readings and sells her handmade magickal crafts through the store. Among Laurie's fame is the story of how she helped Salem police find missing bodies and capture murderers using her psychism and magick, which was featured in an episode of *Unsolved Mysteries.* So Enchanted is a hot spot landmark in Salem itself, which is already extremely busy during this time.

I'm not exaggerating when I say that every day in October, all of us readers would be booked nonstop all day, with some days being eleven hours long. The issue was that during breaks or after my shift, I couldn't switch off my psychic readings, which was the last thing I wanted. It felt as if I was being forced to perform readings even during my off-hours, which intruded upon people's privacy. This is because I spent most of the day with all my psychic faculties completely wide open. I did manage to find a solution. I took a technique I learned from studying under Christopher Penczak and Laurie Cabot and reverse-engineered it. They use a "psychic trigger," which is a special gesture used to prompt the self through Pavlovian response to condition the subconscious to reach the alpha state immediately when triggered. (For my version of this, which I call "Setting a Psychic Prompt," see exercise 18 in *Psychic Witch*.) Since it worked for opening up psychic faculties quickly, I figured something similar could be used to signal to the subconscious that I was back to my mundane perception.

EXERCISE 17

THE SHUT-OFF RING

The inspiration for this method was drawn from the children's novel The Magician's Nephew *by C. S. Lewis. In the novel, the children slip rings on and off to travel between Earth and the Wood Between the Worlds. I decided to experiment using a ring made of hematite, which you can find in almost any metaphysical shop or easily enough online. I chose hematite due to its inherent grounding and protective qualities as a stone. In the following steps, I'll demonstrate using a hematite ring as an example. However, feel free to adapt these instructions to fit any ring or piece of jewelry that you can comfortably put on and take off. I provide this technique as optional for those who read professionally or have extreme trouble muting their psychic perceptions. For more techniques in navigating "volume control" of the flow of psychic information or shutting down afterward, I recommend checking out the exercises in my book* Psychic Witch *that address these issues.*

1. Start by grounding. After grounding, feel the terrestrial energy mixing with your own, imbuing the hematite ring with the energy of groundedness.
2. Keep your breath steady and maintain focus on your intent, ensuring that the energy drawn from the earth remains pure and specific in purpose.

3. Silently utter an affirmation that resonates with your purpose for the ring, such as:

   Hematite ring, guard of mind
   Close the door, secrets bind.
   When you're on, mute the sight
   Quiet the psychic, dim the light.

4. Let this phrase resonate as a fine-tuned energetic vibration that permeates the hematite ring within your cupped hands.
5. Slip the ring onto your finger. As you wear it, recognize the unique energetic signature you've infused into this object, setting it up as a physical cue to help you shift awareness whenever you wear it.
6. You've successfully charged your hematite ring using energy from the earth combined with your focused intent. The ring now holds a specific resonance that can aid you in transitioning to a grounded, everyday state of awareness. Recite the charm every time you put the ring on.
7. When you're about to perform the preliminary exercises prior to a reading, slip the ring off and quietly say:

   Off you slide, the fog now clear
   Psychic senses ready to peer.
   Open the channel, let visions flow
   Guide my mind to what I need to know.

8. Repeat this every time you take the ring off. At the end of your tarot session—after you've done all your closing exercises and regrounded yourself—put the ring back on and repeat the first rhyme. By consistently doing this with the ring, you'll quickly program your mind to know when you're open to psychic perception and when you're intentionally closing yourself off.

3

∞

Contemplation and Meditation

Meditation really captured my interest when I was around fifteen. I didn't exactly fall head over heels for meditation itself, but rather for the concept of it. I had read about meditation as brief mentions in books, and it seemed to pop up in movies and TV shows all the time. Those who practiced meditation appeared to be more spiritually attuned, and that aspect greatly appealed to me. I had spent a significant part of my childhood seeking out anything esoteric or metaphysical, so meditation felt like a natural fit. I was dead set on learning meditation, but I felt a bit lost in terms of how to get started or what approach to take. I didn't know anyone who meditated, and the books I had access to only sort of briefly mentioned it. I decided to check out the closest yoga studio the town over, which was brand new, after I saw an ad in the newspaper that they had a special where you could attend once for free. I collected my bus money and made my way there after an hour of riding. I spent about an hour and a half awkwardly getting my body in positions where I felt like a pretzel and had to strain to hold it. However poorly I may have done so, I still gave it my best shot. I fell in love with the studio, the type of people there, and just the whole vibe in general.

They concluded the yoga session with a non-guided meditation, which ended up being my favorite part. At the end of my free session, the instructor and owner approached me and started chatting and asking me questions since I was the youngest person there. I explained how I couldn't really afford any more classes, so they offered a work exchange to clean their studios after each class I attended, and I enthusiastically agreed. So for about a year I went almost every Saturday to yoga class for the meditation at the end. While I really enjoyed these moments of quiet peace during the meditations, I often wondered if I was doing it right as there wasn't much instruction during this time. To be real, for the bulk of those meditation sessions I was too busy fretting over whether I was meditating correctly to actually relax. Despite being slightly unsure if I was meditating the way I was "supposed" to, I still gave it my best effort. Once I let go of the need to meditate the "right way," I noticed a shift. My visualizations became sharper, and achieving a calm, focused state became easier. My dreams also became more vivid and meaningful. These were the very reasons that deepened my love for meditation. It wasn't merely the concept or the idea of being a meditator; what captured my heart was the benefits of meditation itself.

Through my extensive exploration of metaphysical and esoteric practices since I was that broke but ambitious fifteen-year-old, I have confidently determined that meditation isn't just an incredibly effective technique for psychic tarot readings; it's a cornerstone. It's more than simply a method to induce self-relaxation, though it definitely does that too. Meditation is to psychic ability what sound compression is to music. One of the reasons recorded music sounds smoother is because compression is used by sound engineers. Likewise, meditation makes the perception of psychic ability smoother and easier to work with, quieting what is distraction and amplifying what is important. What's awesome is you can meditate any place, any time, without the need for a yoga studio membership to get started.

While meditation can be a great haven to momentarily escape and recharge from daily life, it shouldn't disconnect us from reality. Instead, it should assist us in engaging with the world in an empathetic way, which builds up our understanding of people and life. Meditation enhances our ability to visualize, serving as a direct mental bridge between our subconscious and conscious minds. In psychic disciplines, the ability to exist in a state of liminality is often discussed—being neither entirely in the spiritual nor the physical world but somewhere in between. Meditation equips us with the balance required to achieve this liminal state, which in turn allows us to draw insight from both our inner world and the reading occurring on the table at the same time.

It's Not About Perfection; It's About Showing Up

Mentioning meditation usually splits the room: folks either adore it or can't stand it. And trust me, I haven't always been saintly about my own practice either over the years. Not every session has been a joy, and I'm far from clocking in monk-level hours. The truth is, there have been times when life got too hectic, or my own mental or emotional hurdles seemed too high to climb, and my practice went out the window. There were stretches where it felt like I was just spinning my wheels, not getting the insights or peace or whatever other results I was expecting. Sometimes meditation became one more thing on an already overloaded to-do list, making it tempting to skip it altogether. So I totally get when people roll their eyes at feeling they have to meditate and the resistance that can arise toward it.

Mastery of meditation doesn't happen overnight but instead takes time and dedication, just like any other skill. It's wise to start slowly and gradually increase each session's duration. Be easy on yourself if you don't experience immediate results in your initial attempts or if you go through periods where you feel like you've suddenly hit a wall. Progress, not perfection, matters on the meditative path. Especially in the beginning stages, focusing on executing everything flawlessly or having vivid visualizations is unnecessary. Instead, approach each session with curiosity and a beginner's mindset, creating an approach of ease and enjoyment. When you start viewing meditation as a fun activity, something you're actually pumped to do rather than a chore, you'll find the resistance melts away. On top of that, the benefits you've been chasing will likely show up much quicker. Sincerity and enthusiasm shouldn't be underestimated. If you're finding that you're resisting meditation, ask yourself how you can get excited about it again. Sometimes stepping back is the best move for gaining a fresh perspective and rebooting your relationship with meditation. Giving yourself a breather might help you recharge and come back stronger.

Troubleshooting Focus

When your thoughts wander during meditation, there's no need for concern about doing it wrong. That mental distraction is part of the meditation. Redirecting your focus is integral to the practice. Each time you redirect your focus after being distracted serves as a mental exercise that enhances your ability to concentrate. This isn't too much different than building muscles at a gym. Every lift against resistance strengthens the muscle involved. It's that resistance that is crucial to building the muscle. Similarly, each return of focus during meditation strengthens your mental faculties. The objective isn't to achieve a thoughtless state but to foster a relaxed, present awareness. In the event of distractions, calmly redirect your focus. The consistent application of this practice will not only improve your meditative state but also contribute positively to your overall focus and peace in daily life.

EXERCISE 18

STRENGTHENING YOUR FOCUS

The following meditation helps to bolster your focus and enhance your concentration skills. Engaging in this meditation regularly can train your mind to remain attentive and present. Keep in mind, just like physical training, honing your focus requires time and regular practice. Be gentle with yourself and celebrate small wins such as noticing a wandering mind and recentering your attention. Over time you will experience a noticeable improvement in your capacity to maintain focus, benefiting your meditation and psychic skills as well as your everyday life.

1. Find a quiet spot free from interruptions. Position yourself comfortably—either cross-legged on the floor or in a chair with feet planted. Maintain an upright posture. Let your hands rest gently on your knees or together in your lap.
2. Close your eyes and inhale deeply through your nose, ensuring your mouth is closed. As you do, sense the air expanding your lungs. Exhale at a measured pace, feeling the air depart your body.

3. Bring your attention to your breath. Notice how it feels as it enters and exits your nostrils. Feel the rise and fall of your chest and abdomen with each breath.
4. Your mind may wander and thoughts may arise. That's okay. The goal isn't to stop thinking. The real target is noticing when your mind has strayed. Once you catch it, just ease your focus back to your breathing.
5. Each time your mind wanders, acknowledge the thought or distraction and then gently redirect your attention back to your breath. The act of recognizing your mind's wandering and bringing it back is the core of this practice.
6. Start with just 5–10 minutes of this breathing focus. As you get better at keeping your attention anchored, feel free to extend the time.
7. To end your meditation, slowly bring your awareness back to your surroundings. Wiggle your fingers and toes, stretch lightly, and, when you feel ready, gently open your eyes.

Troubleshooting Visualization

When I discuss visualization or imagination, I'm not talking solely about "seeing" with the mind's eye. Visualizing isn't just about forming mental images; it's an immersive experience that engages all your senses. Visualization allows you to imagine not only visuals but also scents, tastes, sounds, and even tactile sensations. This multisensory approach turns your visualized scenario into something more concrete and impactful. Immersive forms of visualization like this one have benefits, particularly in the areas of intuition and psychic experiences, helping you fine-tune your intuitive abilities and enrich your psychic experiences by honing your overall sensory awareness and perception.

Visualizing during a guided session or energy practice can be a bit tricky for some individuals. If you're encountering difficulties with visualization, you can explore different methods. One effective approach is to shift your focus toward the sensations and emotions linked to what you're trying to visualize. Instead of trying to vividly "see" an image, pay attention to the emotions and other sensations it evokes. Let's say you want to visualize a serene beach scene. Instead of struggling to create a mental image, fully immerse yourself in the experience of warm sand beneath your feet, the refreshing caress of a cool ocean breeze against your skin, or the soothing sound of waves breaking on the shore. This sensory focus can be just as effective as visualizing, and it may even feel more natural to some. The essential thing is to discover the method that aligns most with your personal preferences, enabling you to establish a strong connection with your inner senses and intuition. The key is to make the visualization experience more sensory and less reliant on clear mental imagery.

Another technique that can be quite effective involves using descriptive words or phrases as mental guides for your thoughts. You can repetitively recite descriptive words or phrases that correspond to what you want to visualize. If visualizing primarily through your sense of sight feels challenging, engaging your other senses or employing descriptive language can offer alternative paths to achieving the same outcome. Just like any skill, visualization improves with practice and consistency. Be patient with yourself; remember, there's no "wrong" approach. The ultimate aim is to involve your mind in a way that enhances your bond with your intuition and psychic talents, and there are plenty of avenues to achieve this.

EXERCISE 19

STRENGTHENING YOUR VISUALIZATION WITH TAROT

This practice is helpful for anyone looking to enhance their ability to visualize. The exercise involves selecting a card from your tarot deck, thoroughly studying its details, and then mentally re-creating it with as much accuracy as possible with your eyes closed.

1. Locate a peaceful and comfortable area where you can be undisturbed. Ensure that you have your tarot deck nearby. Sit down in a relaxed position. With each breath, ease into the moment just a little bit more. Calm your body and mind.

2. Gently shuffle your tarot deck with the intention of strengthening your visualization skills and then draw a card.
3. Spend some time taking in the card you've drawn. Notice the colors, figures, symbols, and patterns. Take in the overall mood and energy of the card. Observe the details—small and large—and remember them.
4. Once you've taken a good look at the card, see how much you remember. Close your eyes and re-create it on the screen of your mind. Start with the larger elements and gradually move to the smaller details. Visualize the colors, figures, symbols, and patterns as vividly as possible. Engage your senses. What do the figures in the card smell or sound like? Is there a specific texture or temperature associated with the image?
5. Once you've visualized the card in as much detail as possible, open your eyes. Notice any elements that you missed during your visualization. Pay special attention to these during your next round of visualization.
6. Repeat steps 4 and 5 several times. With each round, aim to visualize the card with more accuracy and detail.
7. Once you've completed your visualization practice, spend a few minutes in reflection. Did your perception of the card change throughout the exercise? Were there elements that were easier or harder to visualize?

Contemplative Meditation

Contemplation on a theme, idea, or symbol is a form of meditation in itself. This type of meditation involves focusing your attention on a specific concept, allowing you to explore its meaning, significance, and associated insights with depth. Unlike some forms of meditation that strive to clear the mind or maintain mindfulness of the present, contemplative meditation promotes active engagement with a particular focus. This practice proves particularly useful for tarot readers. By contemplating a single card's symbols and themes, a tarot reader can assimilate its essence at a deeper level. For example, a tarot reader might focus on the Fool card. They might consider the symbolism of the cliff, the small dog, the white rose in the Fool's hand, or the Fool's carefree demeanor. Each symbol embodies a variety of interpretations that could unravel new layers of understanding and intuition for the reader. Such contemplation can notably enhance a tarot reader's skills. It enables a deeper understanding of each card, which creates a personal and intuitive relationship with the tarot deck. It can also improve the reader's ability to establish connections between cards in the reading. This allows them to intertwine the symbolic language of the tarot into a meaningful and insightful narrative for the querent.

Contemplation on the Symbolic

The following practices and meditations are helpful for adopting a psychic tarot mindset through contemplation. Contemplation develops a strong connection with the tarot cards and viewing the world through a tarot lens. This connection forms a "language" that bridges you, the cards, and the world. When it comes to psychic ability, the mind relies on its existing knowledge to convey information. In simpler terms, it can only use what is in your mind to communicate its meaning. Dion Fortune, in her channeled classic *The Cosmic Doctrine*, describes the limitations of received psychic information by stating that "perception ceases at the barrier of manifestation."[7]

The "barrier of manifestation" refers to the point where psychic information becomes intangible and incomprehensible within our minds because we don't have a direct frame of reference for it. In other words, our ability to perfectly perceive and understand psychic information is limited to what our minds recognize and relate to. We can only accurately receive and relay psychic information if it matches the knowledge in our internal mental database; otherwise, we can only get a rough approximation, providing a general sense of the message. In other words, unfamiliar concepts or information will only be partially understood or vaguely interpreted. This is why expanding our understanding of tarot's symbolism is crucial regardless of how long

7 Fortune, *The Cosmic Doctrine*, 19.

we've been studying and reading with tarot. It provides much more of a precise framework for interpreting the psychic impressions we receive. The clearer our comprehension of tarot's symbolic language is, the more precise our interpretation of psychic information we receive becomes.

Symbols act as a bridge, helping us understand and communicate complex ideas. They hold rich meanings and can connect different experiences or thoughts through the different dimensions of the inner planes. Everything, from a crystal to a sound, is made of energy. While this energy can take on various forms as a symbol, its essence remains unchanged. Symbols enable us to encapsulate and communicate this energy, demonstrating that everything, in its unique manner, is interconnected and can be conveyed in various manifestations. Tarot is abundant in symbolism, and by delving deeper into this symbolic language and understanding how it connects to both the inner and outer world, we equip ourselves with a broader vocabulary to comprehend the messages conveyed in a tarot reading. Arthur Waite, the co-creator of the Rider-Waite-Smith Tarot deck, explicitly states that

> the true Tarot is symbolism; it speaks no other language and offers no other signs. Given the inward meaning of its emblems, they do become a kind of alphabet which is capable of indefinite combinations and makes true sense in all.[8]

Carl Jung wrote: "As a plant produces its flower, so the psyche creates its symbols. Every dream is evidence of this process."[9] Jung defines the psyche as the entirety of the human mind. In his view, the psyche encompasses a person's conscious and unconscious aspects, thoughts, emotions, and experiences. According to Jung, the psyche possesses an inherent inclination to express itself through symbols. Symbols are considered the native language of the unconscious mind, representing layered meanings that may not be easily conveyed through direct or literal means. The quote suggests that when the deeper aspects of the psyche communicate, particularly in dreams, symbols become the primary medium through which these communications manifest.

8 Waite, *The Pictorial Key to the Tarot*, 5.

9 Jung, *Man and His Symbols*, 52.

By utilizing symbols, the unconscious part of the psyche can tap into the vast reservoir of the personal and collective unconscious, unveiling insights, truths, and connections that might remain elusive through conscious awareness alone. The same principle applies to psychic information. Within our cosmology, the higher self conveys information through the unconscious using the symbolism stored within our psyche's database, and it's the task of the middle self to interpret and comprehend these symbols to the best of its ability.

What distinguishes tarot from many other methods of divination is its comprehensive and concise nature, encompassing a wide range of human experiences, events, emotions, and interactions through its symbols and archetypes. Tarot also allows for personal interpretation and meanings while benefiting from the centuries of collective utilization that has strengthened its presence in our collective unconscious. To think like a tarot reader, it's essential to start observing synchronicities and seeking tarot symbolism in our daily lives. However, this requires a solid foundation in either the traditional meanings of tarot or our own personally developed interpretations. When I discuss thinking like a tarot psychic, I mean being attentive to our experiences, emotions, thoughts—and those of others—and contemplating which card or cards would best represent a given situation if it were to appear in a tarot reading.

EXERCISE 20

THINKING LIKE A TAROT PSYCHIC

This exercise aims to deepen your understanding of tarot symbolism by associating characters and scenes from books and movies with specific tarot cards. By engaging in this practice, you will expand your tarot knowledge and gain insights into the archetypal themes and symbolism represented in various narratives. This is a creative exploration that encourages you to deepen your understanding of tarot symbolism and its application to various narratives.

1. Choose a book or movie that deeply connects with you. It can be a beloved favorite, a recent read or watch, or something you wish to explore further.
2. Think about the characters in the chosen book or movie and consider their traits, motivations, and roles within the story. Reflect on their journeys, challenges, and transformations.
3. Begin associating specific tarot cards with the characters you have identified. Consider the symbolic attributes, personality traits, or key moments that align with the essence of each card. Trust your intuition and personal interpretation of the cards.
4. Move on to analyzing scenes or events in the book or movie. Identify moments that resonate deeply with you, evoke strong emotions, or hold symbolic significance. Connect these scenes to appropriate tarot cards that reflect their themes or lessons.
5. If desired, extend the exercise by exploring how tarot symbolism applies to other elements such as settings, objects, or overarching themes in the book or movie. This will further deepen your understanding of tarot's universal symbolism.
6. Spend some time contemplating the links you've established between the characters, scenes, and tarot cards. Consider the insights and messages that arise from these associations. What new perspectives or understandings do they offer? How does tarot symbolism enhance your interpretation of the book or movie?
7. Repeat this process with events, interactions, and people in your daily life.

Thinking like a Tarot Psychic

WHAT THIS CAN LOOK LIKE

In Guillermo del Toro's movie *Pan's Labyrinth*, Ofelia's experiences are rich with tarot symbolism. Finding herself in a new environment, she navigates both everyday and mystical challenges. Her initial quests, designed to verify her as the reincarnated Princess Moanna of the Underworld, echo the Wheel of Fortune card's themes of fluctuating fate and destiny. When she enters the labyrinth, she faces situations that reflect the symbolism of the Moon card, which deals with illusion, intuition, and subconscious elements. The Faun, or Pan, helps her navigate this mysterious setting. His role closely aligns with the Hierophant, serving as a bridge between spiritual wisdom and everyday life, the otherworld and mundane reality.

Ofelia faces tough obstacles in her quest. Her stepfather, Captain Vidal, serves as the villain of the story and is a dark reflection of the Emperor card, emphasizing his dictatorial and inflexible ways. The escalating tension between Vidal and the rebels draws parallels with the Five of Wands, which stands for conflict and competition. Ofelia's mother, Carmen, yearning for stability and embodying maternal love, aligns with the energies of both the Empress and the Hanged Man, representing nurturing and self-sacrifice. On the other hand, Mercedes, who secretly supports the rebels, can be linked to the High Priestess and the Chariot, representing secrets and determination.

When Ofelia first encounters the Faun, consider the Page of Cups and Two of Wands. These cards capture her childlike wonder and imagination and the grand ambitions she's beginning to develop as she embarks on her magickal quest. As we move ahead to the unsettling Pale Man sequence, the Seven of Cups and the Tower become relevant. These cards symbolize the perilous attraction of temptation and the harsh consequences of danger that can result. As you can see, you could interpret these scenes and characters in multiple ways using different tarot cards. The idea isn't to pinpoint the "correct" card for each moment or character. Instead, the focus is on how the tarot can shed light on different elements of what's happening or who's involved. The process is about reflecting on the tarot and how tarot cards can demonstrate different aspects of the situation or character to create a language between yourself and the tarot outside of the context of a reading.

Tarot Journaling

Keeping a tarot journal benefits both newcomers and seasoned readers. Going back through your entries helps you spot recurring symbols, recurring themes, or significant shifts in your understanding of the cards. This activity lets you see how tarot symbolism has shaped your thoughts and actions over time, giving you keen insights into your own mental and emotional growth. Writing in a tarot journal means actively engaging with the card symbolism; you're not just passively receiving information. This interaction hones your understanding of each card's meanings and symbols. As you keep journaling, you'll start to recognize specific motifs or archetypes showing up in similar scenarios, helping you tailor your understanding of tarot to your personal experiences.

Jotting down your tarot insights also promotes a thoughtful, introspective state within you, which is ideal as a tarot reader. Articulating your thoughts reveals buried emotions and mental patterns, helping you dig deeper into your own psyche. A tarot journal helps you apply the wisdom gained from your readings to everyday life. By reflecting on the messages you receive and how they connect to your personal experiences, you're bridging the symbolism of the tarot with your own thought processes and actions. This not only deepens your tarot practice but also enhances your self-knowledge to understand how your mind works—an invaluable asset in any psychic or spiritual work.

EXERCISE 21

YOUR TAROT JOURNAL

1. Create a sacred space for your tarot journaling practice. Find a quiet and comfortable place where you can focus without distractions. Light a candle, play soft music, or incorporate any other personal rituals that help you enter a calm and receptive state of mind.
2. Select a journal that resonates with you. It can be a blank notebook, a beautifully designed tarot journal, or even a digital journaling platform. Find something that inspires you and feels inviting for self-expression.

3. Before each journaling session, center yourself and set the intention. This can include shuffling the cards, focusing on a question or theme, and pulling a card to provide guidance and inspiration for your journaling session.
4. Write about the tarot readings you've done recently or in the past. Include details such as the date, the question or theme of the reading, the cards pulled, and your interpretations of each card's meaning in relation to the question or theme. Reflect on the insights, emotions, or connections that arose during the reading.
5. Dedicate some time to exploring the symbolism within the tarot. Choose a card from your readings or draw one randomly, and write about its imagery, symbols, colors, and overall impression. Consider the personal significance of these symbols and how they may relate to your current life circumstances and experiences.
6. Journal about any intuitive flashes, messages, gut feelings, and psychic impressions you receive during or after your tarot readings. Trust your inner guidance and let your intuition flow onto the pages. These intuitive insights often hold wisdom and personal revelations.
7. Use your tarot journal as a space to express your emotions, fears, joys, and personal reflections. Write about how the cards align with your current mental state, events occurring in your life, or any challenges you may be encountering. Allow your journal to become a safe container for self-expression and emotional release.
8. Periodically review your journal entries to identify patterns, recurring themes, or milestones in your tarot journey. You'll notice how your understanding of the cards has transformed, the insights you've gained, and the personal development you've undergone. Take note of any synchronicities or moments of clarity that emerge as you look back in your journal.

EXERCISE 22

DAILY DRAW

Incorporating a daily tarot draw into your routine provides a valuable tool for navigating your day with guidance. It acts as a personal psychic companion, offering insights and forewarnings while helping develop your intuitive abilities and enhance your proficiency in interpreting the cards. While this practice may seem simple and more suitable for beginners, it's one of the most powerful methods to familiarize yourself with the tarot's language and enhance your intuitive abilities. Never underestimate how immensely powerful foundational practices can be over time.

To start, at the beginning of your day, give your tarot deck a shuffle, then pose a straightforward question like "What should I prioritize today?" or "Which aspects need my attention?" Following this, draw one card from the deck. Take a moment to contemplate the card and make note of any insights or ideas that arise. Don't worry if these impressions seem random or confusing at first, as they may unveil symbolic messages that become clearer to you later on. That's why it's recommended to keep a journal and record your daily card readings.

Pay attention to any recurring patterns that emerge over time in your daily draws and reflections. Take note of cards that frequently appear. Do specific ones seem to recur? Are there recurring themes or messages that consistently manifest? Do certain numbers, suits, or court cards reappear? These patterns can provide insights into your personal growth and development. By diligently recording your daily draws over an extended period, you may discern patterns within the cards, illuminating the cyclical nature of life and the influential energies at play.

You can also ritualize it a bit by saying a charm as you shuffle your cards. One I like to say is:

I shuffle these cards, their secrets unveil
Seeking answers that their wisdom entails
What destinies await on this chosen day?
What guidance and forces will come my way?

∞

EXERCISE 23

COMPARATIVE TAROT EXPLORATION

While each card carries a broad interpretation, the expression of these meanings can significantly differ from one deck to another. The nuances can greatly enhance our understanding and interpretation of the cards. In this exercise, you'll be exploring these nuances by comparing the same card from two different decks. This comparison can highlight subtle differences and similarities in imagery, symbolism, and the emotions they evoke, giving you a better understanding of the card's meaning. By observing these subtle differences and similarities, you will deepen your understanding of each individual card as well as enrich your relationship with your different tarot decks and the unique insights each one offers.

1. Choose two tarot decks and shuffle the cards of one of them while focusing on your intention to gain insight.
2. Draw a card from your deck and observe it closely. Take a moment to notice its imagery, colors, symbols, and any immediate feelings or thoughts it brings to mind.
3. Set the card aside where you can see it, and now choose a different tarot deck by a different artist.
4. Search through that one to find the identical card that you drew from the first deck.
5. Place it next to the first card you drew.
6. Spend some time contemplating both cards side by side. What do you see as shared aspects between these two cards? Are there shared symbols or colors? Do the cards elicit similar feelings or thoughts?
7. After noting the similarities, shift your focus to the differences. How does the artwork differ? Are there elements present in one card but not the other? Do they evoke different emotions or thoughts?
8. Grab your journal and proceed to jot down your observations, ensuring that you record both the commonalities and distinctions you've noticed between the two cards. Reflect on

your notes. Consider how the different portrayals of the same card might offer different insights or perspectives.

Comparative Tarot Exploration

WHAT THIS CAN LOOK LIKE

To illustrate what this looks like, let's explore the Empress card through two different decks to see how the symbolism shifts for the same card expressed differently. For this, I'll compare the Empress from the Rider-Waite-Smith deck with the Empress of the Marseilles Tarot.

In the Rider-Waite-Smith deck, the Empress lounges in divine abundance. She reclines on a cushioned throne peppered with Venusian symbols and images of harvest. Her head is crowned with twelve stars, linking her to cosmic forces. Pomegranates decorate her robe, serving as a nod to her inherent fertility as well as the cycles of nature; in this vein, think about the myth of Persephone's journey and its relation to the seasons. Around her, fields brim with mature wheat, emphasizing her connection to earth's abundance. A quiet river flows behind her, hinting at her emotional and intuitive layers. A heart-shaped shield, marked with the symbol of Venus, hammers home her associations with love, beauty, and fertility.

Switching gears to the Tarot of Marseilles, the Empress here shows a different kind of regality. She sits erect on her throne and brandishes a shield with an eagle, representing her authority. Her crown, while simpler, is no less significant. It may lack the ornate stars or detailed designs, but its simplicity conveys a direct sense of earthly authority. The environment is sparse, focusing our attention on her role as a discerning ruler. Simplicity can be a virtue when it comes to leadership; it cuts through the noise and commands respect without needing to shout. The Tarot of Marseilles version of the Empress invites us to consider the qualities of governance, leadership, and clarity of purpose.

Both versions of the Empress card captivate us with themes of creativity, abundance, and influence, yet they offer contrasting perspectives on how these themes are embodied. The Rider-Waite-Smith Empress feels almost like a Gaia or Demeter figure, thoroughly enmeshed in nature and its cycles. On the flip side, the Marseilles Empress emerges as a commander, prioritizing governance and order over a connection with the natural world. The Marseilles Empress also embodies the archetypal mother in a different way: she is a matriarch of the people she rules. While both cards express the same overall archetype, that role is expressed differently. The Rider-Waite-Smith Empress overwhelms us with sensory details: the lush fields, the flowing river, the star crown. She embodies an ideal of abundance and emotional richness intimately tied to the earth and its cycles of life. She's much more of a Mother goddess than the Marseilles Empress, who exudes a type of calculated authority. Her sparse surroundings serve to focus our attention solely on her. Her eagle-emblazoned shield and unadorned crown echo themes of strategic leadership and plain-speaking authority. Her version invites us to consider power, wisdom, and governance as equally significant attributes of the Empress archetype. We can see both Empress cards as almost different octaves of the same archetype, with the Rider-Waite-Smith Empress being more about the power of the earth, love, and nurturing, and the Marseilles one being more about the embodiment of queenly energy within society and indirect interactions, as she's looking away from the viewer as opposed to her RWS counterpart.

EXERCISE 24

CARD COUPLING CONTEMPLATION

Just like the previous exercise, this one invites you to explore the dynamic interaction between two cards, shedding light on the complex ways they can influence and shape each other's narratives. The comparison can help you see themes when they pop up in readings as well as nuances between similar-seeming cards. Keep in mind that the focus of this reading is about exploring the relationship between cards. Trust your intuition and allow yourself to be open to the insights that this process brings forth.

1. Select your preferred tarot deck and start shuffling the cards, setting your intention to uncover new insights into the interplay of the tarot's narratives.
2. When you feel intuitively ready, draw two cards from the deck and place them next to each other, allowing yourself to absorb their individual and collective imagery.
3. Start your exploration with the first card. Observe its imagery, symbols, and colors, noting any thoughts or feelings that it invokes in you.
4. Proceed to the second card, repeating the same process of thoughtful observation.
5. With both cards in your awareness, contemplate how they interact. Do they share a common theme? Are there elements that seem to be in conflict? Is there a narrative that surfaces when you consider them together?
6. Open your journal and record your observations, reflections, and any perceived narrative, considering each card individually and together. Review your notes and ponder how the insights you've gained could apply to your own journey or a particular situation in your life.

Card Coupling Contemplation

WHAT THIS CAN LOOK LIKE

To demonstrate what this looks like, I am currently working with the Rider-Waite-Smith deck. The cards that I draw are the Devil and the Lovers.

First, I turn over the Devil card. An ominous figure reminiscent of the classic depiction of the devil presides over this scene. The figure sits on a half cube, perhaps symbolizing an incomplete understanding or limited perspective based on materialism, since the cube is the shape of the element of earth. A man and a woman stand beneath, chained loosely to the cube. The man and woman are eerily similar to the lovers in the Lovers card. Their tails, a flame for the man and a grape bunch for the woman, indicate their primal passions and desires. The card in its entirety paints a picture of bondage, materialism, and the darker aspects of our nature that we are tied to but can free ourselves from, if only we choose to.

Next, I turn over the Lovers card. This card is a stark contrast to the Devil card. An angel with wings spread wide hovers in the sky, while below, a man and a woman stand in the Garden of Eden. This card embodies harmony, unity, and a moral crossroads. It suggests the necessity of making a choice with potential long-term implications—often a choice between virtue and vice.

The Lovers card echoes the concept of connection but in a different context—that of love, mutual respect, and using our free will, unlike the chained companions in the Devil card. Comparing the two, it's intriguing to observe that both cards feature a man and a woman with an otherworldly figure above them. This immediately signals the presence of a relationship or a connection between the two cards. However, the nature of these connections differs drastically. The Devil card represents unhealthy attachments and bondage, while the Lovers card signifies pure connection based on love and respect. Moreover, both cards present a moral crossroads. The Devil card often asks us to examine our life for unhealthy habits, dependencies, or relationships, signifying a need to liberate ourselves. The Lovers card can represent the need to make a choice in accordance with our highest selves, often involving personal values or relationships.

EXERCISE 25

SEEING THE CARDS AS PANELS FOR INTERPRETATION

A helpful way to perceive the interaction between tarot cards in a spread is to imagine them as individual panels in a comic strip. Each card, much like a panel, stands alone in its narrative yet also interweaves seamlessly into the larger, interconnected storyline. This viewpoint can enrich your understanding of the dialogue that occurs within a tarot spread. In a comic strip, every panel carries its own plot point, contributing a unique piece of the overall story. Similarly, each tarot card brings forward a distinct message. However, the card's full significance becomes truly clear when it's interpreted in the context of surrounding cards. Just as the meaning of a comic panel is enhanced by the panels around it, the narrative of a tarot card is influenced by its neighboring cards.

Reading tarot cards in a linear fashion, as you would a comic strip, can help you understand the progression of the reading and the journey it's mapping out. The dynamic interplay between the cards can reveal shifts in energy, highlight points of tension or harmony, and provide a clear timeline of events or inner transformations. Each card's position influences and shapes its interpretation, and viewing them in sequential order can bring to light valuable insights that might remain hidden if cards were read individually and as if they were disconnected. This approach enhances your ability to decode the complex symbolic language of tarot and helps weave together a coherent, insightful narrative from your readings.

1. Lay out your tarot cards in your chosen spread, ensuring they're positioned in a row so that as you gaze upon them it creates a linear storyline like panels in a comic strip.
2. Do a quick scan of the entire spread, as you would when you first glance through a comic strip. Note any dominant energies or themes that immediately catch your attention.
3. Go back to the beginning of your spread and begin to examine each card individually. Think of each card as a separate panel in a comic strip, each with its own narrative or message.
4. While looking at each card, also take into account its neighboring cards. Consider how the energy or message of one card might be influenced by those adjacent to it.
5. Pay attention to the sequence of the cards as you move along the spread. Look for shifts in mood, tempo, or action that could indicate a progression or journey.
6. Once you've closely examined each card, take a moment to step back and view the entire spread as a cohesive whole.
7. Imagine what a transitional tarot card between two adjacent cards in the spread might look like. If you had to fill in a "missing panel" that would make the transition between these cards smoother or more comprehensible, what symbols or themes would that card hold?
8. Now compare your initial impressions from your quick scan with the more detailed understanding you've gained. See if your initial thoughts still hold or if you've discovered new themes that change your understanding of the reading.
9. Take some time to write down your observations, the larger story you've perceived, and any other insights you've gained.
10. Now spend a moment in reflection. Meditate on the broader narrative you've discerned and think about any actionable insights or revelations that have emerged.

∞

Seeing the Cards as Panels

WHAT THIS CAN LOOK LIKE

One instance stands out vividly when I turned to a three-card tarot reading for personal guidance during a challenging time. The cards that unfolded before me were the Five of Cups, the Sun, and the Ace of Wands. In the first card, the Five of Cups, I found myself reflected in the figure mourning over three spilled cups. Similar to the beginning of a film, this card established the narrative of the story that was about to unravel. It painted a picture of my past, one colored by a sense of loss and disappointment. But, as in life, stories evolve and scenes shift. The Sun, the second card, represented a dramatic change of scene in the narrative, mirroring a transition in my own journey. If the Five of Cups was a rainy afternoon, the Sun was the clear, radiant dawn of a new day. The Sun card brought forward a joyful child riding a horse under a glowing sun—a stark contrast to the figure mourning in the previous card. This transition suggested an inner transformation had taken place: the figure had moved past the disappointments represented by the spilled cups, embraced the lessons those experiences offered, and experienced newfound joy and optimism.

The narrative then progressed to the Ace of Wands, signifying another shift in the story's landscape. From the sunflower fields of the previous scene, we are now introduced to a hand emerging from the clouds and holding a budding wand. This transition marked the journey's future stage, representing a promising start infused with creative passion and energy. This card painted a scene where the warm sun had nurtured the growth and maturation of the Ace of Wands, signifying the potential for vibrant beginnings. The joy and vitality of the Sun had sparked a creative rebirth, leading to the passionate pursuits symbolized by the Ace of Wands.

By viewing these cards as distinct scenes within a broader narrative, I was better able to understand the progression of my path. It was helpful to see how each scene seamlessly led to the next, illustrating a clear transition from a period of loss (Five of Cups) to a phase of joy (the Sun) and culminating in a bright future of creative possibilities (Ace of Wands). It was as if the sorrow had been necessary rainfall that watered the ground for the sunflowers to emerge in that card, and then perhaps one of those sunflowers was then harvested for the wand to wield through maturity. Each step of the journey was necessary.

EXERCISE 26

SCRYING WITH THE TAROT

If you're unfamiliar with the term, scrying is an ancient divination technique that usually entails gazing into a reflective surface or object to gain spiritual insights or predict future events. Scrying can be done with clouds, foliage of plants in the wild, or pretty much anything where you can begin seeing images. This practice, used by various cultures globally, is based on the concept that the images in the object disclose hidden information interpretable by the viewer. In tarot card reading, scrying techniques can be utilized to amplify intuition and access the subconscious mind, allowing card images to move or transform in the observer's mind's eye. By liberating their imagination and entering a meditative state, readers can visualize unfolding narratives or watch as static images transform into completely different forms. While scrying is recognized as a psychic art, it equally involves contemplation of what's being observed, especially when it comes to tarot. This dynamic process intertwines intuition and introspection. Scrying facilitates a deeper understanding of what the subconscious brings forward that may not be immediately apparent in the intended symbolism or traditional meanings of the cards.

1. Shuffle your tarot deck with a question or intention in mind, then draw a card.
2. Notice the colors, symbols, and images. Don't rush to interpret them just yet. Instead, allow your eyes to relax and lose focus slightly as you continue to gaze at the card.
3. As you gaze at the card, let your imagination run free. Allow the images to move, change, or evolve in your mind's eye. Don't restrict what you see—the image might morph into a completely different scene, characters might appear and interact, or new symbols might emerge.
4. Pay attention to any feelings, thoughts, or insights that arise during this process. Rather than analyzing these impressions, just observe them as they come.
5. When you feel prepared, gently transition out of your meditative state. Grab your trusty tarot journal and write down what you saw, felt, and thought, as well as any intuitive insights you received. Reflect on your scrying experience. How do the images and feelings relate to your question or intention? Do they give you a new perspective on the card's traditional meaning? Take your time to process and integrate your insights.

Scrying with the Tarot

WHAT THIS CAN LOOK LIKE

One day, while conducting a tarot session, I drew the Ace of Cups card for a querent. Typically, this card speaks to me of the beginning of emotional outpourings, intuition, and spiritual gifts. But that day, as I gazed at the card and allowed my imagination to wander with the visuals on the card, the imagery began to dance and transform. The dove that usually adorned the top of the card hovering over the cup began to morph, its white feathers turning a brilliant shade of yellow. As I watched, entranced, the transformed yellow bird gracefully flew down, alighting just next to an ornate vintage birdcage formed by the water flowing from the cup. The bird looked content, chirping happily, yet it remained outside the cage. I felt compelled to share this vision with my querent, asking, "Does a tiny yellow bird, perhaps next to a beautiful vintage birdcage, mean anything to you?"

The reaction I received was unexpected. My querent's eyes widened with astonishment. They admitted that their beloved canary had escaped a few days prior, and despite searching everywhere, they had been unable to locate it. They were consumed with worry, fearing their pet was lost or worse. But the true surprise was when they mentioned an old, ornate birdcage they had stored on a shelf in their closet, which wasn't the one the canary had vanished from. Guided by the vision, I gently suggested they might want to inspect that particular closet or its surroundings. A few days passed before I received a jubilant call from my querent. Taking my advice to heart, they had found their canary chirping merrily inside the same closet that vintage birdcage was in. While it wasn't directly next to the cage, as in my scrying session with the card, it was in the same closet with the door closed, and they had no idea how it got there.

4
∞

Intuitive Tarot

The term *intuition* often gets tossed around rather casually, without much thought behind the word. Like many other people, I first heard this term within phrases such as "women's intuition" and "mother's intuition." These phrases made it seem like intuitive abilities were something only women or mothers had. This stereotype often surfaced in the tarot shops where I've worked as a reader. While it's one thing to prefer a reader who you feel can relate to your life experiences based on gender, it's quite another to dismiss male readers on the grounds that "men aren't intuitive or psychic," which is something that folks would sometimes have the audacity to tell me. On the upside, I consider it a bullet dodged; it's hard to offer a meaningful reading to someone who isn't open to what you have to say in the first place.

Everyone has intuition because, at our core, we're animals—yes, highly evolved human animals, but animals nonetheless. We often overlook this fundamental aspect of our nature, our primal lower self, which leads us to disconnect from our own intuitive senses. Instinct and intuition are so closely linked that sometimes they're inseparable. Our human instincts, fine-tuned through millennia of evolution, feed directly into our intuitive abilities. When we talk about someone being intuitive in a practical sense, we're really highlighting their natural, instinctual prowess. Phrases like saying someone "took to it like a duck to water" underline this idea; they suggest that just as a duckling instinctively knows how to swim when it hits the water, some people have a natural knack for certain skills or insights.

Kids have a natural knack for intuition, often being more attuned to their imaginative and instinctual sides than many adults. To put it to the test, next time you need some guidance, pull a tarot card and show it to a child you're close to. Ask them about their perceptions of the card, how they imagine the scenario in the image unfolding, and what they predict might happen next. Pay close attention because their fresh take on the card can offer surprising insights. Don't underestimate what comes out of the mouths of babes. This childlike approach captures the essence of intuitive tarot readings, which rely on gut feeling and creativity rather than any formal knowledge of tarot symbolism.

But there's so much more to intuitive readings than just ignoring the companion book that came with your tarot book. As mentioned before, the lower self naturally absorbs energy from our surrounding environment. It processes this energy as emotions felt in the body, physical sensations such as a gut feeling, goosebumps, or the vague feeling that someone is watching you, to relay it to your middle self as information. For these reasons, T. Thorn Coyle aptly refers to the lower self as "the Sticky One" in their book *Evolutionary Witchcraft.*[10] Our lower selves are essentially the energetic lint roller of our selfhood, absorbing all the energetic debris it comes into contact with on an instinctual, emotional, and intuitive level.

Confusing Intuition with Trauma Responses and Biases

Intuition, while a valuable manner for gaining insights, should also be distinguished from other factors that can cloud our judgment. Biases, prejudices, and trauma responses held in our subconscious can unwittingly shape our thoughts and decisions. Especially deceptive are trauma responses, as they can trigger intense emotional responses that can mimic intuition. If an individual has trauma associated with specific scenarios or people, their intuitive clarity may be overshadowed by feelings of fear or anxiety, making it hard to access their true inner wisdom. For example, if you've been cheated on in

10 Coyle, *Evolutionary Witchcraft*, 46.

a relationship, this is going to greatly affect your ability to stay a clear and unbiased conduit to intuition in a reading if the querent you're reading for is discussing the affair they're having, which is a scenario that comes up regularly when reading for the public. In these situations, addressing and healing the root trauma can be beneficial before leaning on intuition.

Biases and prejudices can affect our ability to tap into and trust our intuition. These biases, deeply embedded due to our cultural, social, or personal backgrounds and experiences, can skew our perception and understanding of the world. For instance, most people have an inherently differing yet strong response toward a billionaire versus a homeless person, influenced by preconceived notions, their personal background, and their own relationship with the concept of wealth.

An idea that captures this well is when people give advice or proverbs based on appearance, such as not to trust someone with teeth whiter than the whites of their eyes. This strikes me as a super flawed way to judge someone's character. There's many medical reasons why someone's teeth or eyes may be the color that they are. This says zero about who you are as a person. This kind of snap judgment is in the same ballpark as thinking less groomed people are immoral because "cleanliness is next to godliness" or that tattoos and piercings mean you're a rebel or unprofessional. It blows my mind that people still judge women for their makeup choices or clothes they choose to wear or think you can tell someone's mental or emotional state just by their weight, yet people still do. I've also seen people judging others solely based on a disability, as if it's some kind of character summary, which is another level of messed up. But these are biases and prejudices people often hold, sometimes consciously and sometimes unconsciously.

These sorts of biases make me question the tarot reader way more than any person being judged by their appearance. If they're judging someone's trustworthiness based on the color of their teeth, I can't take their tarot readings or insights too seriously. It's incredibly superficial to assess someone's character based on their appearance. Making a statement like this exposes their limited perspective and makes me wonder what other biases they may harbor that could cloud their judgment or tarot readings. How can I trust their guidance or interpretation of the cards when they're willing to make sweeping judgments based on appearances? It undermines their credibility as a reader in my eyes. Their judgmental attitude raises red flags about their ethical approach to tarot reading and guidance and makes me question whether they can offer advice that's unbiased and compassionate.

By acknowledging and confronting our biases, we can foster a clearer, more accurate worldview and better utilize the insights offered by our intuition and the cards. We need to separate genuine intuition from influences that may obscure our judgment and perception. By fostering discernment and introspection, we can overcome these obstacles and unlock our intuition's full potential in tarot readings and everyday life.

Identifying intuition amidst trauma responses, biases, and prejudices can be complex and difficult, but various methods can aid this process. One approach involves stepping back and critically evaluating feelings and sensations triggered by a specific situation or decision. True intuition often manifests as a serene, clear internal understanding, distinct from a heightened emotional reaction. While both involve emotions, the feelings associated with intuition are usually different in nature. Intuition tends to bring with it a sense of calm certainty and quiet knowing that is solid and steady, unlike the fluctuating intensity that can characterize emotional responses. This nuanced difference can help distinguish genuine intuitive insight from strong emotional reactions. By honing the ability to differentiate between these reaction types, we can better recognize genuine intuition from trauma responses or other emotional reactions.

Another method is practicing self-awareness and introspection. This involves allocating time to scrutinize our biases and prejudices as well as question our own assumptions and beliefs about them. By doing so, we can ensure our intuitive readings are free from personal distortions and truly reflect the wisdom that tarot has to offer to the querent. Recognizing and addressing our biases can make us more aware of how they may distort our judgment and perception. Seeking diverse perspectives and experiences can also be beneficial. This might include immersing ourselves in various cultures, belief systems, social statuses, and thought processes. By expanding our worldview, we can better understand the intricacies of different situations and access our authentic inner guidance more readily.

In tarot readings, it's beneficial to come with an open mind and be nonjudgmental of the person we're reading for, ready to challenge our assumptions and biases. This could involve taking time to reflect on each card's meanings and symbols and assessing our reactions to them. We want to avoid projecting our own qualities, traits, and assumptions onto the person we're reading for, as this could cloud our judgment and perception. By doing this, we can gain much more of a nuanced understanding of the messages the cards convey and more effectively distinguish genuine intuition from other interfering factors. This self-reflection and awareness process is key to our personal and spiritual growth, enabling us to become more conscious, compassionate individuals and insightful tarot readers.

Your Home Frequency

To better understand your emotional and intuitive energy, having a reference point can be useful, especially when it comes to distinguishing a trauma response from an intuitive hit. A technique called "the home frequency," developed by my husband Devin and detailed in his book *The Witch's Book of Power*, is one I frequently use.[11] The home frequency refers to a state where we can access our inner capabilities and embodies a natural way of living magickally. It promotes stability and tranquility, essential elements for our well-being. This state serves as a barometer for psychics and mediums to identify anomalies or deviations. Moreover, it acts as a foundation for different consciousness levels. The home frequency also offers protection by enabling us to identify our own energy and exclude anything foreign. Nevertheless, tarot readers should be mindful that other protective measures should not be overlooked.

11 Hunter, *The Witch's Book of Power*, 31–33.

Tuning in to your home frequency is like checking your emotional and spiritual "home base" before and after you do something like a tarot reading. If you check in with this home base before a reading, it's like setting a stable starting point. This helps you better pick up on any energies or messages coming through the cards because you know where you're starting from. After the reading, checking in again helps you reset. Consider it as a means to purify and reset your energetic state, much like washing your hands before preparing a meal. It removes any residual energy from the reading before moving on with your day. As for protection, knowing your home frequency helps you spot when something's off or if an energy doesn't belong to you. It's similar to being familiar with how your home should appear, enabling you to notice if anything is misplaced or missing. This awareness allows you to take precautions if you sense anything amiss.

EXERCISE 27

FINDING YOUR HOME FREQUENCY

Understanding your home frequency will enhance your abilities as a psychic, intuitive, and empath, helping you distinguish what is and isn't part of your energy or emotions. With time and practice, aim to be able to tune in to this frequency at will just by thinking about it. Be aware that mastering this exercise might take time and practice, but it will enable you to recognize when you're out of alignment with your personal home frequency almost immediately.

1. Begin by finding a comfortable position.
2. Close your eyes and take deep and measured breaths.
3. As you inhale, visualize the divine energy that surrounds us entering and filling your body.
4. On exhaling, imagine all your tensions and negative emotions being expelled from your body.
5. When your mind starts to wander and thoughts emerge, simply acknowledge them and allow them to drift away, like windswept clouds.

6. Recall memories where you've felt confident, happy, loved, creative, powerful, and self-assured.
7. Allow the emotions associated with these memories to bubble up within you.
8. Feel this positive energy flowing through you, washing away any negativity or barriers.
9. Understand that this energy is resetting your vibrations, leaving you feeling rejuvenated and empowered.
10. Visualize this energy reset as a return to your personal factory settings.
11. Consider this energy as your home frequency. Visualize it as a light radiating within and around you.
12. Use your will and imagination to expand this light from your body and aura into your surroundings.

How Intuition Feels

During a tarot reading, you may notice certain physical sensations or feelings that provide valuable insight into the reading. These sensations might include chest pressure, stomach fluttering, or tingling. Each of these sensations carries its own symbolic meaning, helping you interpret the cards more deeply. For instance, tightness in the chest is often associated with emotions that suggest anxiety, fear, or uncertainty, while a fluttering stomach might signify anticipation or excitement. Physical sensations are part of our body's emotional language, giving us a clearer picture of our emotional information during a reading. Recognizing these sensations and what they symbolize is part of developing emotional awareness. This involves mindfulness of our physical responses and the emotions they represent. One effective method to cultivate this awareness is through mindfulness meditation, focusing on these sensations without judgment. Engaging in mindfulness practices enables us to establish a deeper connection with our emotions and the accompanying physical sensations they bring forth. Over time, this heightened awareness can deepen our understanding of ourselves and the messages coming through in tarot readings. As we grow more comfortable trusting our body's intuition and the insights it offers, we also become more confident tarot readers.

To enhance your emotional awareness, you can also focus on your bodily sensations in your daily experiences. The next time you're faced with uncomfortable emotions, pay attention to your body. Are you sensing tightness in your chest, a quickening heartbeat, or a knot in your stomach? While you should be doing this with all your emotions, uncomfortable emotions tend to be the loudest. Through increased mindfulness of these sensations, you can start deciphering the signals your emotions convey and how your body reacts to them. This can be especially helpful in tarot readings, where bodily sensations and emotions can provide insights into the cards' messages and guidance. Through this awareness we become more attuned to our body's emotional language, and over time we understand it better and better.

EXERCISE 28

HOLLOWING YOURSELF TO FEEL YOUR INTUITION

A great practice to strengthen your connection with your intuitive self involves creating a mental state of emotional openness, essentially emptying your mind and setting aside preconceived notions. This approach paves the way for intuition to surface unobstructed. The practice begins with discarding any preconceptions or projections based on external appearances or logical evaluations. By quieting the chatter of the conscious mind, you create a space where intuitive understanding can blossom. In this state of openness, you're unmoored from external perceptions or cognitive biases, enabling you to tap into a deeper level of awareness. From this state, pay attention to the emotions and physical sensations that naturally emerge. These feelings may not align with your conscious expectations, but they are invaluable in offering intuitive insights. They serve as a conduit to your lower self, that instinctive part of you that operates on a deep, intuitive level of understanding.

Despite whether they fit into a logical narrative at that moment, respecting these feelings and sensations is key. This practice not only strengthens your connection with intuition but also sets a solid groundwork for other intuitive pursuits, such as tarot readings. It allows you to see beyond the visible surface and tune in to the energetic and emotional realities that might otherwise stay concealed. This practice proves particularly valuable when working with psychic senses, allowing for greater clarity and precision in interpreting psychic information. When it comes to mediumship, this method becomes absolutely essential. As mediumship requires a deep level of intuitive connection and openness, creating this mental state of receptivity is critical to receive and accurately interpret messages from the spirit realm. The following step-by-step guide focuses on the idea of emptying yourself, allowing you to establish a connection with your lower self and enhance your intuitive abilities. This process emphasizes the concept of becoming empty or hollow, providing a conduit for intuitive messages to flow through without obstruction. It encourages a sense of openness and receptiveness where intuition can freely communicate. Consistent practice will make this process easier and foster a stronger bond with the intuition of your lower self.

1. Close your eyes and notice your breath.
2. Inhale deeply through your nose and exhale slowly through your mouth. This deep, mindful breathing calms the mind and shifts focus inward.
3. As you exhale, envision any preconceived notions, judgments, or assumptions being expelled from your body with each breath. Picture these thoughts being released into the air.
4. As your mind quietens, envision it as an open, expanding space. With each breath, this space grows larger and more receptive.
5. In this state of openness, turn your focus onto any emotions or physical sensations that naturally surface. Don't judge or analyze these feelings; just notice them as they emerge.
6. Recognize these sensations and emotions as intuitive messages from your lower self. What do they convey to you?
7. If you wish to extend this practice, draw a tarot card and observe any emotions or physical sensations that arise. What insights does your lower self offer about the card?
8. Once you're ready, ground yourself again and then gently bring your focus back to your surroundings and open your eyes.

EXERCISE 29

BUILDING YOUR EMOTIONAL DATABASE

The purpose of this exercise is to explore the emotional energy of a randomly drawn tarot card and conjure that emotion within yourself, creating an emotional database that associates each card with specific emotional states. It will deepen your connection to the tarot cards and enhance your emotional awareness. Emotions are complex and can be influenced by personal experiences, so there's no right or wrong answer—only your unique emotional insight.

1. Shuffle the tarot deck with the intention of understanding the emotional energy of the drawn card. Draw a card.
2. Observe the card's imagery, symbolism, colors, and any impressions it gives you.
3. Reflect on the emotions the card evokes in you and the feelings or moods you associate with it.
4. Use your intuition and knowledge of the card's traditional meanings to deepen your understanding of its emotional energy.
5. Bringing your attention inward, close your eyes.
6. Imagine the emotional energy of the tarot card flowing into your being, surrounding you like a warm and comforting aura.
7. Experience and embody the emotions associated with the card without judgment, allowing yourself to feel it intensely.
8. Open your eyes. Reflect on the emotional impressions you've just had.
9. Write down your observations, feelings, insights, personal connections, and any triggered memories from the exercise.
10. Repeat this exercise regularly with a new tarot card each time.
11. Document the emotions you conjured and experienced for each card to build your emotional database. Notice patterns and associations between certain tarot cards and specific emotional states. Use this practice as a tool for enhancing your emotional awareness.

Intuiting Information About the Person You're Reading

Listening to your gut feelings can offer an immediate and direct sense of what is going on with the person for whom you're reading. This intuitive gut reaction often comes as a first impression or an immediate understanding that transcends logic or reason. It can highlight important aspects that need attention, such as potential conflicts, hidden desires, or emerging patterns. These sensations can act as indicators of the emotional and psychological atmosphere in a person's life. Emotions, too, are integral in utilizing intuition during a tarot reading. Empathy helps us tune in to the person's emotional state and gain a better understanding of their experiences through direct experience. Any feelings of joy, sadness, fear, or excitement that surface during a reading can mirror the emotional landscape of the individual you are reading for. These emotions can provide clues to their emotional well-being and can guide the interpretation of the tarot spread. By attuning to your gut feelings, physical sensations, and emotions, you can connect more deeply with the person you're reading for, which allows psychic information to potentially flow more easily.

Intuiting Information About a Person

WHAT THIS CAN LOOK LIKE

A few years back, I was gearing up for a tarot reading with a woman who, at first glance, seemed to radiate happiness and stability. Her contagious laughter filled the room, and her vibrant demeanor painted a picture of someone who had life figured out. Her seemingly endless tales of success and resilience could inspire anyone who listened. As we began the session, I was suddenly hit by a wave of exhaustion. I brushed it aside and continued with the reading, but I couldn't ignore the growing feeling of sadness that enveloped me in her presence. This intuitive sensation was at odds with the cheerful exterior she presented. I felt a clear discordance between what was being projected and what was resonating on an emotional level. As I shuffled the tarot deck,

I trusted my instincts and communicated what I was intuitively perceiving. With gentle care, I relayed my sense of her deep-seated fatigue and concealed sorrow that contradicted her vivacious exterior. Her reaction was immediate. Her smile suddenly faded. With tears in her eyes, she confessed that she had been skillfully hiding her overwhelming feelings of sadness and weariness behind a facade of joy and strength.

The tarot reading that followed astonishingly echoed my intuitive insights. Cards like the Ten of Wands and Four of Cups indicated overburden, discontent, and emotional fatigue, mirroring her internal struggles. With her feelings so accurately reflected in the cards, she felt genuinely seen and acknowledged beyond the mask she wore. The cards offered guidance toward self-care, reaching out for support, and the importance of acknowledging her true feelings. She left the session with a sense of validation and a road map to address her emotional well-being. The reading, complemented by the recognition of her actual emotional state, became the catalyst for her to seek professional help and prioritize self-care. This experience shows how trusting these intuitive insights can peel back the layers to reveal a deeper understanding beyond surface appearances.

Intuiting a Card's Meaning Among Countless Potentials

Intuition acts as a guiding light within the broad spectrum of meanings that tarot cards encompass. Considering that each card holds countless interpretations, understanding their messages can feel akin to traversing a complex maze, yet it's within these paths of interpretation where our intuition can shine a light on the most fitting route. Our intuition is akin to an internal compass, guiding us toward the interpretation most compatible with the situation. By paying attention to the intuition of our emotions and physical sensations, we can sift through countless potential meanings and pinpoint the message that truly aligns with the reading's energy. This process leans on our natural ability to perceive beyond the physical world's appearances, sensing the interwoven energetic and emotional layers of our reality. As we nurture our relationship with our intuition, we develop a unique intuitive language. It's through this personal language that the tarot conveys its wisdom in deeply personal and meaningful ways. In other words, you'll start linking certain feelings and sensations with different concepts that offer insight into the reading. This process can clarify what a drawn card signifies versus its other potential meanings. Let's consider a past reading of mine to illustrate how this might look.

Intuiting a Card's Meaning

WHAT THIS CAN LOOK LIKE

A tarot reading I conducted for a querent in Los Angeles stands as a great example of the critical role of intuition in tarot interpretation. This reading showcased how intuition can not only enrich the tarot reading process but also reveal incredibly precise and personally relevant insights. As we initiated the reading, I intentionally aligned with my home frequency. Deep, mindful breaths helped ground my energy, and I set the intention to be a clear conduit for the reading that was about to unfold. As I shuffled the tarot deck, a distinct sensation appeared—an almost effervescent tingle radiating from my heart center—an undeniable signal that my intuition was primed and ready to guide me. Upon laying out the cards, a flood of emotions rushed through me. The Two of Swords made its presence known. Usually signaling a moment of decision or a crossroads, this card, in this context, brought forth an unexpected feeling of tranquility. This suggested to me that, though at a crossroads, my querent possessed a deep inner peace regarding their path. The Seven of Cups appeared, typically indicative of illusion and choices, yet as I touched this card, a clear and sharp sensation coursed through my gut. Instead of the card's typical interpretation of confusion or illusion, my intuition guided me toward a different understanding. This sensation of clarity suggested my querent, rather than being lost in an illusion of indecision, was realizing the importance of not limiting their ambitions or dreams.

The King of Pentacles emerged as the next card I drew. As I focused on this card, a grounding sensation washed over me—a sense of being deeply rooted. This suggested to me a strong foundation in my querent's life and a readiness to expand upon it. Using these emotional and bodily cues as guidance, I allowed my intuition and imagination to paint a vivid picture, providing a context for my querent's situation, which suggested a decisive moment where they had the choice to leave behind an unsatisfying past and venture toward their true passion. The Two of Swords, coupled with the tranquility I felt, pointed to my querent's peace regarding an imminent decision. The Seven of Cups, along with the gut feeling of clarity, hinted at their capability to see past illusions and recognize the importance of not limiting their dreams. The King of Pentacles, paired with the grounding sensation, symbolized their readiness to grow upon an already strong foundation.

Connecting the Puzzle Pieces of Intuition with the Cards

The intersection where intuition meets the symbolism of tarot cards is nothing short of remarkable; it's where it really becomes powerful. Here your intuition serves a dual role: it helps you understand the querent's circumstances and navigates you through the potential meanings of the cards. This is a conversation involving your intuition, the querent's energy, and the tarot's symbolic language. As a child, my initial attempts at readings were rather clumsy. I grappled with understanding the mechanics of tarot and struggled to create coherent readings. However, the process was essential, as working with tarot cards can kindle and enhance one's intuition. There's a transformative element to engaging with tarot—an effect that perhaps is tied to the collective energy, or egregore, associated with the tarot, which is a type of thoughtform I will explore in more depth later. Despite early struggles, the journey of working with tarot turned out to be a catalyst for intuitive awakening and understanding. Here's the story of my first accurate reading, which was due to tapping into my intuition without even realizing it yet.

Connecting the Puzzle Pieces of Intuition with the Cards

WHAT THIS CAN LOOK LIKE

Way back during my freshman year of high school, a friend approached me and asked for a tarot reading. Eager to practice my burgeoning skills, I readily agreed. We nestled in a quiet outdoor spot during our lunch hour and I began the session with the shuffling of the tarot deck. As I started laying out the cards, something about her energy felt different to me. Without a clear reason why, I playfully asked if she had gotten a haircut or changed anything physically. Her response was a simple no, which left me puzzled as the subtle change in her energy was palpable. Trusting my intuition, I pressed on. As the cards unfolded, I fell into my usual routine, buried in the guidebook, parroting the meanings of each card in an almost mechanical fashion. Then something extraordinary happened. The Empress card, pregnant on her throne; the Sun card, depicting a gleeful child on a white pony; and the Six of Cups, with its nostalgic innocence and memories of simpler times between two children, seemingly whispered an intertwined narrative. At first it seemed ridiculous, but trusting the sudden intuitive spark, I hesitantly voiced my interpretation. "I'm not sure why, but these cards seem to be hinting toward pregnancy. Perhaps I made a mistake somewhere."

I half expected her to laugh off my audacious prediction, but her serious expression told a different story. My friend confessed that she was, in fact, pregnant but for obvious reasons was keeping it a secret. The revelation left me speechless as this was something entirely new and delicate to handle for me. But she trusted me with her secret, confiding that she had been seeing someone privately for the past year, and a late period followed by a pregnancy test confirmed her fears. It was an incredibly overwhelming and humbling moment for both of us. I realized then that something magickal had happened during that reading. The cards, quite literally, had spoken to me. I could discern patterns, relationships, and messages from them. It was as if a veil had been lifted from my mind. I could finally engage with the tarot on a deeper level. That moment solidified my bond with the tarot deck I had used for the reading. The human emotions and situations depicted in this deck resonated with me, and, for the first time, I felt I could comprehend the depth of the tarot language.

But the revelations of the day were not over yet. Driven by the wisdom of the cards and a surge of intuitive guidance, I found myself advising my friend on how to approach her situation, especially in breaking the news to her conservative parents—and, to our surprise, the advice worked! Everything eventually fell into place for her, much to our relief. This experience marked a significant turning point in my journey with tarot. I had started the day as a novice reading out of a guidebook but ended it with an understanding of the intuitive depths tarot could reach. I felt like I had transformed from a mere fledgling card reader parroting meanings into a conduit for meaningful, intuitive advice. This was my first instance of harnessing the tarot's power and using it to provide relevant, impactful guidance, and it certainly wasn't the last.

EXERCISE 30

EMPATH DEVELOPMENT WITH TAROT

This exercise is an approach you can use to evaluate and enhance your intuitive skills, which involve sensing and understanding other people's emotions, by working with the tarot deck. This allows you to strengthen your empathic skills and also test to see how your development is progressing. This cooperative style of practice not only increases the fun factor but also allows you to sharpen your empathic intuitive skills.

1. Start by thoroughly shuffling your tarot deck. Draw a card from the deck but do not look at it yet.
2. Try to intuitively pick up on the emotions and vibes that the card carries.
3. Start asking yourself questions such as "What feelings am I getting from this card?" and "What kind of energy is the card radiating?"
4. After reflecting on these questions, flip the card over to see if your intuitive guesses align with the card's imagery.
5. To further test your empathic accuracy, repeat the process with multiple cards.
6. To make the empath test more exciting, team up with a partner. In this version, your partner should look at a card and mentally channel the emotions and energy it conveys. As the participant, your goal is to tap into the emotional energy your partner is feeling and guess the card based on those sensations.

CHAPTER FOUR

The Ideomotor Effect and Pendulums

A pendulum, particularly in divination or dowsing, is a small weighted object suspended from a string or chain and able to swing freely in all directions. The weighted object can be crafted from various materials like crystals, metals, or wood. The string or chain's length varies, but many users prefer a length that allows the pendulum to swing effortlessly just above a surface when held by a relaxed arm. Often employed for spiritual guidance, decision-making, or sensing energetic fields, the pendulum's movements are thought to be influenced by subtle energies, unconscious physical movements, or spiritual beings. These movements provide responses to asked questions or proposed tasks. Typically, these responses are interpreted according to previously established swing directions, such as back and forth, side to side, or circular motions.

Pendulums provide a tangible way to connect with one's intuition. This connection is largely due to a fascinating phenomenon known as the ideomotor effect or response. The ideomotor effect refers to involuntary and unconscious motor behavior—in other words, our bodies making subtle movements without our conscious control or even awareness. In the context of using a pendulum, the ideomotor effect is at play when the pendulum moves or swings seemingly on its own, though it's actually being influenced by tiny, subconscious muscle movements in the hand of the person holding it.

This interaction between our subconscious and physical bodies suggests that the pendulum isn't operating independently but instead is reflecting deeper intuitive knowledge of our body's wisdom that may not be immediately accessible to our conscious minds. By tapping into this inner wisdom, a pendulum becomes a conduit for the user's lower self to communicate and answer questions that the conscious mind might struggle to articulate. Using a pendulum is a way to listen to your own intuition through your subconscious mind. It allows your lower self to speak through the ideomotor phenomenon, bypassing the chatter of the conscious mind to access deeper truths.

Pendulums and Their Application in Tarot

Pendulums can be a beneficial tool during a tarot reading, offering additional depth and enhancing the insights obtained. One of the key ways pendulums can assist is by aiding clarification. There can be times when a tarot card's message may seem ambiguous and not be straightforward. Here, a pendulum can step in. You can gain a clearer understanding of the card's specific meaning within the context of the reading by using it to ask yes or no questions regarding the card's potential interpretations. Pendulums can also be used to select the cards for the reading. Some tarot readers hover the pendulum over a laid-out deck, watching for a particular movement that they've designated as a sign to choose a card. This approach allows the subconscious mind to play a role in the selection process, possibly infusing more intuition into the reading. Pendulums can serve as tools for confirming readings. Think of them as offering a second opinion. If you've interpreted a tarot reading in a specific way, you can use a pendulum to verify if this interpretation aligns with your intuition. Pendulums are also considered sensitive to energy, though really it's just a way to tap into your body's knowledge via your lower self's intuition. Some tarot readers use pendulums to measure the energy surrounding a specific card. This helps discern whether the card's influence in the reading is strong or weak.

EXERCISE 31

CONNECTING WITH AND USING A PENDULUM WITH TAROT

Here we'll establish your unique communication style with a pendulum, an essential first step in harnessing this intuitive tool.

1. Begin the exercise by deciding on specific movements of the pendulum that will signify yes or no. You could interpret this as a clockwise spin for yes and a counterclockwise spin as no, or maybe a side-to-side swing indicates yes and a back-and-forth motion is no.

2. Once you have defined these movements, verify your communication style with the pendulum. To get the hang of it, you can start by asking the pendulum some easy yes or no questions that you already know the answers to. For example, you might ask something like "Is the sky blue?" or "Is today Wednesday?"
3. Observe the pendulum's responses to these questions. If the movements of the pendulum match with the yes or no movements you defined earlier, then your communication style has been successfully determined. If not, repeat steps 1 and 2 until the responses are consistent with your definitions.
4. Shuffle your deck as you would normally. While shuffling, focus your energy and intentions on the deck, asking it to work in sync with the pendulum.
5. Draw your tarot spread as usual. Each card serves as a focus point for your intuitive energies. Don't interpret the cards yet.
6. Hold your pendulum above the deck. Ask it to align its energies with the deck by saying something as simple as "Pendulum, please align your energy with this tarot deck to reveal deeper insights." Observe if the pendulum displays your predefined yes movement, signaling a successful energy alignment.
7. Move the pendulum above each card in the spread, one at a time. For each card, you can ask yes or no questions to delve deeper. For instance, for the Lovers card, you could ask, "Does this card indicate a decision I have to make soon?"
8. Sometimes the pendulum's answer may imply that a further layer of understanding is needed for a specific card. If so, draw a clarification card and hold the pendulum above it, repeating the inquiry process. For example, if the pendulum signals yes when you ask if the Death card signifies a literal end, you might ask, "Is this end related to a job?" when you hold it over the clarification card.
9. Once you've gone through each card and feel satisfied with the depth of insight gained, thank both your tarot deck and your pendulum for their guidance.

EXERCISE 32

FEELING THE TIMELINE DURING A TAROT READING

One of my absolute favorite techniques during a tarot reading uses a mixture of intuitive and psychic abilities through clairtangency. It's the perfect example of how intuition and psychism work in tandem. I see clairtangency as the sense that bridges the psychic clairs with intuition. During this technique, you'll be using your intuitive faculties to gain psychic information. In other words, you're going to be tapping into your lower self to perceive psychic information. By psychic, again, I mean information that isn't present in the environment but pertains to instances where there's absolutely no way you could gain that specific information by any external means. This technique takes a lot of practice, but once you get the hang of it, it's a game changer. With it you'll be able to focus on specifics to make precise predictions.

Earlier—in exercise 16, Establishing Your Energetic Space—we projected energy as glowing light to draw our neon signs and claim our energetic space. We're going to be projecting that same energy to "draw" in the space before us and really zoom in on detailed information. As mentioned, this is particularly helpful when a querent wants a specific timeframe. I've never used this at the beginning of a reading or early on. Usually I employ this technique once the reading has been going on for a while, if not at the end. One reason is that these types of details won't come without getting the broader information first. Just like painting or drawing, you want to focus on the main outlines before going in to do detail work. The other reason is that halfway through your reading, you should be in a pretty good psychic flow. For this exercise, I'll use timing as an example, but there's so many other creative ways to utilize this technique during a reading.

1. Extend the finger of your dominant hand and visualize drawing a glowing horizontal line in the air before you. This line represents the span of your life.
2. At both ends of this horizontal line, draw vertical lines. These act as markers for the start and end points of your life's events.
3. As you contemplate the tarot reading and the specific event you're interested in, such as the onset of a new romantic relationship, make a request to your higher self. Ask for insight into the timing of this event.

4. Along your glowing horizontal line, draw additional vertical lines at intervals, increasing each interval by five years. These markers now subdivide your timeline into segments.

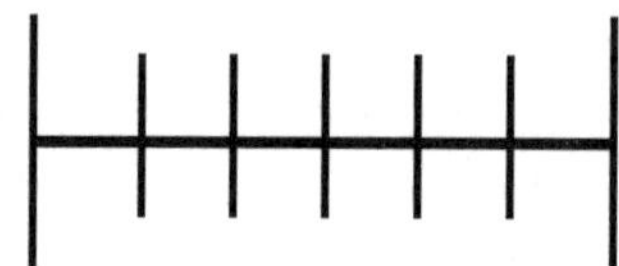

5. Use your nondominant hand to gently touch the timeline you've created, feeling it with your palm and fingers.
6. Pay close attention to tactile sensations as your hand glides over the various points. Look out for areas that feel different, such as warmth, a tingling, or a pulse of energy.
7. When you locate an area that feels different, use your thumb and pointer finger as if pinching that segment of the timeline, then unpinch your fingers to zoom, just like you'd zoom in on a touchscreen.
8. As it zooms in, the segment between two five-year markers now expands to show finer divisions of time.
9. On this zoomed-in segment, draw five more vertical lines to divide this section into individual years.
10. Once again, run your nondominant hand along these new markers. Notice any shifts in tactile sensations and focus on the line that feels distinct.
11. Zoom in one last time. Within that year, create four vertical markers to represent the four seasons—spring, summer, autumn, winter.
12. Pass your hand once more over these seasonal markers. Detect which season elicits a distinct sensation.
13. Relay your prediction, being clear that it's what you're picking up and not a prophecy set in stone.
14. Take a moment to thank your higher self for the guidance. Gently dissipate the glowing timeline with a wave of your hand.

∞

5

∞

Getting Out Of Your Own Way

The biggest obstacle in reading tarot that we have is ourselves. Questioning ourselves and our own ability is healthy to a degree. It keeps our egos in check. There's a point where every tarot reader will feel impostor syndrome, the feeling that they're a fraud or not a real tarot reader; I haven't met a single one who can honestly say they've never felt that at one time or another. My husband refers to this as the "itty bitty shitty committee" that likes to take up space in our head and fill us with doubts about ourselves and our abilities. Most of the time those voices are liars. They're a form of self-sabotage that come from feelings of inadequacy. So let me be crystal clear: there's no definitive path to becoming a real tarot reader. It's a misconception to believe that obtaining certification, attending tarot classes, gaining recognition, or immersing yourself in tarot communities alone will legitimize you as a tarot reader. Improving your tarot reading skills may involve various techniques, but ultimately you determine your own legitimacy as a tarot reader. Your proficiency as a tarot reader is measured by your ability to connect and read with the cards and offer helpful guidance that changes people's lives for the better, not by any other means.

Some people might feel a bit insecure about being unfamiliar with traditional card meanings and be overly reliant on intuitive interpretations of the cards. On the flip side, others might feel insecure about only knowing traditional card meanings and feeling disconnected from intuitive or psychic insights and interpretations during a reading. If this is you, I encourage you to spend time working on the area you're feeling insecure about.

Tarot is a lifelong study and exploration, and there will always be gaps in our knowledge. If there's a topic I'm not well versed in, instead of feeling like I'm inadequate as a tarot reader for not knowing these associations, I'll take time to read, reflect, and study the subject deeper until I feel familiar and comfortable with it. Once I'm comfortable with a concept I'm exploring, it's up to me to decide if I want to incorporate this new understanding into my tarot readings.

Impostor syndrome can also pop up its ugly head when we are overly familiar with a specific deck but unfamiliar with others. Some folks may know the Thoth deck like the back of their hand but feel they can't read with a Rider-Waite-Smith–based deck as the associations and card titles are often different. Likewise, a lot of Rider-Waite-Smith readers can look at a card from that deck and tell you exactly what the card means, but if you show them the same card from a Marseilles-based deck (especially a pip card), they are at a loss for what it could possibly be about. There also have been times where I'll be talking to another tarot reader and they'll mention a card by name, say the Seven of Cups, and I have no idea which card they're talking about in the moment, but if I saw the card visually, I would know exactly what the card means at first glance. If any of these resonate with you, you've got a couple of choices. You can either come to terms and learn to be comfortable with the fact that you have your comfort zone of tarot, the decks and areas that you are perfectly fine sticking with. Or, what I recommend is that you could slowly begin learning other decks and their cards with daily exercises like the ones I provided earlier such as the daily draw, comparative tarot exploration, and card coupling contemplation (exercises 22–24). In the end, the limitations of your knowledge are only the ones that you set on yourself.

When it comes to impostor syndrome about your psychic and intuitive abilities, I want to reemphasize that questioning what you receive every now and then is healthy and normal. This creates a sort of checks and balances as well as a sense of discernment. It's only a problem when that inner doubt becomes a constant occurrence. No amount of studying tarot meanings on its own will increase your ability of psychism. To become skilled, you'll simply have to dig in and get some practice under your belt. There's really no other shortcut. Experience comes with time and repetition. For the majority, it's a slow journey rather than an instant transformation. That's why it's a practice, just as you would practice any other art form. It's very rare, if ever, that a person will pick up a violin and play perfectly after only a few tries. Instead, the violinist will keep at it, knowing that the horrible noises coming from the violin will eventually become beautiful music over time with practice.

Take a Deep Breath

If you take a moment to reflect on any of your feelings of inadequacy as a reader, you'll likely find that they're all rooted in fear. Usually, fear of what others think. Whether that's about meeting the expectations of the person you're reading for, fear of conducting a reading that is inaccurate and will lead the querent greatly astray, or fear of not being as legit as other tarot readers or psychics. That last one, comparing yourself to other tarot readers or psychics, is one that I see so many fall prey to. In tarot, as in life, your main competition should be your own past performance. Aim to be a better reader today than you were yesterday. Tarot readers that you feel are better than you should be framed as inspiration for your own progress. Comparing your progress and ability to others is one of the fastest ways to hinder your own growth and advancement. We are all different. We all have different backgrounds, different relationships with our own intuition, psychic ability, spirituality, and divinity. There's no one set of standards or goals to meet for everyone. Therefore comparing yourself to others will only hurt your own progress. Your own connection to the cards is actually your superpower. It's what will make you, as a tarot reader, unique. The uniqueness of perspectives and relationship with the tarot and your own psychism will provide insight and guidance that no one else can, just as another tarot reader will be able to provide insight and guidance that you can't.

Psychic immersion, the second exercise in my book *Psychic Witch,* is a solitary adaptation of an exercise I would perform in my psychic development classes. Essentially, I would have people partner up with someone that they don't know and tell them to just pretend to be an all-knowing psychic. I would encourage them to have fun with it and be silly, without focusing on being accurate. I would then ask them to give the other person a psychic reading while they were in this role-playing mode. Consistently and overwhelmingly, the majority of the psychic insight they'd give the other person was accurate. There's a few reasons for this. The first is that they were essentially given a permission slip to be wrong. When the fear of accuracy is absent, people get out of their own way, and allow themselves to just be in the flow of their own natural psychism and intuition. That is how powerful fear is when it comes to blocking ourselves.

Approaching the tarot with fear and self-doubt restricts our capacity to receive accurate and insightful guidance, whether that's fear of the cards themselves or fear of being wrong. For many people who've come from a religious or cultural background that views the tarot or psychic ability as evil, this block toward the tarot and psychism buries itself deep into their subconscious and is something that needs to be actively addressed and worked through. Benebell Wen puts it perfectly when she writes in her book *Holistic Tarot* that

> fear is dangerous, not the tarot. The tarot represents the spectrum of the human condition, the good, the evil, the light, and the dark. Do not fear the darker aspects of the human condition. Understand them. The tarot is a storybook about life, about the greatness of human accomplishment, and also the ugliness we are each capable of.[12]

This fantastic quote invites us to approach the tarot with an open mind and a willingness to explore all aspects of the human condition. Engaging in this process sheds light on our unique traits, skills, and shortcomings, giving us a more holistic understanding of ourselves. It urges us not to shy away from the darker or uncertain aspects of the tarot but to seek understanding and growth from them.

With openness and curiosity, we amplify our receptivity to the tarot's insights as well as those within ourselves. Studying the cards' meanings and

12 Wen, *Holistic Tarot*, 12.

symbolism establishes a firm knowledge base, which in turn refines your interpretive abilities. However, beyond sheer knowledge, it's extremely helpful to trust your intuitive and psychic connections when working with tarot. If a message initially puzzles you, allow yourself time for reflection and lean on your intuition for guidance. Psychism often comes through in the form of symbolism; however, symbolism is, well, symbolic. We can receive accurate psychic information, but if we don't know how to interpret that information and be clear in what symbolism we're receiving versus how we're interpreting it, we're positioned to misinterpret that information and give inaccurate information during our readings.

When the Unlikely Is Exactly Right

During a tarot reading for a woman, the conversation shifted when she asked if I could attempt mediumship to reach her late aunt. I let her know that I hadn't picked up on any specific spirits around her but was willing to try, emphasizing there were no guarantees. I closed my eyes, trying to tune in, but all I got was emptiness; no human spirits showed up. She then offered her aunt's name as a focal point. I focused again, but the only thing I kept seeing was the image of a cat.

"I'm sorry, but I can't connect with your aunt," I told her. "All I keep getting is a vision of a cat." Her eyes went really wide. After gasping, she said, "*That's her*! *That's my aunt*!"

I'm sure I was looking at her like she was an alien. She burst into laughter and explained that her aunt was a die-hard cat enthusiast who had said she'd come back as a cat to keep an eye on her. Her aunt had even told her to look out for a feline presence as a sign. This was a great lesson for me when it came to not holding back and sharing even what seems like off-target psychic information during tarot readings. What you might consider random or feel unsure about could be the key to unlocking guidance or confirmation for someone else. It might be the most important piece of information of the whole reading for them. If we hesitate to share, we'll never know its importance. Worst-case scenario, the client won't understand the message. Best-case scenario, you might just connect someone with their aunt who's a cat.

∞

Clearly Discerning the Symbol from the Interpretation

When we give psychic readings, it can sometimes feel like we're playing a game of charades and Pictionary all at once. In charades you act out a word or phrase using only body movements and noises—no talking allowed. In Pictionary you sketch your chosen word or phrase until someone guesses what you're drawing. Similarly, when receiving psychic information, the messages and insights can come through in many different ways and often require some interpretation and translation. Trust yourself and your psychic connection when interpreting the messages and insights that come through during a reading. Allow yourself to be open to the different ways that information may come through, whether it be through symbols, feelings, or even a sudden insight. Trusting your gut can help you gain a more precise grasp of the meanings and insights that are coming through.

To build your muscles for understanding and conveying psychic or intuitive information accurately, you'll first need to understand yourself and how your mind works. This means getting in touch with your own intuition, internal database of psychic imagery, shadow self, and understanding when your mind is wandering or thinking about random things. Keep an eye on the insights that surface during your meditations and everyday experiences, and focus on strengthening your relationship with your inner wisdom. Once you're more at ease with your intuitive skills, you can start sharing psychic information with other people. Start with friends and family members who are open to receiving a reading, and practice conveying the messages and insights that come through in a clear and understandable way. Try to remember to separate what you're receiving from how you interpret it and to communicate this distinction clearly to those receiving the reading. As time goes on, you'll get a better handle on how you personally receive psychic information. This will smooth the way for you to decode and communicate these insights to other people.

When it comes to doing psychic or intuitive readings, understand the role of the ego in accurately conveying information. Though tuning in to a higher source often means setting your ego aside, that ego is crucial when it comes to turning those divine messages into something concrete and understandable. The ego is part of the middle self, which is the bridge between our higher and lower selves and the way we interact with others. Your ego helps translate the spiritual insights you receive into terms that are clear and relatable for the person getting the reading. That's why we should strive to work on balancing our higher and lower selves so that we can clearly receive the information and then use our ego as a tool to convey it accurately. Just don't let your ego get out of balance; that's where the pitfall lies.

Like a spider, the middle self weaves together the threads of the higher self and the lower self into something that can be understood by your conscious mind and by others. Without your ego, you'd lack the means to decipher the spiritual messages you get, let alone explain them in a way the person asking the questions would grasp. To be a skilled reader, I believe it's important to have a healthy relationship with all three aspects of your soul—higher, lower, and middle. When we do this, we bring all parts of ourselves to the tarot reading.

Clearly Discerning the Symbol from the Interpretation

WHAT THIS CAN LOOK LIKE

I once performed a mediumship reading for someone's loved one who had passed where I saw diamonds buried underground, and while it would have been easy to jump to conclusions, I knew it was important to take a moment to really tune in to the message and convey it in a way that was clear and helpful by dissecting the imagery. I relayed what I saw by saying,

> I'm seeing diamonds, and they appear to be underground. Emotionally, I feel this is very important to your deceased. However, as I'm looking at this image closer, it looks like they're planted under soil almost like seeds. Earlier I had sensed that he came from a farm or ranch setting, so the way that I interpret this is as a pun of 'rich soil' and a strong emphasis on the quality of land being a strong priority in his life, or he may have concerns about a specific plot of land, perhaps regarding his farm.

This interpretation turned out to be correct and provided valuable insight and guidance to the person I was reading for. Keep in mind that the accuracy of a reading heavily depends on how well we understand and articulate the messages we get. By carefully tuning in to the message and being explicit about the symbols and our interpretations, we can give readings that are both precise and impactful.

When we receive complex and confusing images during a psychic reading, trust the information we're receiving and interpret it with caution and clarity. I recall a time when a querent came to me seeking guidance on their career. I tuned in to see what information I could receive about their work, and what I saw were images that were difficult to interpret and left me feeling confused. I saw a large Tesla coil with energy running all around it, followed by a microchip, which left me feeling even more uncertain about what the images meant. But I realized I needed more details, so I turned inward to dig deeper. As I tuned in, I saw an image of an orchestra at an opera, with everyone motionless except for the conductor. I realized that the conductor was the key to interpreting the images I had seen.

I conveyed this message to the querent with caution and clarity, saying,

> I'm seeing a large Tesla coil with energy running all around it, but I'm also seeing a microchip. Let me try to gain more clarification . . . Okay, this is even stranger. I'm seeing an orchestra at an opera or something, but everyone is motionless except for the conductor, and I feel there's an emphasis on that.

After the session, the querent confirmed that they worked on semiconductor microchips with lasers, which validated the accuracy of the images I had seen during the reading. I learned from this experience how crucial it is to be careful and explicit when sharing the insights I get, and to seek further details when needed. It also highlights the previous quote by Dion Fortune I shared about how if we have no frame of reference for the psychic information we're receiving, the psyche will do its best to approximate it in ways that make sense to us—or, in this case, the person I was reading for.

The Death card is a perfect example of the importance of interpreting the cards with care and compassion. While some people may fear the Death card and assume that it signifies physical death, this isn't usually the case. The Death card symbolizes transformation and change, signaling the close of one life chapter and the kick-off of a new one. When interpreting the Death card, it's essential to convey its meaning clearly and compassionately, taking into account the unique circumstances and perspective of the person receiving the reading. For instance, a reader might say something like, "The Death card, while it may sound scary on the surface, represents an inevitable change or transformation in your life. It indicates you're in a transitional phase, shedding something that's no longer beneficial for you. This may be difficult or challenging, but trust that this change is ultimately for your highest good." By separating the card's traditional meaning from the person's potential fear response to seeing it turn up in their reading, the reader can provide guidance that can help the person navigate this period of change with courage and wisdom.

Psychic Amnesia

As a tarot reader, I've come across what I call "psychic amnesia" during readings for others. This is when the person you're reading for may not fully connect with the information presented during the reading, but it usually becomes clear to them later on. It's similar to those times when you're showering and, out of nowhere, the solution to a nagging issue just hits you. The same thing can happen with tarot readings! Now, don't worry—just because what you're saying doesn't immediately click with them doesn't mean that you as the tarot reader are doing something wrong. Various factors can trigger this phenomenon. Sometimes querents get fixated on one particular point in the reading and miss the rest of the message. At times, the emotional impact of a reading can be so intense that it becomes difficult to concentrate on the details being shared.

There are ways to combat psychic amnesia and help your querents fully connect with the information being presented. First and foremost, you'll want to make sure the person you're reading for is in a comfortable and relaxed state before the reading begins. Take a few deep breaths together, maybe light some candles, and set the intention for a clear and insightful reading. I also ask querents to not cross their arms or legs, as this is both energetically and psychologically indicative of guarding one's own energy. During the reading, speak clearly and concisely, and avoid using overly complicated language or concepts. Make sure to check in with your querent throughout the reading to ensure they're following along and understanding the information being presented. After the reading, take a moment to recap the key points and answer any questions the querent may have. Giving them a written recap or an audio recording of the session can be useful for later reference. It's smart to touch base with the individual a few days after the reading to find out if they've had any more insights or have lingering questions about the session. A successful tarot reading is all about clear communication and connection.

Being psychic can sometimes feel frustrating, especially when you provide accurate information during a reading that the recipient can't immediately grasp or make a connection with. However, even if a querent doesn't instantly understand or resonate with the information given during a reading, it doesn't imply the reading was off the mark. Trust in the messages you receive and present them to the querent as clearly as possible. Encourage them to mentally record the information and mull it over. Like an annoying fly buzzing around, doubt can be a distraction, diverting your focus from the reading at hand. Brush it aside and have faith in your psychic abilities and that the querent will understand the messages in their own time, even if they can't fully comprehend it in the moment. From personal experience, I can say that even the most skeptical querents have returned, acknowledging the accuracy of past predictions, after some time has passed. And who knows, they may come back for another reading, carrying a newfound respect for your psychic precision.

When the person you're reading for doesn't resonate with your insights, it's normal to second-guess your abilities. Even the best psychics experience this. Keep the vibe alive and share what you're picking up, even if you're a bit uncertain. That one detail you're unsure about might be the key to a big realization for them. Sure, you might miss the mark at times. We're all human, and nobody is perfect. Go easy on yourself. Keep faith in your skills and trust that your psychism will steer you the right way. Even if the insights you provide don't immediately resonate, they might prove beneficial for the person you're reading for at a later time. Trust in the potency of your connection and the energy you're channeling. Make sure to share this information, even in the face of doubt. The details you're unsure about sharing could end up being the most impactful for them. I usually give a heads-up that I could be off the mark or that I might not interpret the message perfectly, but I emphasize that it's what I'm currently picking up.

I once shadowed over one of my psychic mentors while she was conducting a reading. The person said, "I can't see how that could possibly be" in response to psychic information that my mentor was relaying to her. Without missing a beat, my mentor quipped back, "Of course you can't see it; that's why you're having a session with me. My job is to tell you what you can't see." While I can't imagine ever talking to someone I was reading for in this manner, she definitely had a point with that statement, and it's well worth considering.

When a Querent Closes Off During a Reading

It can be disheartening when the person being read rejects or denies some of the information presented during the session and completely shuts off from engaging in the reading. As an empathetic reader, you invest your energy and intuition into providing the best possible guidance. You genuinely want to help and offer meaningful insights into their life or situation. So, when they shut down or resist a particular message, it can feel like your efforts are being dismissed or unappreciated. Bear in mind that each person has their reasons for reacting as they do. They might not be ready to confront certain truths or may feel uncomfortable facing certain aspects of their lives. It's not necessarily a reflection of your abilities as a reader at that moment but more about their individual emotional state and readiness to process the information.

When this happens, stay grounded and maintain confidence in the energy and impressions you receive. The information you pick up during a reading comes from a place of intuition, empathy, and connection to a higher consciousness. Again, trust in the process and the guidance you are receiving. Even if the person doesn't acknowledge the accuracy of the reading immediately, it doesn't diminish the authenticity of the messages you conveyed. In some cases, the person may reflect on the reading later and realize the validity of the insights you shared. They might come to understand that their initial resistance was due to fear, denial, or uncertainty. Some folks who come for readings require a bit of time to absorb the information and decide how it aligns with their life situation. Your role as a reader is to offer guidance and support and relay what you're receiving, but it's ultimately up to the individual to decide what they do with the information provided. You cannot force someone to accept the messages or act upon them. Your best move is to be kind and open-minded, making it a comfortable zone for them to sift through their emotions and thoughts.

When a Querent Closes Off During a Reading

WHAT THIS CAN LOOK LIKE

Allow me to share an experience about a reading many years back wherein the person I was reading for refused to believe that her son was using heroin. Normally I won't read for people who aren't in the room and haven't given their consent, but everything in me told me to do so when this querent asked if I could do a reading about her son, so I trusted my intuition and proceeded. Throughout the reading, needles consistently emerged in my mind's eye, and odd aches nagged at my arm. The tarot spread was dominated by swords cards like the Three of Swords, Eight of Swords, and the Four of Swords, which depicts a figure lying down with eyes closed under the swords. As I scryed into the cards, the swords all turned into syringes. Despite having never met her son, my gut insisted that he was on heroin. However, the woman staunchly believed her son was only using substances other than heroin, asserting that he harbored a strong aversion to needles.

This disagreement led to a commotion, and she demanded a refund from the store where I was conducting readings.[13] However, a year later she returned, revealing she had discovered her son was indeed using heroin after unearthing a stash of used needles in her home. Because she had kept the possibility in mind post-reading, she was able to intervene and get him help. This experience underscores the importance of trusting our intuitive reception, regardless of immediate disbelief or adamant denial from those we're reading for. Sometimes the provided information requires time to fully assimilate.

Being the bearer of uncomfortable news, particularly when it involves something as difficult as drug addiction, is a daunting task nobody looks forward to. There will be instances when the messages we receive during a reading are strikingly clear, compelling us to deliver them, no matter how uncomfortable that task is. Delivering challenging information with tact and sensitivity may not be the most appealing aspect of our role, but it's undeniably part of being a responsible and ethical reader. It's critical to manage delicate information with care to avoid unnecessarily alarming those we read for, especially on the off chance that we might be mistaken.

13 Every now and then you'll have someone demand a refund; don't let it get you down—every situation will be different, and you will have to rely on your own sense of the person and situation as to granting it or not. In the case of this reading, I decided to go ahead and let her have the refund.

As readers, our responsibility lies in relaying information in a manner that is both helpful and empowering. While the impulse may be to share every detail obtained during a reading, approach the information with sensitivity and discernment. After all, our aim is to assist and guide those we read for, not to instill fear or leave them feeling helpless because our ego wants us to take pride in "saying it exactly as it is." Harsh truths rarely benefit anyone because at best it often closes them off to what you're saying and at worst causes harm to them. The truth can be the truth without being harsh. This doesn't mean that you need to sugarcoat everything you say, but tact and compassion go a long way. Our goal should always be to help people, not hurt them, with what we receive. I've also regularly found that when people tell you to give it to them straight and not hold back or sugarcoat anything because they can handle it, they rarely actually understand all of what that entails.

When Your Reading Is Wrong

Acknowledging the occasional misstep or inaccuracy can be challenging. As a psychic reader, it's natural to desire consistent accuracy; who wouldn't want to predict the future flawlessly? However, this is where the ego begins getting in our own way, and a balanced blend of humility with confidence is key in tarot reading. During a reading, make a distinction between the inherent meanings of the cards and your personal interpretation of them. This approach can help circumvent misunderstandings and inaccuracies. Make sure to point out that your interpretation isn't set in stone. You might receive symbolic insight and interpret it one way, but it might mean something else to the querent and how it fits into their life. By setting this expectation, the individual is more likely to be open to the insights provided, even if they don't instantly grasp their significance. No one has all the answers. Sometimes we'll miss the target, and that's completely fine.

Understand that not all insights will be immediately clear to them. Therefore, advise them to "put it in their pocket" and allow ample time to reflect on the reading, assuring them that they can return to you for any questions or further clarification. Becoming a proficient psychic tarot reader requires more than merely shuffling a deck and relying on good fortune. It involves honing your psychic abilities, deeply familiarizing yourself with your cards, and communicating effectively and honestly. Even the best readers sometimes make mistakes. Don't let the worry of messing up hold you back.

EXERCISE 33

AUTOMATIC WRITING WITH TAROT

Automatic writing is a powerful practice for tarot readers, particularly when reading for oneself. The challenge of self-reading in tarot often lies in separating our conscious biases, hopes, and fears from an objective interpretation of the cards. Here, automatic writing assists by allowing us to bypass our conscious layer of thought, effectively tapping into our subconscious to receive unbiased guidance. When confronted with a card that's difficult to interpret within the context of a reading, automatic writing can act as a gateway to deeper insights. By focusing solely on the card's imagery, symbols, what you feel, and by allowing intuition to flow freely in the writing process, you may find yourself articulating thoughts and perspectives that conventional interpretative thought might miss. It serves as an exercise in enhancing psychic and intuitive skills and getting out of your own way. As you surrender conscious control and let your intuition guide your hand across the page, your connection with your subconscious mind and your higher self becomes stronger. I recommend starting with pen or pencil and paper first with automatic writing, but you may also want to try typing at some stage in the process and see if one method works better for you.

1. Choose a tarot deck that you feel a strong connection with. This deck will be the medium through which your subconscious thoughts and feelings will be expressed.
2. Set a clear intention for your automatic writing session. This could be to seek guidance, clarity, or messages from the universe or your subconscious mind.
3. Shuffle your tarot deck. As you shuffle, keep your intention in mind. This will energetically align the cards with your purpose.
4. Draw one or more cards.
5. Take a few moments to observe the cards. Let your eyes wander over the imagery and symbolism. Instead of relying solely on

traditional tarot meanings, allow any thoughts, feelings, or impressions to arise naturally.

6. With your cards as inspiration, begin to write. This should be a free-flowing process without conscious direction. Allow the symbolism of the cards to guide your pen. Do not worry about grammar, sentence structure, or coherence at this stage.
7. As you keep writing, you might notice that your words start to develop their own natural rhythm or unique style. They might be poetic, cryptic, or deeply personal. This is your subconscious mind expressing itself.
8. Once you feel you've written enough, stop and review your automatic writing. The insights it provides could relate to your current situation, reveal subconscious desires, or uncover hidden aspects of your personality.

Automatic Writing with Tarot

WHAT THIS CAN LOOK LIKE

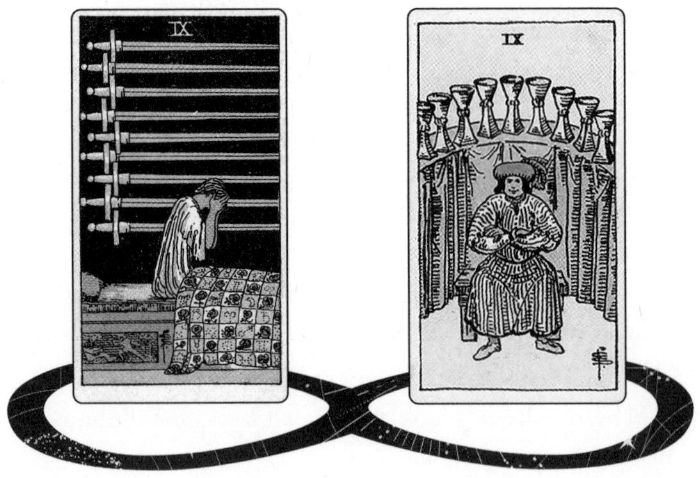

I recall a particular time when automatic writing significantly aided me during a self-reading session. I was grappling with a major personal decision and found myself torn between two conflicting feelings. Seeking guidance, I turned to my tarot deck. As I shuffled the cards and drew two for advice,

I was confronted with the Nine of Swords and the Nine of Cups. The juxtaposition was jarring. The Nine of Swords, symbolizing anxiety, fear, and sleepless nights, indicated the presence of deep-seated worries and mental turmoil. Conversely, the Nine of Cups, known as the wish card, embodies contentment, satisfaction, and emotional fulfillment. The stark contrast left me wondering: Should I succumb to my anxieties or seek contentment and trust in the process? Unsure of how to interpret this disparate pairing, I decided to delve deeper through automatic writing. Taking my journal, I grounded myself and transitioned into a meditative state.

With both cards' imagery vividly in my mind, I began to write, letting the cards' symbols and energies guide my hand. The words that flowed began crafting a narrative that underlined the balance between our fears and aspirations and the challenge of emotional equilibrium. My writing suggested that the energy of the Nine of Swords, while daunting, could be channeled as a motivator to strive for the contentment represented by the Nine of Cups. Instead of being consumed by fear, I could use it as a catalyst to pursue emotional satisfaction. The more I wrote, the clearer it became that the cards were not opposing forces but rather signposts on a journey toward emotional balance. They offered a road map to navigate between anxiety and fulfillment.

EXERCISE 34

TAROT VOICE REFLECTION

This exercise is a great way to boost confidence in your tarot-reading abilities, foster intuitive connections, and move past any mental blocks you might experience when interpreting a card for your situation. By pretending to read for someone else and recording your interpretations, you can detach yourself from any biases or preconceived notions. This free-flowing, candid approach often leads to surprisingly accurate insights. This exercise allows you to step out of your own way and just let your intuition speak. It can break down barriers of doubt or uncertainty and help you build trust in your ability to read and interpret tarot. This exercise offers additional benefits when revisited after some time has passed. Listening to the recording later can reveal further messages that you may not have initially noticed. Plus, as your memory of the exact words you spoke fades, it starts to feel more like you're receiving a reading rather than giving one. This aspect enhances your ability to gain fresh insights from the recording.

1. Begin by grounding yourself and tuning in to your intuition. Take your tarot deck and shuffle it with the intention of seeking guidance.
2. Draw a card. In this exercise, imagine that the card is for another person even though the reading is meant for yourself.
3. Set up a voice recorder or simply use any recording app on your phone.
4. Start the recording and begin talking about the card. Don't overthink it; just let your words flow. If you're stuck, start by describing the imagery on the card and what it could represent.
5. Continue talking for one whole minute. Say whatever comes to mind, allowing your intuition to guide your interpretation. The idea isn't to worry about getting it right or wrong but to really connect with your intuition through the card.
6. After you've wrapped up, give the recording a listen. Approach it as if someone else is offering you advice in a reading. You might find yourself pleasantly surprised by the accuracy and depth of the insights that emerge.
7. Practice this exercise regularly. As you gain confidence, slowly extend the duration of your speaking sessions, progressing from one minute to five and eventually ten minutes.
8. Once you're confident with single card pulls, start practicing with multiple cards and eventually full spreads.

Tarot Voice Reflection

WHAT THIS CAN LOOK LIKE

To provide you with a real-life example of the previous exercise, a friend of mine graciously agreed to let me perform a tarot reading for her and share it with you. It illustrates what a five-minute interpretation of a card might sound like when using a voice recorder. I've transcribed my analysis verbatim to help you see how the exercise flows when put into practice. The card that came up for her was the Strength card. Here is my five-minute-long discussion about the card, captured exactly as I spoke it:

> Um, okay, so I've pulled the Strength card for you. The Strength card, a potent representation of courage, patience, control, and compassion, is the eighth card in the major arcana. In tarot numerology, the number 8 is often associated with strength, power, and balance. It's a number that signifies drive, ambition, and the ability to achieve great things, which seems fitting for this reading. Immediately, the lion draws my attention. Traditionally associated with raw emotions, passions, and base instincts, the lion is being gently tamed by a serene woman. This powerful image speaks to the delicate balance between power and gentleness, strength and kindness. It suggests not a suppression of these potent emotions, but rather their skillful management.
>
> As I focus on this depiction, I'm feeling a sense of respect for the courage it takes to face our inner beasts. This card might be hinting at a time in your life where you're dealing with intense emotions or facing a challenge that incites powerful responses. The Strength card presents a lesson: courage and understanding, rather than brute force, are required to handle such situations. Look closely at the woman's expression: it's calm, serene, reflecting inner tranquility amidst potential turmoil. It resonates with a quiet strength, reminding us that our ability to maintain peace within, despite external circumstances, is the true mark of strength. When I connect with this image, I sense a feeling of reassurance, suggesting that you too can find such serenity within yourself, no matter the challenge.
>
> Overhead, the lemniscate, or infinity symbol, represents the limitless potential of spiritual growth that comes from mastering our instincts and emotions. I want to also add that it's an eight on its side, which is the number of this card. The infinity symbol seems to suggest to me at this moment the idea of continual movement and progress.
>
> Now, let's delve into the colors. Warm yellows and golds dominate the card, colors of vitality, optimism, and clarity. When I immerse myself in these colors, I feel a rush of energy and positivity—an emotional cue suggesting an optimistic outlook is needed in your situation. The card's color palette promises that clarity will come and that the situation can foster spiritual growth and renewed vitality.
>
> The Strength card's message deepens as we understand its imagery. Your journey might involve developing patience and understanding—not only toward others but also toward yourself. It's about recognizing that true strength comes from within, from overcoming personal

trials. In practical terms, this card nudges you to remain patient and calm in the face of adversity and to extend compassion when challenged. True strength lies not in brute force but in the will's resilience and character. Your inner strength can conquer any obstacle. This deeper insight from the Strength card presents a call to acknowledge your inner strength and approach challenges with patience and compassion. As I meditate on this card for you, the overwhelming feeling is one of empowerment. I hope these insights resonate with you and provide clarity and strength for the challenges you're facing.

Neuroplasticity and Affirmations

Neuroplasticity refers to the brain's innate ability to adapt and evolve based on the thoughts it consistently entertains. This concept holds immense significance when considering the impact of affirmations. Affirmations are concise, positive statements individuals repeat to themselves when aiming to foster personal growth, alleviate stress, and boost self-confidence. Typically, these statements are geared toward countering negative thoughts and nurturing a positive mindset. The remarkable aspect of neuroplasticity is its pivotal role in habit formation, which is essentially the core objective of affirmations: shaping positive mental habits. The underlying principle here is that with each use, the brain's plasticity enables the strengthening of neural pathways. Consequently, each repetition of an affirmation reinforces the neural connections associated with the positive belief being affirmed. This practical application aligns with the widely acknowledged neuroscience maxim "Neurons that fire together, wire together."[14]

Neuroplasticity's remarkable ability extends to empowering cognitive reappraisal, a conscious mental strategy where we intentionally shift our perspective on a situation to manage our emotions. This concept becomes particularly relevant when we delve into the practice of affirmations. Through the regular practice of affirmations, we actively reconfigure our neural pathways, striving to convert our pessimistic thoughts and convictions into optimistic ones. As our brains adapt and evolve in response to this practice, it becomes increasingly effortless to align with the affirmations we're diligently repeating. On the flip side, consistent negative thoughts can also wire together beliefs in the brain. However, affirmations serve as a counteractive force. The potency of spoken words surpasses the influence of mere thoughts. That's because it's the power of thought that is also externalized. Through the establishment and nurturing of positive beliefs and attitudes via affirmations, we can mitigate the adverse impacts of stress. Affirmations offer more than just a fleeting sense of well-being. They actively contribute to stress reduction and the cultivation of self-assurance, significantly enhancing our mental health. What's particularly intriguing is their ability to yield long-term benefits for our brain's well-being.

A beneficial aspect of affirmations lies in their ability to help shape our self-concept and identity, both vital aspects of mental well-being. Our brain isn't static. It's in a perpetual state of adjustment where it's constantly modifying its structure and function to align with our self-beliefs. Therefore, the consistent practice of positive affirmations can stimulate adaptive changes in the brain that echo and fortify a positive self-image and identity. Due to neuroplasticity, our brain is designed to improve at tasks it performs repeatedly. This principle applies to emotional regulation as well. If we practice affirmations geared toward managing our emotions, our brain will, with time, enhance its ability to regulate emotions effectively.

14 Hanson, *Hardwiring Happiness*, 10.

As tarot readers, using affirmations can be instrumental in strengthening your psychic abilities. A consistent practice of affirming their intuitive prowess and psychic skills can stimulate and reinforce the associated neural pathways, making them more potent and readily accessible. This process, coupled with stress management and positive self-perception fostered through affirmations, can amplify your psychic potential. The emotional regulation provided by neuroplasticity can enable tarot readers to quiet that self-doubt in one's psychic abilities.

EXERCISE 35

PSYCHIC AFFIRMATION CARD DRAW

The following exercise offers an effective strategy to weave tarot and psychic affirmations into your daily routine, leveraging their collective force to enhance your psychic abilities. The process involves drawing a daily tarot card for guidance and another card for a corresponding affirmation from this book's appendix A. This creates a synergy of intuitive insight and positive reinforcement. Repeating these affirmations, especially in front of a mirror, helps strengthen neural pathways associated with the psychic abilities you aim to enhance, courtesy of neuroplasticity. This technique isn't a one-off exercise. This is something you'll want to practice consistently.

Regular engagement with this exercise will result in changes that are initially subtle, but over time they become more pronounced and transformational. The aim extends beyond enhancing psychic abilities; it's about cultivating self-trust, uncovering your inner wisdom, and building a resilient, positive mindset. This exercise also helps conquer any confidence issues you may have regarding your psychic abilities. Consistently practicing tarot reading and affirmations serves as a gentle nudge of your inherent capacity to tap into universal wisdom. The fortification of these neural pathways can notably boost your confidence, enabling you to trust your intuition and psychic insights. Over time, you'll not only enhance your psychic abilities but also foster an unshakable belief in your capability to access and harness these intuitive skills.

1. Following your contemplation of the daily card, reshuffle your deck with the specific intention of identifying an affirmation

that enhances and harmonizes with the energy of your daily card. Then draw a second card.

2. Refer to the appendix to find the affirmation that corresponds to the second card you drew. This affirmation is designed to work in tandem with the message of your daily tarot card, strengthening your psychic abilities.
3. Close your eyes and repeat the affirmation to yourself several times, allowing its message to seep into your consciousness. Try to visualize the affirmation's energy merging with your daily card's energy.
4. Afterward, stand in front of a mirror, gaze into your own eyes, and articulate the affirmation audibly.
5. Following this, record the daily card and affirmation card you've drawn in your journal, along with the corresponding affirmation. Take a moment to write down any impressions, feelings, or insights that arise while you engage with the cards and affirmation.
6. Finally, make it a habit to consistently repeat your affirmation throughout the day, particularly during moments of solitude or meditation. If possible, try to repeat it aloud. This vocalization, coupled with mirror practice, will help to reinforce neural pathways associated with this affirmation, enhancing your psychic abilities through the power of neuroplasticity.

EXERCISE 36

ORACLE CLARIFIERS

Instead of drawing clarifying cards if a card doesn't make sense in a reading, a technique I like to use is having a second deck that isn't tarot but is instead a single-symbol oracle deck. By fusing the language of symbols from both decks, you will unlock a precision that brings depth and focus to your divinatory practice.

1. Choose a single-symbol or single-word oracle deck that complements the tarot. Look for clear symbolism and avoid

cluttered or ambiguous imagery for a seamless integration of insights in your readings.

2. Familiarize yourself with the chosen oracle deck. Read the provided interpretations or establish your associations with the symbols to deeply connect with the oracle cards and their language of symbols.
3. Begin your tarot reading as usual, shuffling the tarot deck and drawing cards for your spread. These cards will provide initial insights into the querent's situation or your sought guidance.
4. After completing the tarot spread, shuffle the single-symbol oracle deck with a clear intention. Use the oracle cards to bring additional clarity and focus to the messages from the tarot cards, enhancing the depth of your readings.
5. Draw oracle cards from the chosen deck, one for each tarot card in your spread. Place the oracle cards on top of or beside the corresponding tarot cards in the same order to establish a powerful connection between the two systems of divination.
6. Interpret each tarot card together with its corresponding oracle card. The single symbol or word on the oracle card will offer specific insights and focus your interpretation on the particular area of life or situation represented by the tarot card.

6
∞

The Inner Planes and Internal Tarot Temple

In occultism there is a concept known as the inner planes. These are realms of subtle reality that intertwine with and surpass our tangible, waking world. We frequently tap into our own individual spaces of the inner planes without realizing it, typically during dreams, but they can also be reached through meditation, trance, and ecstatic practices. The inner planes serve as a source of information, wisdom, and guidance. They also provide a platform for direct interactions with our spiritual allies, including spirit guides, deities, and a myriad of other entities. The term *plane* can be somewhat misleading. While it's easier for us to understand these planes as if they're stacked like books or how they're illustrated in models, these are just simplified depictions for our convenience. In reality, all these planes coexist within the same space simultaneously.

Think about a really solid object, like a crystal. Even inside the crystal, its atoms and molecules that compose it aren't touching each other but have space in between. They're always moving and vibrating in their own little areas. Now consider this space filled with something else—let's call it astral matter. It's like an invisible sea that penetrates and fills up all the gaps within solid things. So, while you might see a crystal as just a crystal, in another way of thinking, it's also a crystal floating in this invisible sea of the inner planes that intertwines with it in the same space. Occultist Dion Fortune provides another insight, noting that these planes represent different states or conditions of being. This concept becomes clearer when considering the multidimensional nature of humans. Our existence comprises a physical body, emotions, mind, and spirit, all of which inhabit the same space simultaneously. This suggests that various states of being are present within a single entity at any given moment. It also means that we have the potential to directly access these inner planes within ourselves. This concept parallels Carl Jung's concept of the personal unconscious, which he considered our individual sphere within the collective unconscious. He similarly saw the collective unconscious as a force that intermingles with and surpasses nature, which we have direct access to through our own psyches.

One of the best methods for engaging with the inner planes is to establish your own inner temple. Specifically, we'll be setting up an internal tarot temple. This internal tarot temple will serve as your personal spiritual space within the inner planes, designed for psychic work with tarot cards. Your internal tarot temple will have a standard structure, including various rooms dedicated to different tarot-related topics, but it will also be personalized to reflect your tastes, spiritual journey, and individuality. Essentially, it's a collaboration between your conscious imagination and your unconscious psyche, making it a unique and private sanctuary.

Rest assured that nothing can enter your internal tarot temple without your explicit invitation, making it a completely private and safe space for your spiritual work. Even if you don't initially visualize the internal tarot temple with complete clarity, don't worry. Just set your intentions with focus and continue to work with it. Over time, as you interact and strengthen your relationship with it, it will become more concrete and vivid. If you already work with an inner temple, such as the one I teach in chapter 6 of my book *Mastering Magick*, just add this onto it as a whole different area of your inner temple that you can access.

The Neverending Story and the Inner Realms

Michael Ende's fantasy classic *The Neverending Story* draws powerful parallels with the occult idea of the inner planes, which isn't surprising as the author was greatly interested in occultism and anthroposophy. Both occultism and *The Neverending Story* explore the power of human consciousness, imagination, and existence. In *The Neverending Story*, Fantastica (or Fantasia in the 1984 film) is a boundless realm, shaped by human dreams and hopes. A notable part of the book, not shown in the film, has the main protagonist, Atreyu, discovering a secret from Uyulala, a voice without form. Uyulala reveals the existence of an "outer world," in reference to our physical world, implying Fantastica is the inner world.

The health of Fantastica is deeply connected to human emotions and dreams. As humans neglect their dreams, "the Nothing"—symbolizing hopelessness and a dry imagination—begins consuming Fantastica. This mirrors the inner planes, which reflect humanity's collective mental state. Negative thoughts can cause turmoil, while positive energy brings peace. Venturing into these realms is also an introspective journey. Bastian's travels in Fantastica represent his exploration of his psyche, leading to personal growth. Likewise, the journey through the inner planes in esoteric traditions is a path of self-discovery and reflection. Travelers seek to understand themselves and the universe. Both Fantastica and the inner planes emphasize creation. In Fantastica, Bastian learns he can reshape the world with his imagination. Similarly, occult beliefs state that we can influence and create within the inner planes to impact our physical reality.

Benefits of Your Internal Tarot Temple

Your internal tarot temple also offers a designated internal sanctuary to retreat to after intense readings or during periods of spiritual turmoil. This retreat can assist in managing your energy, recharging, and maintaining your emotional and psychic well-being. The safe confines of your internal tarot temple can provide an ideal space for shadow work using tarot. Engaging with challenging cards or readings can reveal unexplored aspects of yourself, fostering personal growth and a more nuanced understanding of yourself and others. Frequent engagement with your internal tarot temple will heighten your intuition and enhance your psychic abilities over time. This will lead to more insightful and precise readings as you become more attuned to tarot's energies and symbols. The more you work with these energies, the more tangible and vivid these internal landscapes become, especially during your tarot readings. The visual and sensory richness of your internal tarot temple can help refine your visualization skills.

Your internal tarot temple is purposefully designed to incorporate symbols, images, and elements associated with tarot. As your internal tarot temple aligns with your energy and psyche, it enables a deeper connection with the cards, allowing for a more personal interpretation of their symbolism. Carl Jung believed in universal and archetypal symbols shared by all through the collective unconscious. The tarot deck is abundant with such archetypal figures, each carrying symbolic meaning. Within your internal tarot temple, you can actively engage with these figures through a process similar to what Jung called active imagination. These dialogues offer an opportunity to understand the energies and lessons these figures represent, adding depth to your interpretations and expanding your understanding of the cards. Beyond archetypes and symbols, the inner planes are a realm where you can directly interact with spiritual guides, your higher self, or other benevolent entities. These connections grant additional insight, clarity, and support for your readings. Regular visits to the temple and mindful interactions with your spirit guides can enhance this spiritual connection, resulting in much clearer guidance and an intuitive understanding of the tarot's messages during readings. If a tarot reading seems particularly difficult to interpret, retreating to your internal tarot temple can provide fresh perspectives and insights to help decipher the meanings. The temple's serene, focused environment can aid in unraveling complex or puzzling card arrangements, possibly through discussions with your tarot spirit guide, which we'll get to later in this book.

Think of inner temples on the inner planes, like the internal tarot temple, as being somewhat reminiscent of the enchanting portrayal of a castle from Diana Wynne Jones's novel *Howl's Moving Castle*, which you might recognize from the Hayao Miyazaki and Studio Ghibli movie adaptation. Both one's inner temple and the castle are complex, almost living structures that surpass physical constraints, reflecting the vastness of the human mind and spirit. The iconic castle from Jones's novel and Miyazaki's film is an abstract masterpiece of rooms and spaces that warp in size and configuration. Much like inner temples, the castle's interior is larger than its exterior, symbolizing the endless potentials, emotions, and thoughts within our psyche. This parallels how mystics and occultists view and work with inner temples: as an expansive sanctuary accessed within the mind that extends beyond their physical boundaries.

The castle and one's inner temple are both influenced by the states of their occupants. As Howl's mood shifts, the castle's layout rearranges, reflecting the wizard's emotional states. Similarly, the configuration and ambiance of an inner temple can change based on the emotional and psychic well-being of its creator. If the practitioner is calm, the inner temple may appear tranquil; if they're distressed, it may reflect turmoil. In both instances, the inner environment serves as a mirror reflecting the mental and emotional landscapes of the individual. Their tastes, styles, and psyches significantly influence these spaces. Howl's castle bears his eccentricities, just as a practitioner's inner temple manifests their unique preferences, artistic style, and magickal affinities. Both the moving castle and inner temples are deeply personal spaces that require consent for entry. In Jones's narrative, only those permitted by Howl can enter his castle. This magickal boundary protects the space from unwanted intrusion, which is a concept ubiquitous in occultism, where inner temples are sanctuaries accessible only through invitation. This feature emphasizes the sacredness and personal nature of these spaces. Both the moving castle and inner temples function as hubs connecting to various other dimensions or planes. Howl's castle has doors that open to diverse locations. Similarly, inner temples often have portals that lead to different areas of the inner planes, symbolizing access to various aspects of the self, spirit allies, universal archetypes, or spiritual realms.

Some Considerations Before We Begin

As stated before, your internal tarot temple is a personalized space designed to facilitate deeper understanding and connection with the mystical energies of the tarot. It's an extension of your mind and spirit. As such, it's entirely tailored to your own needs and abilities. For many, this space might be a vividly complex sanctuary explored through detailed visual imagery. For some, the temple might be better experienced through sound, sensation, role-playing, emotion, narration, physical movement, writing, or sketching.

If you happen to have ADHD, aphantasia, or struggle with concentration and visualization, I haven't forgotten about you. It's not just about seeing the temple with your mind's eye; it's more about feeling and connecting with it in a way that works best for you as you follow along and then eventually explore and work with your internal tarot temple. For instance, if you find it easier to connect with auditory stimuli, consider using sound to build your internal tarot temple, though a combination is probably the best. You can create or choose specific sounds that encapsulate the energy of each part of the temple, such as the different chambers. Envision crackling flames for wands or the soothing rush of wind for swords.

Alternatively, you could focus on the tactile. Imagine the warmth you might feel in the wands chamber or the cooling sensation as you step into the room of swords. Feel the grounded earthiness of the pentacles room or the enveloping softness in the cups chamber. If you're more inclined toward physical movement or role-playing, embody the energy of each suit. Create different areas in a room to represent each chamber, and move through them in a way that corresponds with the suit's energy. The crucial aspect here is to completely engage in the experience, similar to participating in physical theater or live-action role-play.

A narrative approach can be particularly helpful if visualization is a challenge. Describe the internal tarot temple to yourself, painting a picture with your words as though you're telling a story, and describe to yourself what you're doing within it. The kinesthetic approach allows you to embody the energy of each suit physically. This could be as simple as changing your posture to match the energy of the room—a strong, assertive stance for the wands chamber or a relaxed, flowing posture for the cups room. If you lean toward the visual side, consider creating or commissioning artwork that represents the rooms of your temple. Having a visual reference can help make the space feel more tangible and provide a focal point for your exploration. Through journaling, you can engage with the energies, symbols, and concepts associated with each suit. Even if you aren't an artist, sketching lets you physically draw out your inner tarot temple, creating a tactile and visual representation to refer back to; plus it holds the energy that you put into its creation.

Starting your journey with the internal tarot temple might seem overwhelming at first, but again, mastering this is not a race. Don't feel intimidated. While we'll briefly explore the whole temple in one sitting, you don't have to do it that way. Instead, break it down. Focus on one room or aspect at a time. This allows you to explore in manageable segments, reducing feelings of overwhelm and aiding in maintaining focus. Active engagement can further enhance your experience. If sitting quietly isn't your forte, incorporate movement into your practice. Walk around as you contemplate a certain room or suit, or use physical objects as symbolic representations for different elements of the temple. This engagement of your body can help fully connect your mind to the experience. Supplementing your exploration with tools such as a fidget spinner or a stress ball can prove to be a boon, especially for individuals with ADHD. By offering a secondary focus, these tools can support your concentration and engagement, making the journey more immersive.

Guided meditations can serve as a powerful resource to help you maintain focus and structure in your exploration. Whether it's a guided meditation designed specifically for the internal tarot temple, a recording of your own detailing each room, or listening to this in audiobook form, the guidance will act like a personal tour guide for your journey, providing structure and focus. Expressing your thoughts through journaling is another effective way to delve deeper into your exploration. Writing about each room and the energies, feelings, or ideas it evokes can give you a more grounded experience. This tangible interaction allows for a connection with the temple and offers a record of your mystical journey. Timers can be an instrumental part of your practice. Setting a timer gives you a manageable chunk of time to explore your internal tarot temple. Starting with short intervals, like five or ten minutes, and gradually increasing the time as you become more comfortable with the practice sets a gentle rhythm to your exploration. Your internal tarot temple will become more familiar with each visit.

Even if short, regular visits can simplify the process over time. It's like learning an instrument or a new language: frequent practice enhances your skill and comfort. By incorporating these methods, your exploration of the internal tarot temple will become a dynamic and engaging experience, tailor-made to resonate with your needs. It's all about finding what works best for you. There's no "wrong" way to construct or navigate your internal tarot temple; it just needs to work for you. The key is to engage your senses to tap into deep wells of power and insight within and beyond you and deepen your connection with the tarot. It's not about accessing and exploring it exactly as I share. As long as you're accessing the inner planes through your internal tarot temple in a way that suits you best, you're on the right track.

In the next exercise, I'll provide an example of how your internal tarot temple could look and be structured. This is designed to give you a clear concept of its potential setup. The primary feature of your temple should be a central room designated for tarot reading and psychic growth. Five additional rooms should be connected to this central hub. These rooms represent the four suits of the minor arcana, each with its unique chamber, and a fifth room that is associated with the major arcana. All of these rooms need to embody the distinct characteristics of their respective suits, and they should house life-size representations of each card. After completing this exercise, you're welcome to keep it as it is or modify your tarot temple to better align with your personal tastes and symbolic associations. This space should feel intimately customized to you. Over time, it should evolve organically with you as you work with it more and more.

I suggest that prior to engaging in the next meditation, you take a moment to acquaint yourself with the steps involved by reading through it first. This will facilitate a seamless and uninterrupted flow throughout the process. The meditation I am about to present is divided into six distinct exercises, each designed to guide you through the exploration of your internal tarot temple. You have the flexibility to use these exercises independently whenever you revisit specific aspects of the temple.

EXERCISE 37

JOURNEYING INTO YOUR INTERNAL TAROT TEMPLE

Close your eyes and gently draw in a deep, calming breath. As you inhale, embrace the tranquility of this moment. Exhale and release any stress or tension that may be clinging to your body. Picture a glowing pathway of golden light unfurling before you, inviting you forward. This path guides you to the threshold of your unique sanctuary on the inner planes: the internal tarot temple. Imagine standing at an imposing door, flanked by two pillars, one of obsidian on the left and another of moonstone on the right. Moving with intention, you open the door and step into the central chamber of the tarot temple, a haven of wisdom and insight. The serene silence of the space envelops you. The air brings along calming and fragrant scents that you find enjoyable. As you breathe in the soothing scent, let it lull your spirit deeper into the heart of this sacred sanctuary.

Arching high above you, the ceilings are adorned with shimmering mosaics. Beneath your feet lies a smooth marble floor patterned like a chessboard, tiling the ground. On the sturdy walnut tables spread across the room rest ornate tarot decks alongside an array of divination tools. Perhaps you see crystals in myriad hues, gently swaying pendulums, or scrying bowls brimming with still water. The chamber is graced with lush tapestries and verdant terrariums, adding earthy layers to this mystical setting. Allow your eyes to wander across the vibrant scenes depicted on the tapestries and the miniature havens of lush greenery within the terrariums. Absorb the sight of the ferns, ivy, and moss, their vibrant energy rejuvenating your spirit. Statues, each symbolizing a facet of tarot's wisdom, grace the room.

In the middle of the chamber, there's a circle of plush velvet cushions that encircle a crystal ball placed on a rosewood pedestal. Here, in the temple of tarot, you are attuned to the pulse of spiritual energy that hums through the room. Feel this tranquil energy resonate within you. As you look around, you notice five majestic doors encircling the room. Each door is carved from a distinct type of wood and embodies the essence of a tarot suit. The first, made of robust oak, represents the suit of pentacles. Its handle, shaped like a pentacle, resonates with the energy of earth, stability, and prosperity. Next, a door of ethereal silver birch symbolizes the suit of swords. Its handle, shaped like a sword, vibrates with the energy of intellect, communication, and conflict. A door of fiery red cedar pulses with the ambitious energy of wands. Its handle, shaped like a leafy wand, glows warmly. Another door of lacquered driftwood, bearing the emblem of cups, exudes emotional resonance, compassion, and intuition. The final door, grander and larger, is made from starlight ebony. It's dedicated to the major arcana, the keys to life's mysteries, and its handle is shaped like an infinity symbol. Each door invites you into a unique realm of exploration, carrying a distinct vibrational frequency that echoes the energy of the respective suits. For now, remain in the central room, where you are held captive by its mesmerizing beauty. The internal tarot temple is your space for contemplation, education, and mystical resonance. Take some time to explore and feel the tranquility of this central room.

EXERCISE 38

THE CHAMBER OF PENTACLES

When you're ready, inhale deeply and let your gaze fall upon a door made of sturdy oak, its surface embedded with emerald green gemstones. The handle, shaped in the form of a pentacle, invites you to explore the realm of the suit of pentacles. As you push open the door, the scent of fertile earth and blossoming flowers welcomes you—a sensory representation of the pentacles' association with earth, abundance, and physical well-being. The walls of the pentacles chamber boast majestic murals of every card in the suit of pentacles. From the diligent figure in the Eight of Pentacles honing his craft to the generous figure in the Six of Pentacles sharing his wealth, each mural is a life-sized lesson in prosperity, security, and physical abundance. The murals seem to almost come alive as you delve deeper into the chamber, the figures' movements slow and graceful, their expressions ones of determination and contentment. Their stories of hard work, diligence, and the joy of tangible success resonate in the very air of the chamber.

At the heart of the chamber, a grand, richly laden banquet table spans the room's width. The table is resplendent with a bounty of food and drink, an homage to the earth's abundance and the pentacles' association with material wealth. Surrounding the table are lush potted plants and fruit trees heavy with ripe, fragrant fruits—tangible evidence of the earth's generosity. Sunlight pours in through clear glass windows, spotlighting an abundance of jade plants and money trees. Their vibrant green leaves seem to shimmer with prosperity, reflecting the earthly riches associated with the pentacles. In a corner of the room you'll see an array of beautifully handcrafted tools. Among them you'll see a mason's chisel, a gardener's trowel, and a weaver's spindle. Each tool symbolizes the respect for hard work and craftsmanship that is so central to the suit of pentacles.

The chamber of pentacles is a warm celebration of the earth's abundance, a testament to diligence and a sanctuary of physical well-being. Here, the value of hard work and the joy of tangible success is embraced and revered. As you absorb the powerful stories of the grand murals and the tangible abundance within the room, you feel a sense of security, of groundedness, ready to channel the earthly wisdom of the pentacles into your journey. When you feel prepared, simply turn toward the door through which you entered and step back into the central chamber of the tarot temple.

EXERCISE 39

THE CHAMBER OF SWORDS

From the central chamber, approach the majestic door crafted from silver birch, emblematic of the suit of swords. Feel the cool touch of the sword-shaped handle. As you push it open, a rush of fresh, crisp air greets you, the faint scent of parchment and ink lingering subtly within it, whispering tales of intellect and communication. Step into the chamber, a grand space that feels like stepping inside an antique library of all the world's knowledge, its walls and high arched ceiling decorated with expansive murals of each card from the suit of swords. From the Two of Swords depicting a blindfolded figure at a crossroads to the triumphant figure on the Six of Swords journeying toward calmer waters, each mural is a masterpiece, a life-sized tableau that feels as though you could step right into the scene. As your gaze sweeps the room, the murals seem to shimmer, an optical illusion creating a sense of the images whispering, their figures moving, their stories unfolding in real time. Each card is a living testament to the triumphs and trials of intellect, decision-making, and assertive communication.

In the heart of this chamber, a great crystal obelisk reaches toward the ceiling. Its icy clarity represents the sharp, discerning quality of the mind associated with the swords suit. The obelisk's pointed tip seems to pierce the air above, slicing through the ether, embodying the precision and clarity of thought that this suit symbolizes. Scattered across the chamber, you notice high shelves holding countless scrolls and tomes. Their parchment pages rustle like the soft whisperings of the air element, representative of the suit you stand within. A vast desk rests at the room's center, quills and ink pots arranged neatly upon its polished surface, inviting you to partake in the art of communication and put thought into tangible form. Transparent gossamer curtains hang at the chamber's tall windows, billowing gently in the breeze that seems to be constantly present in this room. This ephemeral wind carries with it soft whispers, an echo of every thought, every idea, that has taken flight within this sacred chamber.

High above, a skylight reveals an ever-changing canvas of clouds, the embodiment of the air element associated with swords. At times the clouds are sparse and serene; other times they assemble into towering, brooding dark clouds, embodying the myriad expressions of thought, from tranquility to tempest. Throughout the room, stands of yarrow and marjoram sway gently, their fragrances mingling with the scent of parchment. Known for their association with mental clarity and courage, these plants are the tangible symbols of the swords' essence. This chamber, dedicated to the suit of swords, is a place where thought takes flight, where the keen blade of intellect slices through confusion, where words, thoughts, and decisions wield the power of creation and transformation. As you take one last sweeping look at the grand murals, reflect on the lessons of each card and its imprint upon your heart and mind, enriching your journey with the wisdom of swords. When you are ready, leave the chamber of swords, closing the silver birch door gently behind you, and return to the central tarot temple.

EXERCISE 40

THE CHAMBER OF WANDS

Set your sight on the door of fiery red cedar that embodies the suit of wands. When you reach out to the door's handle, shaped like a wand sprouting leaves, you find it is warm to the touch. As the door swings open, an almost palpable surge of energy meets you, an invisible wave of warmth and enthusiasm. The scent of smoldering cedar and sprightly citrus fills the air, embodying the passion and zeal of the wands suit. The chamber of wands is a testament to the spirit's unyielding drive and determination. The walls bear vibrant murals of the suit of wands' cards, each a life-size manifestation of the card's energy. From the focused figure in the Two of Wands gazing out toward the horizon with a world in his hands to the charismatic leader in the King of Wands, each mural emanates a brilliant radiance, reflecting the wands' vivacious spirit. As you step further into the room, the murals appear to flicker and dance, as though each figure is lit from within by a flame of willpower. The images' motion embodies the dynamic energy of the suit of wands, their vibrant colors echoing the suit's association with fiery ambition and creativity. In the heart of the chamber, a large torch, its fire burning bright and steady, stands resolute and undying. This vibrant beacon of unwavering flame is a symbol of the indomitable willpower that defines the suit of wands.

Large windows, framed with drapes of fiery orange and sunflower yellow, welcome sunlight to pour in, filling the room with an invigorating brightness, a nod to the suit's fiery association. The torch's placement in the room signifies the beacon of determination one must hold high to navigate the path toward their goals. Around the chamber, pots of vibrant sunflowers and red hibiscus bloom fervently. Their rich hues reflect the fiery essence of wands, the plants a living testament to the suit's potent energy and vibrant life force. The chamber of wands is a radiant celebration of passion, determination, and action. It's a place where willpower ignites, ambitions take flight, and creativity blossoms like the radiant flowers around you. As you drink in the sight of the wands' grand murals and feel the room's pulsating energy, your spirit feels invigorated, ready to channel the wands' fiery wisdom into your journey.

EXERCISE 41

THE CHAMBER OF CUPS

When you are ready, return to the embrace of the central tarot temple, leaving the fiery passion of the wands chamber behind. Now your attention is drawn toward a door crafted from driftwood, its surface worn smooth by the ocean's caress: a perfect embodiment of the suit of cups. The handle, beautifully carved into the shape of a chalice, seems to shimmer with the hues of a calm sea as you push it open. Stepping into the cups chamber is akin to being enveloped in a comforting embrace. The air feels softer here, imbued with the scent of sea mist and blooming jasmine, a sensory whisper of the suit's association with emotions, intuition, and love. The chamber walls bear breathtaking murals of the suit of cups' cards. From the tranquil figure in the Four of Cups contemplating his choices to the joyous celebration in the Three of Cups, each mural is a life-sized homage to emotional richness. The figures in the murals appear so real, their expressions so vivid, that one could almost hear their laughter, their sighs, their thoughtful silences. The murals seem to shift subtly as you move deeper into the room, their colors deepening and brightening in a fluid dance, embodying the fluid nature of emotions, the ebb and flow of feelings. Right in the heart of this chamber stands an impressive fountain. The fountain's waters are gracefully cascading into a spacious basin designed in the shape of a chalice. The water's melodious babble fills the room, a serene symphony that reflects the soothing, healing properties of the suit of cups.

This chamber is dappled in soft light, filtering through stained glass windows that depict scenes from the cups cards. The hues of tranquil blues, serene greens, and warm rose tones imbue the room with a comforting luminescence, an ever-changing dance of colors that reflects the spectrum of human emotions. In a quiet corner, an inviting chaise lounge is nestled beside a window, draped in soft fabrics of sea green and lavender. This corner invites contemplation and exploration of one's feelings and intuition. The chamber is graced with flourishing pots of lotus and moonflowers. Their intoxicating fragrances waft throughout the room, further nurturing the sense of serenity. Each bloom, in its own way, mirrors the spiritual awakening, intuitive understanding, and emotional depth symbolized by the cups. The chamber of cups is a soothing sanctuary of emotions, a place that whispers of love, encourages intuitive exploration, and nurtures inner growth. As you absorb the emotional narratives of the grand murals and the calming aura of the room, your heart feels at peace, your intuition awakened, ready to carry the wisdom of cups into your journey. When you're ready, return back to the central chamber of the tarot temple.

EXERCISE 42

THE CHAMBER OF THE MAJOR ARCANA

Now your attention is drawn toward the grandest door of all: a door made of ebony. The handle, carved into the symbol of a lemniscate, the infinity symbol, beckons you toward the realm of the Major Arcana. The door itself is adorned with an illuminated depiction of the Wheel of Fortune symbol from the Rider-Waite-Smith deck.

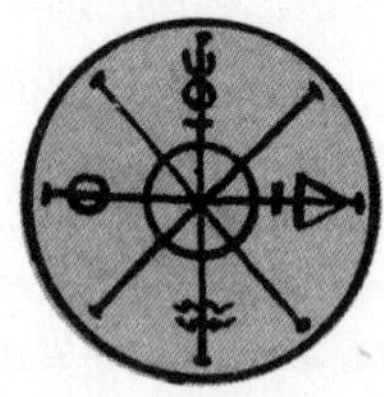

As the door opens, you are welcomed with an aura of ancient knowledge. The rich air is filled with frankincense and myrrh. It conjures a sense of timeless ambiance that hints at the presence of universal truths waiting to be uncovered. The chamber dedicated to the major arcana is

an awe-inspiring cosmos unto itself. The chamber's walls are adorned with majestic murals depicting the major arcana cards in larger-than-life detail. From the innocent Fool embarking on his journey to the ascended figure in the World, each mural is a visual narrative of life's grand stages and the soul's spiritual journey. The murals pulse with a mesmerizing vitality, the figures moving in slow, purposeful motion, revealing their stories in a way that speaks to the very core of your being. The colors shift and flow, reflecting the transformative journey of spiritual evolution signified by the major arcana.

At the heart of this grand chamber, a mesmerizing holographic orrery spins slowly, depicting the planets and their celestial orbits. The celestial model serves as a reminder of the universal truths and mysteries that the major arcana encompasses, our connection to the cosmos, and the grand design of existence. Tall stained glass windows stretch up to the ceiling, where a transparent dome reveals an ever-changing view of the heavens. Constellations and celestial bodies move across this window to the cosmos, their dance a testament to the balance and revelatory mysteries of the universe. Throughout the chamber, clusters of crystals glimmer with luminous light, their facets reflecting and refracting the room's luminescence, composing a ballet of light and shadow. Each crystal amplifies the chamber's energy, reinforcing the connection between the material and spiritual realms, a key aspect of the major arcana.

The chamber of the major arcana is a captivating voyage into the profound enigmas of life, a tribute to the soul's odyssey, and a joyful recognition of the link between the tiny and the vast. Submerge yourself in the splendor of the murals. Absorb the room's wisdom. Take a moment to experience the interconnected oneness with the cosmos. You are poised to embark on your spiritual journey through the major arcana, aligned with your own life's course. When you're ready, make your way back to the central tarot temple, take a deep breath, and slowly open your eyes. Carry this tranquility with you—the wisdom of the tarot and the connection to the divine and the material realms. The path to the temple of tarot is always open, waiting to welcome you back into its sacred embrace.

Tarot and Active Imagination

Active imagination is a technique developed by Carl Jung to consciously explore and interact with the unconscious mind. Jung emphasized that it's something we do by ourselves, without external guidance or influence.

It involves focusing on inner imagery, such as symbols or archetypes, and actively engaging with them. Through this process, a dialogue is established between the conscious and unconscious minds, revealing hidden meanings and messages. Jung also utilized active imagination to delve deeper into dream symbols, encouraging individuals to actively engage with dream imagery for a better understanding of the dream for personal interpretation and understanding.

Mary K. Greer points out that while Jung's approach was more passive, focused on exploring the psyche and one's complexes, our current practice of immersing ourselves into the inner planes is more active.[15] When we enter our internal tarot temple, we consciously summon specific symbols, archetypes, and energies that the tarot is based on to engage with directly. We maintain focus and allow the structure and scenes to remain stable in our minds, akin to lucid dreaming, whereas with Jung's technique you allow the whole thing to go wherever your unconscious wants to wander, as if it were a dream you were actively observing but were passive in regards to any goal or purpose other than introspection. What we are doing is much more like lucid dreaming in this regard than dreaming as passive observers. In the next exercise, we will utilize our internal tarot temple to gain insight directly from the tarot itself.

EXERCISE 43

DIRECTLY EXPLORING A CARD

Close your eyes and take a deep, calming breath. Feel the peace of the moment as you inhale. As you exhale, let go of all your stress and tension. Picture the bright path of golden light opening up in front of you, leading you to the front of your internal tarot temple's doors, flanked by pillars made of moonstone and obsidian. Open the door and enter the temple. Identify the suit of the card you seek clarity on. Look around the room and find the corresponding chamber door. If it's a major arcana card, seek the door with the Wheel of Fortune glyph inscribed on it and the door handle shaped like the symbol of infinity. Approach this door and

15 "Active Imagination vs. Guided Imagery," Mark K. Greer's Tarot Blog, https://marykgreer.com/2019/02/10/active-imagination-vs-guided-imagery.

feel its texture under your fingertips as you push it open. Step into the chamber. The grand room is adorned with life-size murals of every card in the suit. Search the murals for the card you want to understand. If you're using a specific deck you want to gain clarity about, allow the mural to reflect that card's artwork. Once you find it, stand before it. Reach out and place your hand on the mural. Suddenly, it becomes a vibrant portal. Step into it. You are now part of the card's scene.

Take in your surroundings. Notice the landscape, colors, animals or figures, if there are any. Pay attention to any sounds, scents, or sensations. If there are figures, approach them. They radiate wisdom and understanding. Ask your question clearly in your mind, directed at them. "What does your card signify in connection to my present circumstances?" or "What insight do you have for me?" Allow their response to form. It might come as words, feelings, images, or even changes in the scene itself. Take your time to understand their message. You might ask the figures what certain symbols within their card mean. Once you feel you have gained the insight you sought, thank the figures. Step back toward the portal. As you pass through it, you find yourself once more in the suit's chamber. Pause for a while to contemplate your encounter before departing from the chamber, gently shutting the door as you exit. Return to the main hall of the temple, carrying with you the wisdom of your journey. Make your way toward the temple's majestic entrance. As you cross the threshold, feel yourself gradually returning to the physical world and open your eyes when ready.

Directly Exploring a Card

WHAT THIS CAN LOOK LIKE

To illustrate what this experience is talking about, I'm going to do it and then explain what I experienced.

I pulled a tarot card at random to get some advice on a book idea I've been kicking around in my head. The card I pulled was the Three of Pentacles. I entered my internal tarot temple as normal, and this is what I experienced:

> I move toward the doorway bearing the emblem of the pentacles. I reach out and touch the symbol, feeling its cool, sturdy relief under my fingertips, radiating the energy of groundedness and material achievement. Easing the door open, I step into the realm dedicated to pentacles. Among the captivating murals, my attention is arrested by the Three of Pentacles from the Rider-Waite-Smith deck, the card I pulled earlier. The image is of a craftsman working intently on a cathedral

under the watchful eyes of two observers, one of whom holds the cathedral's blueprints. I reach out and touch the mural. An energy pulses beneath my hand, and the mural becomes a gateway. As I step through, the scenery around me transforms. Suddenly, I am standing within the echoing halls of the cathedral, the very scene from the card. The craftsman from the card is before me, his attention concentrated on the stone he is chiseling. The observers stand close by, attentively watching his work.

My question is clear in my mind as I approach: "What wisdom do you have for me about writing my book?" Addressing the craftsman first, he takes a moment from his work, wiping the sweat off his brow before speaking of the necessity of practice, skill, and unwavering dedication. His words ring true, reminding me that my writing will flourish with steadfast diligence and commitment. Turning to the figure clutching the cathedral's blueprints, he emphasizes the importance of a detailed plan, a clear vision for the work, and the benefit of seeking constructive feedback. His words resonate deeply with me, as these are all challenges I often face when working on my books. His insights emphasize the significance of meticulous planning, establishing a solid structure, and maintaining organization, while also fostering a willingness to embrace constructive feedback throughout my writing journey. The last figure, the third man in the card, speaks of the value of collaboration, mutual respect, and understanding. His insight highlights the importance of working in harmony with others and considering diverse perspectives in my writing process. Their collective wisdom provides a well-rounded perspective that illuminates my situation. Grateful for their insights, I thank them and step back toward the now familiar luminescent portal. I pass through it and find myself back in the realm of pentacles.

EXERCISE 44

INTERNAL TEMPLE SPREAD

In this tarot spread, we will explore five chambers within your internal tarot temple, each representing a different realm of experience: pentacles, swords, wands, cups, and the major arcana. By drawing five cards, you will gain insights into the current lessons and opportunities for growth within each chamber of your inner world.

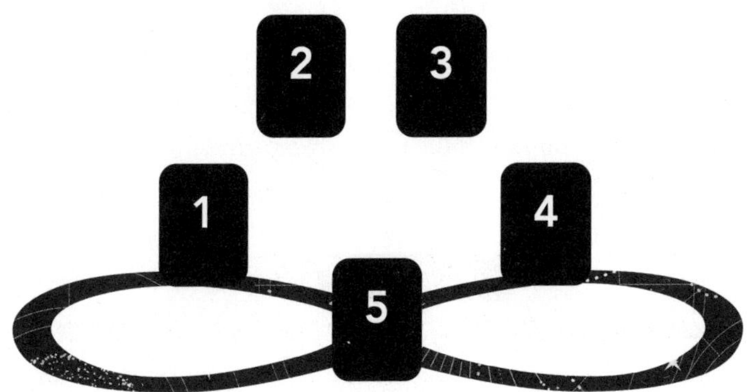

1. **Pentacles Chamber**—Draw a card to explore the realm of material and earthly matters. This chamber represents your relationship with finances, career, physical health, and overall material stability. The card will reveal the lessons you can currently learn and the practical steps to improve your connection with the realm of pentacles.
2. **Swords Chamber**—Draw a card to delve into the realm of thoughts, intellect, and communication. This chamber represents your mental state, beliefs, and communication patterns. The card will offer valuable insights regarding the lessons you can glean concerning mental clarity, decision-making, and the art of effective communication.
3. **Wands Chamber**—Draw a card to uncover the realm of inspiration, creativity, and passion. This chamber represents your drive, enthusiasm, and creative pursuits. The card will offer guidance on the lessons you can currently learn to ignite your inner fire, pursue your dreams, and channel your passion.

4. **Cups Chamber**—Draw a card to explore the realm of emotions, intuition, and relationships. This chamber represents your emotional well-being, intuition, and connections with others. The card will reveal the lessons you can learn to deepen emotional understanding, nurture your intuition, and cultivate meaningful relationships.
5. **Major Arcana Chamber**—Draw a card to connect with the realm of destiny and higher spiritual lessons. This chamber represents significant life events, soul lessons, and spiritual growth. The card will offer insights into the major themes and transformative opportunities currently present in your life journey.

EXERCISE 45

EXPLORING THE WISDOM OF THE CHAMBERS

Now that you have gained insights from the internal temple spread, it's time to embark on a transformative meditation journey. This exercise will guide you to visit each chamber individually in meditation, regardless of whether the tarot card matches the suit of the chamber. For example, if you drew the Two of Swords for the chamber of wands, ask for the chamber of wands' insight into that card. Through this journey, you will open yourself to the unique perspective and wisdom that each chamber holds.

1. Enter your internal tarot temple.
2. Begin with the pentacles chamber. Visualize yourself stepping into this realm of material stability and abundance. Ask the room to show you insights from its perspective based on the tarot card you drew. Embrace any visions, feelings, or sensations that arise, allowing yourself to learn the lessons of grounding, prosperity, and practicality from this chamber.
3. Move on to the swords chamber. Enter the realm of thoughts and intellect, inviting the room to share its wisdom with you, regardless of the tarot card's suit. Embrace any mental clarity, ideas, or revelations that come your way. Absorb the wisdom of

mental flexibility, effective communication, and adept problem-solving.

4. Journey into the wands chamber, the realm of inspiration and passion. Allow the room to present its insights to you, even if the tarot card didn't match the suit. Experience the creative energy, motivation, and enthusiasm that emanate from this chamber. Embrace the lessons of creative expression, ambition, and personal power.
5. Transition to the cups chamber, where emotions and relationships reside. Let the room reveal its perspective to you, based on the tarot card you drew. Experience the realm of love, intuition, and deep connections. Absorb the lessons of emotional healing, empathy, and nurturing.
6. Finally, approach the major arcana chamber, representing destiny and spiritual growth. Regardless of the suit in the tarot card, seek wisdom from this chamber about significant life events and soul lessons. Embrace any insights and revelations about your spiritual journey.
7. After visiting all five chambers, take a moment to integrate the experiences and lessons from each realm. Reflect on the wisdom you have gathered and how it can positively impact your life, as well as your interpretations of the tarot.

V
THE HIEROPHANT

7

∞

Your Tarot Spirit Helper

Consistently throughout history we have seen the idea of multidimensional benevolent nonphysical entities assisting humans. This concept and the practice of working with spirit guides experienced a surge of popularity and revival during the nineteenth and twentieth centuries with the rise of Spiritualism. In Spiritualism, psychics and mediums often spoke about their spirit guides who helped them not only on their own spiritual journeys but also in conducting their psychic and mediumship readings. Spirit guides do not belong to a distinct category of spirits; instead, they represent a role that various types of spirits can assume in their connection with you.

Spirit guides are immensely helpful in enhancing psychic abilities. They exist on the inner planes, which means they are already present and can assist you in comprehending the information you receive with greater clarity. They can help strengthen your connection to the inner planes, where this information originates from. Regardless of your spiritual path, anyone and everyone can work with spirit guides. I cannot stress enough the significant improvement I experienced in my tarot readings when I began incorporating and working with my tarot spirit guide. During the readings, my spirit guide helped me access information that might have been challenging to receive solely through my own psychic abilities. Moreover, they aided in directing my attention toward specific aspects and communicated with me directly through my clair senses.

Discerning Spirit Guides

Every spirit you encounter has its own agenda, and it's crucial to ensure that their motives align with your highest good when working with them. Some spirit guides are assigned to us from birth, while others cross our paths during our journey. A genuine spirit guide serves as a companion on your spiritual evolution, offering assistance and guidance for your personal growth. The distinction between a spirit guide and other spirits or allies lies in their selfless nature. Unlike other spirits with whom you may collaborate for various purposes, spirit guides do not seek anything in return because their primary role is to aid and mentor you. This doesn't imply that other spirits are inherently negative or that you should refrain from interacting with them. It simply highlights the unique quality of spirit guides and their specific intention to support you as part of their own mission of spiritual evolution.

When working with spirits, watch out for the accuracy of their information. A spirit guide will never mislead you or provide you with bad information. However, it's possible to initially misinterpret their guidance, which is why developing a strong relationship with them through ongoing interaction is extremely beneficial. As the term implies, a spirit guide's primary role is to provide guidance, not to foster a codependent or parasitic relationship where you become reliant on them. Instead, a spirit guide will always encourage your personal growth and development, including your spiritual journey. This means they will often guide you toward connecting with your own higher self and discovering your own truths. A spirit guide will never ask you to harm yourself or others, nor will they provide information, insights, or feedback that belittles yourself or others. They will always respect your boundaries and never ask you to violate or override your own free will or that of another. They will never seek adoration, worship, or offerings for their assistance. That said, it's a common practice to demonstrate respect and gratitude toward your spirit guide. This can be as simple as expressing thanks or as symbolic as offering gifts such as lighting a candle, presenting flowers, or offering a glass of water. The key distinction here is that these gestures are not seen as payments or obligations. Instead, consider your relationship with your spirit guide as you would with a cherished friend whom you value and appreciate.

EXERCISE 46

MEETING YOUR TAROT SPIRIT GUIDE

Begin by finding a comfortable and quiet place to sit or lie down. Close your eyes and take several deep, calming breaths. Inhale through your nose, filling your lungs with air, and exhale through your mouth, releasing any tension or stress. As you relax, imagine yourself standing before the grand door of your inner tarot temple once again. The pillars of obsidian and moonstone flanking the door seem even more majestic. You gently push the door open and step into the central chamber. The familiar fragrance of sandalwood and lavender welcomes you, soothing your senses. Feel the temple's tranquil energy resonate within you. Visualize yourself in the center of the room beneath the high, shimmering mosaics. Take a moment to feel the temple's calming energy, the mystical aura of the place enveloping you in a warm embrace. Take a few more deep breaths, allowing this peaceful energy to flow through you.

In the heart of the temple, imagine a circle of light appearing before you, growing larger and brighter. This light is a portal or doorway to your spirit guide who will aid you in understanding the wisdom of the tarot. Step into this circle of light. As you do, feel yourself being gently lifted, as though you are floating on a current of warm, supportive energy. You are being transported through the realm of spirit, moving toward your guide. After a moment, feel yourself gently landing. As the light around you dims, find yourself in a serene grove surrounded by majestic trees. The air here is cool and fresh; the sound of a babbling brook nearby is a soothing melody. This is a sacred space, a meeting place for you and your guide. As you stand in this sacred grove, call to your spirit guide. Say silently, "I call upon my tarot spirit guide. Please come forward and connect with me." Pay attention to the space around you. Look for any changes, any movements.

Your guide may appear in the form of a human, an animal, or even a mythical being. It may be a spirit guide you already work with or it could be one you're just meeting now for the first time. It may also be a feeling or a sense of presence. Don't be alarmed if you cannot see them clearly. Spirit guides often communicate through feelings, intuition, and symbolic imagery. Ask your spirit guide their name. Listen for a name or a word. It may not come immediately, and that's okay. Trust in the process. If a name does not come to you now, it may reveal itself later when you're ready to receive it. Ask your guide for a symbol that represents their essence and will help you connect with them in the future.

Pay attention to any images or symbols that come to your mind. Trust what comes. It's okay if it isn't clear right away. Take a moment to thank your guide for their presence and their help. Express your gratitude for their willingness to aid you in understanding the wisdom of the tarot. Know that your spirit guide is always there, ready to assist you whenever you need them.

When you're ready, return to the circle of light. Feel yourself being lifted once again by the energy current that carries you back to the tarot temple. Feel yourself gently landing in the central chamber. Take a moment to sit and reflect on your experience, the meeting with your guide, the name, and the symbol that were revealed. Finally, take a deep breath and slowly open your eyes. You are back in the physical world, carrying with you the tranquil energy from the tarot temple and the connection with your spirit guide. Visit your tarot temple regularly; with each visit, the presence and guidance of your spirit guide will become clearer and more tangible. Take some time now to write down your experience, noting any details about your guide's appearance as well as the name and symbol they shared. These details will serve as valuable tools in your ongoing journey with the tarot. It's okay if the spirit isn't completely clear during the meditation. If you didn't see it, just have a sense that it's there. Revisit your tarot temple regularly, and you will begin to see, feel, and understand your tarot spirit guide more each time. Be patient with the process and trust in your journey.

How To Call On Your Tarot Spirit Guide

In Michelle Welch's book *Spirits Unveiled*, she provides clear advice on how to connect with your spirit guide. She's absolutely correct when she writes that

> assuming you have identified a spirit guide you want to get to know better, the best way to begin to connect with your spirit guide is to simply think of them. It sounds simple because it is. Remember that your guide is always accessible to you, but often you are unaware of its presence. However, when you consciously think of your guide, it is an invitation to them for more direct communication. They are always ready and willing to assist you; you only have to ask.[16]

16 Welch, *Spirits Unveiled*, 20.

Connecting with a tarot spirit guide—like my own, which appears as a barn owl—starts off subtly. At first their guidance might feel so faint that you question if it's just your imagination or coincidence. But as you invest time in the relationship, their messages get clearer and more direct. You become more attuned to their presence, picking up on their cues more easily. A big part of establishing this deeper connection involves using their name and focusing on their appearance or any unique symbol they've given you. It's like a password that ensures you're really communicating with your guide and not some other spirit trying to interfere.

EXERCISE 47

WORKING WITH YOUR TAROT SPIRIT GUIDE

Like any other time before doing a tarot reading, you will want to complete the preliminary exercises before proceeding with this exercise (see the list on page 36). I recommend performing this exercise in solitary readings for yourself to begin with. As you get more comfortable with it, begin incorporating it into readings for others.

1. Recall your tarot spirit guide's name, appearance, and symbol. If you struggle to see or sense them, use your imagination to project their image into the room. Visualize them sitting across from you, their presence reassuring and comforting. This act of imagination helps to create a thoughtform, a psychic construct that helps anchor their energy in your space.
2. Once you feel the presence of your guide, articulate your intention for the reading. For example, you could say, "I call upon (guide's name) to guide me in this tarot reading. Please illuminate the cards with your wisdom and provide clear and insightful messages."
3. As you shuffle your tarot deck and lay out your spread, maintain a state of openness and receptivity. Your tarot spirit guide's guidance will come through your psychic clair senses.

   CLAIRVOYANCE: You might see images, symbols, or colors related to the cards you've drawn. Look for any visual cues that stand out.

CLAIRAUDIENCE: Listen for any words, phrases, or sounds in your mind. These could be direct messages from your guide or sounds that have symbolic meaning.

CLAIRTANGENCY (PSYCHOMETRY): You may gain insights or impressions from touching the cards, feeling the energy that each card holds.

CLAIRALIENCE (CLAIRSCENT): Pay attention to any scents or smells that come to you during the reading. These scents can be associated with specific cards or provide additional insight into the reading.

CLAIRGUSTANCE: You might taste something in your mouth that isn't physically present. These tastes could hold symbolic meanings that could help you interpret the cards.

4. At this point you can ask your guide any questions about the cards. You can request them to clarify certain card meanings or ask them to fetch specific information.
5. Reflect on the messages received. How do these insights interact with the cards you've drawn? Take your time to understand and integrate these messages.
6. When the reading concludes, express your gratitude to your tarot spirit guide for their guidance. Visualize your guide's image gently fading as they return to their realm, leaving their wisdom and energy behind.

Working With Your Tarot Spirit Guide

WHAT THIS CAN LOOK LIKE

A few years back, I was conducting a tarot reading for a new friend I was just starting to get to know. She was facing a significant career decision but chose not to disclose the specifics, leaving it to the cards and my intuition to reveal her situation. She just wanted to see what the cards had to say. As we made ourselves comfortable for the reading, I prepared to call upon my tarot spirit guide. I visualized the image of a barn owl, with its friendly, apple-shaped face and wise eyes mirroring ancient knowledge. Soon enough I could sense the familiar energetic warmth of the barn owl's presence filling the room. I laid out a few cards: the Eight of Cups, the Ace of Swords, and the Wheel of Fortune emerged. The Eight of Cups, symbolizing her present situation, suggested a deep longing for something more despite her attachment to her current job. The Ace of Swords, indicative of her potential future, pointed toward a fresh start or a change in perspective. The Wheel of Fortune, reflecting her hopes and fears, signified inevitable changes and her apprehension about the unknown.

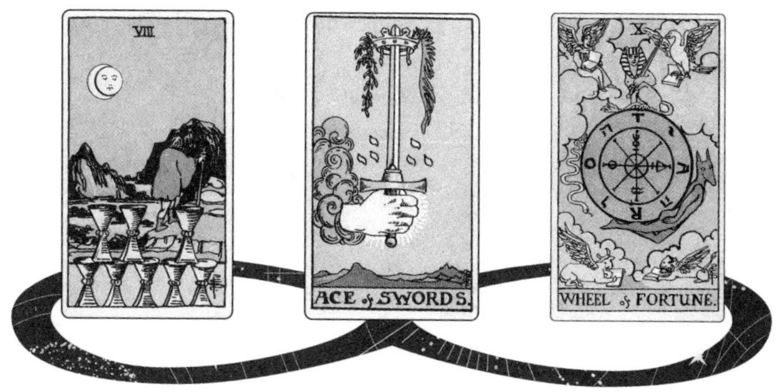

As I began interpreting the traditional meanings of the cards, I noticed within my mind's eye the barn owl flying toward a small potted plant in my room—a resilient species that thrives in urban environments, symbolizing sustainability and adaptability. This led me to intuit that her career decision could be tied to the outdoors or nature somehow. The Eight of Cups card felt warmer under my fingertips (clairtangency), suggesting a message. I followed the sensation and began to feel a sense of accomplishment as an emotion within my body. The barn owl seemed to underscore the emotional growth tied to embracing changes. While reflecting on the Ace of Swords, I noticed a refreshing scent of crisp, clean air filling the room (clairalience), reinforcing the promise of a fresh start that the Ace of Swords traditionally symbolizes. The Wheel of Fortune card initially confused me. Then, unexpectedly, I tasted a unique tang of citrus in my mouth (clairgustance). The barn owl seemed to suggest that her life would be a blend of challenges and rewards with the forthcoming change. Suddenly the barn owl flew toward a poster on my wall of a beautiful, thriving forest, which seemed to confirm my intuition that the career choice she was contemplating was indeed something dealing with nature. So I told her that I was getting the sense that nature or being outside was somehow central to this reading and asked her if that had anything to do with the decisions she was facing. She confirmed this and told me that it was a job in the field of environmental science. As you can see, the guidance from the barn owl enriched my reading. Each card's message became more personalized, carrying wisdom. To her surprise and comfort, she found the reading accurately reflected her situation, and it gave her the courage to accept the new job.

My experience working with my barn owl spirit guide during tarot readings really drove home how valuable a spirit guide's insights can be. My understanding of the cards just seemed to get deeper and more nuanced when the owl chimed in. I found that the owl's guidance not only made the reading more accurate but also led me to discover things I might not have realized on my own. When I do a reading with the barn owl, it feels like our consciousness sort of syncs up. Sometimes it's hard to tell where my own intuition ends and the owl's guidance begins. We come together in a way that combines its wisdom and my psychic skills, making the whole reading just click. Paying close attention to my psychic senses is crucial. Having a spirit guide like the barn owl helps me fine-tune my clairvoyant, clairaudient, and other psychic abilities. It's a great partnership that takes my readings to a whole new level and makes them incredibly personal.

EXERCISE 48

FEATHER FLIGHT SPIRIT GUIDE TAROT SPREAD

In this exercise we'll seek to strengthen communication with our tarot spirit guides through the universal symbolism of a single feather. Feathers have long held significance as messages from the higher realms, bridging the earthly realm with that of spirits. With the feather flight spirit guide tarot spread, we embrace this powerful imagery to deepen our connection to our tarot spirit guide, create a tangible and spiritual experience with them, and observe how our guide communicates with us.

∞

1. **Calling On Your Tarot Spirit Guide.** Find a tranquil outdoor space where you can feel the presence of nature. Close your eyes, take a deep breath, and envision a magnificent feather gently floating down from the sky, symbolizing your connection with your tarot spirit guide. Watch as the feather hovers to each spot in the spread, sort of like the feather in the movie *Forrest Gump*. As you hold the tarot deck in your hands, set the intention to build a stronger connection with your tarot spirit guide and invite their presence to guide you through the reading.

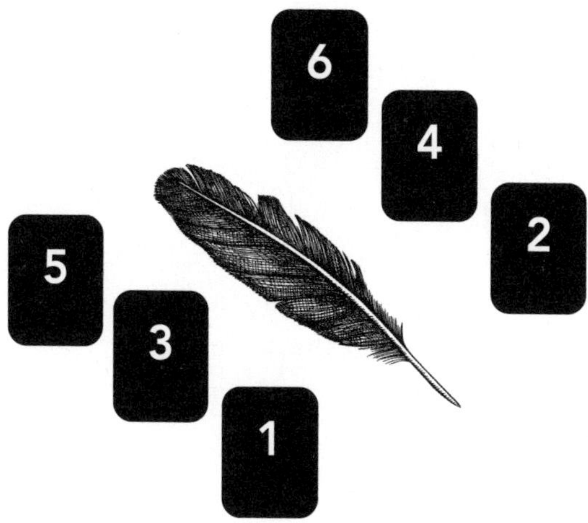

2. **Card One: Feather Unfolding (Tarot Spirit Guide Connection).** Shuffle the tarot deck while focusing on the beauty and wonder of the unfolding feather, representing the unfolding bond with your tarot spirit guide. When you feel ready, draw the first card, envisioning the feather gently whispering the message from your tarot spirit guide. This card will reveal the guidance and advice your guide wants to convey to deepen your connection.
3. **Card Two: Winds of Challenge (Obstacles to Overcome).** Draw the second card, imagining the feather encountering gusts of wind and turbulence. This card represents the obstacles and

challenges that may be hindering a clear connection with your tarot spirit guide. Embrace these challenges as opportunities for growth and strengthening your bond.

4. **Card Three: Feather's Flight Plan (Guidance).** Draw the third card, picturing the feather gracefully navigating through the winds and finding its path. This card offers guidance from your tarot spirit guide to overcome the challenges and build a stronger connection. Trust in the wisdom and support your guide provides.
5. **Card Four: Feather's Landing (Focus Areas).** Draw the fourth card, visualizing the feather gently landing in a specific place. This card will indicate the areas of your life or aspects of your tarot practice that your tarot spirit guide wants you to pay attention to. Embrace these areas as focal points for enhancing your connection and understanding of the tarot.
6. **Card Five: Guiding Current (Additional Support).** Draw the fifth card, imagining a supportive current of air lifting the feather higher. This card reveals the external support or resources available to you in your journey of connecting with your tarot spirit guide.
7. **Card Six: Feather Soar (Elevated Connection).** Draw the final card, picturing the feather soaring high in the sky, carried by the winds of your tarot spirit guide's guidance. This card represents the potential for an elevated connection with your guide and the positive outcome of your efforts to build a stronger bond. Embrace the potential for insights and a deeper understanding of the tarot's wisdom.
8. Take some time to reflect on the messages received from each card and their connection to the creative imagery of the feather flight. Trust your intuition and allow your tarot spirit guide to speak to you through the tarot cards and the symbolism of the feather. Express gratitude to your tarot spirit guide for their loving presence and support as you embark on this journey of building a stronger connection.

Feather Flight Spirit Guide Tarot Spread

WHAT THIS CAN LOOK LIKE

Here's an example of me performing this spread and an explanation of what I saw on the screen of my mind's eye as I tuned in to each card. In the feather unfolding position, which focuses on the relationship between me and my barn owl spirit guide, the Magician card showed up. As I looked at the card, I pictured a forest lit in an almost magickal light. My barn owl was there, moving between mirrors hanging from trees. The mirrors seemed to challenge what was real and what was not, making me think more deeply about everything. This setup really seemed to resonate with the Magician's themes of transformation and creative potential. Seeing my barn owl interact with the mirrors got me thinking maybe this is a sign that I should deepen my bond with my spirit guide through creativity and imagination. Instead of sticking to familiar patterns, I could start to explore new, imaginative forms of spiritual connection. Whether it's creative rituals, different types of meditation, or even artistic expression, the Magician and my barn owl are nudging me to expand my spiritual toolkit. This feels like a direct invitation to deepen our connection by embracing the unexpected and the magickal in our ongoing spiritual dialogue.

In the Winds of Challenge position, which is all about what might be blocking my connection with my barn owl spirit guide, I pulled the Four of Cups card. As I looked at it, I imagined myself standing beside a quiet, moonlit lake. My barn owl was perched on an old tree branch nearby, looking pretty deep in thought. The Four of Cups is generally a card about contemplation but also about emotional stagnation, and that got me thinking—maybe the thing blocking me and my barn owl from connecting more deeply is my own tendency to get stuck in my head, overthinking things or becoming too introspective. The quiet lake and my owl's introspective mood seemed like a wake-up call to stop navel-gazing and start actively engaging more with my spirit guide. Instead of just contemplating the mysteries, maybe it's time to dive in and explore them deeper together. This could mean taking more direct steps to communicate with my guide or opening up to messages and signs in my day-to-day life.

In the Feather's Flight spot, which shows how to get past the blocks in my relationship with my barn owl spirit guide, I drew the High Priestess. As I focused on the card, I pictured myself following my barn owl into a cave full of ancient symbols. The deeper we went, the more it felt like the symbols were talking to us in some way. This connected strongly with the High Priestess's vibes about trusting intuition and digging into deeper knowledge. If the Four of Cups was about me getting too stuck in my own head to connect with my barn owl well, the High Priestess seemed to say the way through is to start trusting my gut feelings more, and not just in a "this feels right" way, but in a deeper "this resonates with ancient wisdom" kind of way. It's almost like the High Priestess and my barn owl were teaming up to say, "Listen to your inner voice, and pay attention to symbols and signs. They can guide you through the blocks you've been feeling." Basically, it's time to lean into those more intuitive, esoteric forms of understanding to make my connection with my barn owl spirit guide even stronger.

In the Feather's Landing position, I drew the Eight of Pentacles and found myself in a calm space filled with the gentle light of candles, with tarot cards neatly laid out in front of me. My barn owl perched nearby, watching every move with keen eyes. The Eight of Pentacles seemed to emphasize the idea that each tarot reading, even daily single-card draws, should be treated with the same level of attention and care. The presence of my barn owl seemed to echo this sentiment, urging me to slow down and fully engage with each card's imagery, symbolism, and message. It was as if my spirit guide was saying, "This is a form of art, and art cannot be rushed. Allow yourself the space to sink deeply into the moment, understanding that each card drawn is an opportunity for growth and deeper connection with your spiritual self." It's clear my barn owl spirit guide wants me to take my time with each tarot reading, making sure I approach every card, every spread, every intuitive pulse with thoughtful consideration.

In the Guiding Current position, I drew the Wheel of Fortune. My vision placed me and my barn owl high above, perched on an enormous turning wheel. As we rotated, it hit me that while change is an ever-present factor, the cycle itself can also be a guide. The Wheel of Fortune emphasized that just as there are external forces influencing the wheel's turn, there are also external sources of wisdom and guidance in my life. It felt like a nod toward tapping into outside resources, whether that be mentors, books, or supportive communities. It was as if the wheel itself was advising me to diversify my sources of wisdom and lean on collective knowledge to help me grow spiritually. Importantly, it reassured me that even though the cycle of life includes ups and downs, there's an abundance of external guidance available to help me navigate it.

In the Feather Soar position, I pulled the Nine of Swords. Instantly I was walking through a maze under the moonlight, my barn owl's hushed voice serving as my guide. The card itself is often about confronting inner worries or fears, and here it signaled that the payoff for facing these fears head-on would be a stronger, more intimate connection with my barn owl spirit guide. Each whisper from my barn owl felt like a nudge, steering me away from mental traps and toward a clearer emotional state. It's like my barn owl was saying, "Overcoming your inner struggles isn't just good for you, it's good for us; it deepens our connection." This card wasn't just about personal growth; it was a green light telling me that a richer bond with my barn owl was not only possible but also directly linked to my willingness to tackle my internal challenges.

EXERCISE 49

UNDERSTANDING YOUR TAROT BIRTH CARD

Understanding your tarot birth card can offer insightful guidance on your life journey. This concept, introduced by Angeles Arrien and further popularized by Mary K. Greer, connects your birth date with a card from the major arcana. Your birth card can symbolize your inherent strengths, potential challenges, and personal themes. Moreover, integrating insights from your tarot spirit guide can deepen your understanding and interpretation of this card. Let's walk through the process of determining your birth card using Pamela Colman Smith's birthday as an example. She is known as the illustrator of the widely recognized Rider-Waite-Smith deck, and I'm not the least bit surprised that she's an Aquarius.

1. Write down the birth date in the MM/DD/YYYY format.
   In this case, we are using Pamela Colman Smith's birthday, February 16, 1878, so it will be written as 02/16/1878.
2. Break down each element of the birth date into single digits and add them together:

   Month: 0 + 2 = 2

   Day: 1 + 6 = 7

   Year: 1 + 8 + 7 + 8 = 24

   FIRST: Combine the results from step 2:

   2 (month) + 7 (day) + 24 (year) = 33

   THEN: Reduce the sum from step 3 to a single digit or a number that corresponds to a major arcana card:

   3 + 3 = 6

3. Connect the single-digit number to its corresponding major arcana card. In this instance, the number 6 corresponds to the Lovers.
4. Ask your tarot spirit guide for their perspective on the significance of your birth card in your life. Reflect on the typical symbolism of the card, along with the guidance provided by your guide. Ask your guide how this card can symbolize your inherent strengths, potential challenges, and personal themes.

EXERCISE 50

UNDERSTANDING YOUR YEAR CARD

The process of identifying your tarot card of the year can provide a wealth of insight into the upcoming challenges and blessings that you might encounter. Just as the individual cards of the tarot deck tell a story, so too does the energy of the year ahead. As a remarkable example, we'll calculate the tarot card of the year for the year 1910, which is notable in history as well as significant in the tarot world. It was during this year that the renowned Rider-Waite-Smith deck became a hit and soon-to-be classic.[17]

1. Start by adding together the digits of the given year, 1910, like this: 1 + 9 + 1 + 0 = 11.
2. Take the number of the birth card, the Lovers (number 6), and add it to the total you got in the first step: 6 (birth card number) + 11 (sum of the year's digits) = 17.
3. If the total from the previous step isn't a single-digit number or doesn't correspond directly to a major arcana card (like the number 21 does), you'll need to reduce it further to a single digit or to a major arcana number.
4. Your next task is to match the resulting number from the previous step to its corresponding major arcana card. Here, the number 17 corresponds to the Star.

17 "Rider 'Roses and Lilies' Deck (1909)," Waite Smith—A Tarot Revolution, https://waitesmith.org/index.php/decks/rider-roses-lilies-deck-1909/.

5. Now that you've identified your tarot card of the year, meditate on its symbolic meanings and messages. Ask your tarot spirit guide for additional insight and clarification about what this card might mean for you in the context of the year.
6. Ask your tarot spirit guide how the energies of the card are unfolding in your life during this time. Record what you receive in your journal and revisit it on New Year's Day to compare what you received with how the year unfolded.

Birth and Year Cards

WHAT THIS CAN LOOK LIKE

The Lovers tarot card symbolizes love, harmony, decisions, and partnerships. These elements closely parallel the life of Pamela Colman Smith, or "Pixie," as she was often called. Her collaborations were key to her career, particularly her work with Arthur Edward Waite on the famed Rider-Waite-Smith Tarot deck. This cooperation showcases the unity represented by the Lovers card. The card also signals the importance of choices. Pixie decided to chase her artistic dreams at a time when societal norms discouraged women from doing so. This bold step echoes the bravery symbolized by the Lovers. The card also represents the balance of opposites, a theme that resonates strongly with Smith's life. She seamlessly melded the tangible, practical aspects of her craft as an illustrator and writer with the metaphysical, conceptual nature of her spiritual interests in occultism and esoteric mysticism. These domains are often considered to be opposing—one being grounded in the physical world and the other in the spiritual/metaphysical world. Smith's ability to meld these contrasting fields in her work showcases her harmony with the essence of the Lovers card. Lastly, the Lovers card highlights a journey of self-discovery and acceptance, reflected in Pixie's commitment to her art despite societal pressures.

We can look at the relationship of the year 1910 in Smith's life with the Star card in two different ways. One evident approach would be to examine the deck she introduced to the world, while another avenue would involve delving into her personal life during that period. The Rider-Waite-Smith deck beautifully embodies the essence of the Star card, offering hope, insight, serenity, and a spiritual guidance. Smith, with her knowledge of mystical traditions (along with ideas from Waite), infused the deck with rich symbolism, making the once cryptic language of tarot accessible to all. It's like they took the healing, optimistic energy of the Star and sprinkled it throughout the entire deck. Ruled by innovative Aquarius, the Star card reflects the deck's groundbreaking nature, being one of the first to illustrate the minor arcana with detailed scenes that told their own unique stories. It also brought forward a lot of Eliphas Levi's and the Golden Dawn's esoteric associations in an extremely innovative and new way. This revolutionary approach to crafting the tarot didn't just popularize tarot; it made it a tool for everyone, ensuring that its wisdom and guidance were readily available to any seeker.

However, the year 1910 seemed to mark a turning point in the life of Pamela Colman Smith. In the initial stages of her career, Smith achieved notable success, in part due to her collaboration with Alfred Stieglitz, a distinguished figure in the art sphere. Stieglitz acknowledged Smith's artistic capabilities and guided her onto a path that led to fame. Nevertheless, as 1910 unfolded, Stieglitz's artistic preferences transitioned, mirroring the shift in the art world toward post-impressionism. His focus gravitated toward

European modernists, known for their sensual interpretations of art, creating a departure from Smith's spiritual and symbolic approach.

This change marked a critical juncture in Smith's professional journey, aligning with the Star card's symbolism in tarot—a card depicting hope, healing, and spiritual rejuvenation. Despite the release of the Rider-Waite-Smith deck, which irrevocably transformed the practice of tarot reading, Smith herself started to withdraw from the public arena. In a manner resonating with the Star card, she sought solace in spiritual exploration, distancing herself from the recognition and fame she had once found. This period of introspection and spiritual searching culminated in her conversion to Roman Catholicism in the subsequent year, a transformative step in her personal and spiritual journey. This conversion not only solidified her commitment to her newfound spiritual path but also marked a clear separation from her prior artistic and occult affiliations. Smith's life in 1910 embodies the Star card's message, marking a phase of renewal, healing, and embracing a new spiritual direction amidst significant changes and challenges.

Dream Incubation

Dream incubation is a technique that aims to receive guidance or answers through dreams. This process involves setting a specific intention or question before sleeping. The practice derives its name from ancient customs where individuals would sleep in sacred spaces, such as temples, hoping to experience divine dreams that could impart answers or bring healing. In this sense, they would have their question that they'd "incubate" in their dreams. In essence, dream incubation is a purposeful way to interact with our subconscious mind, inner realms, and psychic abilities. It treats dreaming not just as a passive event during sleep, but as an active domain of consciousness where we can seek guidance and insight. The belief underpinning this practice is that dreams are neither random nor meaningless but intimately linked to our inner selves and the larger universe.

As previously mentioned, dreaming offers a direct connection to our inner realms and spirit allies. In the dream state, our conscious mind is at rest while our subconscious mind is active. This state makes us receptive to subtle energies and messages from the spirit world. This connection isn't confined to our personal psyche but expands to a larger spiritual landscape within the inner planes, home to our spirit allies. These allies can be seen as either facets of our unconscious mind or as distinct spiritual entities. For me, that differentiation isn't important; what is important is the result from interacting with them. They can offer guidance, wisdom, and insights into our lives, providing answers to our questions, solutions to our problems, and guidance on our journey. We can also ask for further insight from our spirits about a tarot reading we've done for ourselves or received from another. By setting an intention or posing a question to our tarot spirit guide before we sleep, we signal to our subconscious mind, the collective unconscious, the inner planes, and our spirit guide that we are ready to receive their wisdom.

EXERCISE 51

DREAM INCUBATION WITH YOUR TAROT SPIRIT GUIDE

This dream incubation journey involves seeking clarity through a connection with your tarot spirit guide before dreaming. Tarot spirit guides serve as a link to higher wisdom and the depths of the subconscious mind, enhancing your understanding of tarot readings. Dreaming is a natural setting for such encounters, as it allows for permeable barriers of conscious thought, leading to insights and answers. Instead of calling your spirit guide to provide you with guidance from the inner plane into the outer world, you're going into the inner planes through dreaming. The process requires trust, patience, and curiosity, with experiences being unique to each individual. Dream interpretation may demand practice due to the symbolic or abstract nature of insights, and it's essential to remain patient and repeat the process if necessary. The tarot spirit guide may not always appear directly in dreams but may instead subtly influence dream content to provide guidance and clarity. The communication may not be explicit, but guidance is always present.

1. Set aside some quiet time before going to bed, using this opportunity to relax and clear your mind. This can be achieved through meditation, gentle yoga, or simply sitting in a quiet,

comfortable spot. The aim here is to slow down your mind in preparation for the dream incubation process.

2. Recall the tarot reading you wish to gain further clarity on. Look over the cards, remembering their positions in the spread and your initial interpretations. Reflect on any doubts or questions you have about this reading.
3. Establish a clear and concise question or intention related to the tarot reading, then call upon your tarot spirit guide and pose your question to them. Visualize their appearance, symbol that they gave you, and their name. Your intention might be something like, "Dear tarot spirit guide, please reveal the deeper meaning of the Tower card in my past reading" or "Dear tarot spirit guide, please show me how to apply the advice from my tarot reading to my present situation."
4. Solidify your intention by writing it down on a piece of paper. Keep this paper under your pillow or near your bed. If it feels right, you may also place your tarot deck that you used for the reading in the same location.
5. Once you are ready to sleep, visualize your tarot spirit guide appearing in your dream. Imagine them as vividly as possible, perhaps offering you guidance, advice, or answers in response to your question.
6. After setting your intention and visualizing the dream, allow yourself to fall asleep naturally. Trust that your subconscious mind will continue to work on your question as you sleep.
7. Upon waking, make an immediate effort to recall your dreams. It can be helpful to keep a dream journal nearby to record any details you remember as soon as you wake up. Reflect on these details, looking for symbols or themes that could offer answers to your question.

EXERCISE 52

DRAWING THE RIGHT QUERENTS

Your tarot spirit guide can act as a scout, bringing you and those who'll benefit most from your readings together. This spiritual guide bridges the gap between the physical and the spiritual worlds, helping you connect with individuals who truly need your tarot insight. This connection is intentional, driven by a combination of energy and necessity. Those seeking clarity, guidance, or confirmation on their life's path are gently guided toward you. This serendipity is harnessed through your tarot spirit guide's influence, allowing you to offer meaningful and impactful readings to those who are drawn to your service.

1. Close your eyes and call upon your tarot spirit guide with genuine intention. Ask them to assist in attracting individuals who would benefit the most from your tarot readings.
2. Surrender any personal desires or expectations and trust that your spirit guide knows the perfect people to draw toward your readings.
3. Repeat a powerful affirmation together with your spirit guide, such as: "For the highest good of all, with the guidance of my spirit companion, I attract those in need of wisdom and healing through tarot who will listen and benefit from the readings."
4. Visualize your spirit guide as a radiant, guiding light extending their energy outward. See this beacon of light reaching out to those who would benefit from your tarot readings.
5. Feel yourself aligning your energy with your spirit guide, working together as a team to connect with the people in need of your tarot insights.
6. Become a receptive channel for your spirit guide's wisdom and guidance. Embrace the flow of energy as they attract the right individuals toward you.
7. Trust that meaningful synchronicities and encounters will occur as your spirit guide aligns your paths with those seeking tarot readings.

8. Regularly communicate with your spirit guide, expressing gratitude for their assistance in bringing the right people to your tarot sessions.

An Imaginary Friend or a Spirit Guide?

When you initially begin your journey with a spirit guide, it's quite normal for the interaction to resemble that of an imaginary friend. Nevertheless, this shouldn't be interpreted as the spirit being unreal or purely a product of your imagination. As explained, psychic ability and imagination often have striking similarities, as they both rely on the same mental faculties and brainwave states. Dion Fortune nailed it when she wrote:

> To say that a thing is imaginary is not to dispose of it in the realm of mind, for the imagination, or the image making faculty, is a very important part of our mental functioning. An image formed by the imagination is a reality from the point of view of psychology; it is quite true that it has no physical existence, but are we going to limit reality to that which is material? We shall be far out of our reckoning if we do, for mental images are potent things, and although they do not actually exist on the physical plane, they influence it far more than most people suspect.[18]

The more you engage with your spirit guide, the better you become at discerning whether you're simply creating something in your imagination or utilizing those same pathways to receive genuine information. This is precisely why practices like meditation, self-reflection, journaling, and enhancing self-awareness prove valuable in the development of psychic abilities. These practices assist in gaining insight into the functioning of your own mind, enabling you to differentiate whether the information you receive arises from your inner psyche or external sources. By honing your discernment, you can deepen your connection with your spirit guide and gain greater clarity in receiving meaningful insights.

18 Fortune, *Spiritualism in the Light of Occult Science*, 91.

EXERCISE 53

STRENGTHENING THE PRESENCE OF YOUR TAROT SPIRIT GUIDE

The presence of your tarot spirit guide is a personal experience. This exercise aims to strengthen your connection with them through imagination, visualization, and intention. The more you engage in this practice, the more integrated their thoughtform may become, providing you with guidance and comfort on your spiritual journey.

1. Begin your day with a calming meditation. Visualize your tarot spirit guide appearing beside you, radiating a comforting and supportive energy. Set the intention to carry their presence with you throughout the day.
2. As you get ready for the day, recite affirmations that affirm your connection with your tarot spirit guide. Speak aloud or silently to yourself, acknowledging their guidance and protection as you navigate the day's events.
3. Throughout the day, before making important decisions or facing challenges, pause for a moment. Imagine your tarot spirit guide by your side, offering their wisdom. Seek their guidance through visualization, asking questions, and sensing their responses.
4. When stress or anxiety arises, close your eyes briefly and imagine your tarot spirit guide wrapping you in a comforting embrace. Feel their calming energy as they help you center yourself and find inner peace amidst the chaos.
5. During lunchtime or breaks, take a walk in nature. Imagine your tarot spirit guide exploring alongside you, whispering insights about the natural world and encouraging you to connect with the energy of the environment.
6. At the end of the day, sit quietly and reflect on the experiences you had with your tarot spirit guide. Journal about the moments you imagined them being present, the messages they conveyed, and the emotions they evoked.

∞

7. Close the day with a gratitude meditation, expressing thanks to your tarot spirit guide for their constant support and presence. Visualize them embracing you with love and gratitude, anchoring their thoughtform deeper into your reality.

EXERCISE 54

ASPECTING YOUR TAROT SPIRIT GUIDE

This exercise is more advanced and should only be attempted when you feel completely comfortable and confident in your connection with your tarot spirit guide and trust them completely. You'll want to have a strong foundation in working with them and be sure of the energy you are inviting. If you ever feel uneasy or unsafe during the exercise, it's crucial to stop immediately and reconnect with your own energy. Approach this practice with respect and a willingness to learn and grow on your spiritual journey. By invoking your tarot spirit guide and harmonizing energies, you can fortify your bond with your spiritual ally, fostering a deeper partnership in your metaphysical path.

During the exercise, you'll be inviting your tarot spirit guide to overlight you, where you blend your energies with theirs and imagine seeing through the eyes and feeling through the body of your spirit guide, which can grant you a different perspective and heightened intuitive abilities. You're essentially wearing them as an energetic mask or suit. This could be considered a form of "aspecting," a term adopted simultaneously in the 1980s by Ivo Dominguez, Jr.'s tradition Assembly of the Sacred Wheel and Starhawk's Reclaiming tradition from Roger Zelazny's 1960s science fiction novel Lord of Light. *Aspecting is where you take on an aspect of a spirit without having a full possessory experience. I've found the practice I'm about to share can lead to more unique insights into the tarot cards and the messages they convey. You'll interpret the tarot cards from your spirit guide's perspective, offering fresh insights, symbolic meanings, and alternative interpretations, ultimately leading to a more comprehensive understanding of your reading. Embrace this empowering experience as an opportunity for personal and spiritual growth. It's essential to trust yourself and your relationship with your tarot spirit guide before attempting this practice.*

1. Mentally call upon your tarot spirit guide by name and visualize their symbol or representation.
2. Imagine a radiant light surrounding you, representing your tarot spirit guide's energy. Visualize this light merging with your own, creating a blend of energies. Feel their presence gently enveloping you like a protective and supportive costume.
3. Visualize yourself and your tarot spirit guide as one unified being. Imagine looking through their eyes and feeling through their body. Sense their wisdom, intuition, and psychic abilities merging with your own, enhancing your perception and understanding.
4. With your tarot spirit guide's energy flowing through you, shuffle the tarot cards while remaining in their presence. Draw the cards for your reading, feeling their guidance and insights influencing your choices.
5. As you lay out the cards, interpret them with your tarot spirit guide's perspective. Trust your intuition and any thoughts or emotions that arise while connecting with their energy. Feel the added depth and clarity in your psychic insights during the reading.
6. After the reading, take a moment to thank your tarot spirit guide for their support and insights. Reflect on the experience and any unique perspectives or messages you gained through their guidance.
7. When you're ready to conclude the exercise, visualize your energy separating from your tarot spirit guide's energy. Allow their presence to gently withdraw from your energetic costume, returning you to your individual self.

VI
THE LOVERS.

8
∞

Psychic Tarot

In my early twenties, I wasn't too serious about my psychic abilities or spiritual path. I set aside my initial love of it in favor of partying and socializing. Yet, during a house party, an unexpected psychic vision altered my perception of my own psychic strengths and their importance. While I had navigated psychic phenomena before, mastering them was still a work in progress, especially in terms of honing them for intentional use rather than letting them happen haphazardly. That evening, as music and casual conversations filled the air and a drink rested in my hand, an intense, unwelcome vision jolted my awareness. I saw the alley that we walked through to get to the party; I heard muffled cries; I felt the panic of an unseen struggle. Almost at the same time, a voice—crystal clear and impossible to ignore—advised, "Leave now; don't go alone. Don't walk." The experience differed from the usual psychic background noise I had become accustomed to on rare occasions. It was a resounding, urgent warning.

My heart pounding, I surveyed the room. Friends and acquaintances were deep in chatter, blissfully ignorant of my internal crisis. The vision had presented a direct message specific in its intent and immediate in its demand for action. I swiftly approached the close friend I'd arrived with, who I'll call Susan for the sake of this book, taking her away from the crowd. Without going into details—knowing her staunch atheism would likely make her skeptical—I insisted we needed to leave immediately. The urgency in my voice was enough; though visibly confused, she agreed to go. Another friend wasn't as receptive. He brushed off my warning and continued to enjoy his drink.

I asked him to send a text later to confirm his safe arrival home. Hurried farewells were exchanged, and Susan and I left. Ignoring our usual preference for walking, we hailed a cab to take us back to our apartment. The message was clear in its directive, and I wasn't about to test its accuracy by dismissing it.

When morning light filled my room, my phone buzzed with incoming messages that quickly dispelled any remnants of sleep. Groggy and hungover, I grabbed my phone. A sinking feeling took hold as I scrolled through the texts. My friend who had opted to stay at the party had been assaulted in a dimly lit alley adjacent to the house, precisely the kind of space I'd visualized the previous night. He and the friends he was with had experienced a frightening struggle, further aligning with the vision and sensations that had overwhelmed me. It was unsettling to confront the pinpoint accuracy of my psychic warning, particularly in how closely it correlated with my friend's nightmarish ordeal. This experience was more than enough to shake me out of any lingering casual attitude toward my psychism. They were tools—ones that needed careful honing, respectful consideration, and, above all, serious attention when they sounded an alarm.

The unsettling event was a pivotal moment that propelled me into a more disciplined exploration of my psychic capabilities. My approach shifted from viewing them as quirky side notes to recognizing them as important abilities. These abilities offered tangible protection for me and those I care about. My experience wasn't unique; it echoed the long history and wide reach of psychic phenomena across different societies. These instances of psychic abilities have happened to countless people around the world and still do. Whether it's an intuitive nudge or a vivid vision, people from varied backgrounds report experiences that have been instrumental in avoiding harm or making impactful life choices. These abilities don't discriminate; they manifest regardless of age, cultural background, or socioeconomic status.

Susan and I eventually split up as friends, and it felt like a piece of me was missing. To get an idea of her, think of Janeane Garofalo's character Heather Mooney in *Romy and Michele's High School Reunion*. Susan was the real-life version: chain-smoking, clad in perpetual black, tons of black eyeshadow and eyeliner, which we jokingly referred to as her raccoon eyes, and she was always ready with a cutting one-liner. I loved her. She was my ride-or-die for every wild adventure. For years, if you saw one of us, the other was sure to be close by. Unfortunately, drugs entered the picture, and the friendship crumbled under the weight of choices I couldn't support and severe personality changes. People would still ask about her long after we had gone our separate ways, a testament to how tightly our lives had once been entwined. I imagine she fielded the same questions whenever she appeared solo as well, a visual imbalance where there used to be an unbreakable duo.

Time marched on. I ended up living just outside Yosemite in a charming small town called Mariposa. One day, out of the blue, Susan consumed my thoughts. The radio seemed to conspire in this fixation, playing nothing but songs that were her old favorites. That night she visited me in a dream. In a confined room, amid a blazing argument, she suddenly broke the tension, saying, "I don't want to fight anymore." We hugged, and as we made peace, she bid me goodbye. I woke up with the dream still vivid in my mind, compelling enough to share with my roommates, who had known Susan as well. Then, almost as if scripted, I got a message that same evening. "Did you hear about Susan?" it read. My skin tingled at the eerie timing. "She's gone. She took her own life last night." The synchronicities were too poignant to ignore, making me wonder whether the threads of our once-intertwined lives had reached out one last time to say goodbye and make amends on the inner planes. My psychic sensitivities couldn't help but resonate with the timing, the songs, the dream—all conspiring to mark the end of an era and the loss of a soul with whom my life had been so deeply connected. Psychic abilities are not just quirks; they are intrinsically linked to the rhythms and relationships that shape our lives.

Embracing the Term *Psychic*

I'm not some unique case; you have psychic abilities too. Many people feel uneasy about the term *psychic*. This hesitation is usually due to the negative stereotypes linked with the word and the exaggerated portrayals found in popular media like movies and TV shows. Hollywood's portrayal of psychics as mystical individuals with supernatural abilities has led to a distorted understanding of what psychic abilities truly entail. Being psychic isn't supernatural; rather, it's a natural ability that every single person is born with. Anyone who engages in mediumship, which we'll explore later on, knows that spirits communicate directly through the clair senses. As spirits before, during, and after incarnation, we all possess these abilities. Psychic abilities operate both as a spiritual language for decoding energies beyond our physical senses and as a conduit connecting our daily experiences to the inner planes.

The words we use can significantly shape our perceptions and understanding. Avoiding the term *psychic* because of its stigmas and stereotypes can unintentionally lead us to neglect or overlook the full range of our innate senses. Just as with the concepts of affirmations and neuroplasticity, our words hold immense power. Embracing the term *psychic* and reshaping its understanding can be a first step toward recognizing and harnessing our inherent psychic abilities. By redefining *psychic* to denote the innate human capacity for enhanced perception, empathy, and understanding—the language of the spirit—we allow ourselves the opportunity to tap into these often latent abilities. Once we acknowledge our psychic potential, tools such as tarot cards offer a practical way to bring that ability into sharp focus. The tangible nature of tarot cards provides a physical point of concentration, helping us channel and refine our psychic energies more effectively.

Developing Psychic Sensitivity

As cliché as it sounds, developing and maintaining psychic abilities is a journey, not a destination. This process, much like nurturing any other skill or talent, demands continuous effort, attention, and introspection. Psychic abilities can strengthen over time with consistent effort, but they can also fade into dormancy if not exercised regularly. The initial phase of this psychic journey typically involves recognizing the existence of psychic abilities within us. Once we acknowledge this, the next stage involves cultivating and refining these abilities. This can often involve tuning in to our clair senses—clairvoyance (clear seeing), clairaudience (clear hearing), clairalience (clear smelling), clairgustance (clear tasting), and clairtangency (clear feeling). These are very similar to our physical senses, but instead, they detect subtle, nonphysical energies and information. After we've unlocked our psychic abilities, we need to keep honing them to stay sharp. Regular practice becomes crucial at this stage. Similar to how a musician must continually practice to improve and maintain their skills, we must also regularly exercise our psychic abilities to keep them strong and clear. Practical steps to nurture our psychic abilities could involve setting aside time each day for meditation, regularly performing readings for ourselves or others, participating in exercises aimed at strengthening our psychic senses, or just making a conscious effort to trust and listen to our intuition in everyday life. If you've gotten this far into the book and have followed along, you're already primed for this work.

Clairvoyance

Most folks picture clairvoyance when they hear psychic powers. It's the most well-known of the psychic senses. Clairvoyance, often called clear seeing, is the skill of picking up pictures, symbols, or even whole scenes in your head that offer special insights. It's like having a private cinema screen in your head, where you are capable of projecting images, symbols, and seeing complete scenes on it. This could manifest as visualizing a tarot card before it's drawn or envisioning a scene that directly answers a friend's pressing question. You know how you get lost in a book and the scenes just start unfolding in your mind's eye? That's exactly what clairvoyance feels like. Incorporating clairvoyance into your tarot practice can provide additional visual context and symbolism, thereby enhancing your interpretation's depth. Clairvoyance can also be external, whereby you literally see energy, lights, shadows, or figures with your external eyes as if it were an energetic overlay of physical reality.

To enhance your clairvoyance during tarot readings, gently rest your gaze on each card, absorbing the details, colors, symbols, and scenes, while noting any spontaneous visual impressions that arise. Occasionally shift your focus from the deck to a blank surface or close your eyes briefly to strengthen your inner visualizations. Pay close attention to the visuals that appear in your mind's eye, as they can offer deeper insights into the reading. To further develop your clairvoyant abilities, regularly practice guided imagery exercises such as guided meditation or simply conjuring up simple shapes or objects in your mind's eye and seeing how long you can hold them. This will improve your ability to perceive nonphysical symbols and images. For external clairvoyance, learn to use a soft gaze to better see energy fields, practicing by focusing on a windowpane and then shifting your view to objects beyond the glass, training your eyes to smoothly adjust focus. Apply this technique in readings by treating the client like the window, allowing your vision to softly look through and beyond them.

Clairaudience

Clairaudience, or clear hearing, refers to the psychic ability of perceiving sounds, voices, or music that is imperceptible to the normal sense of hearing. It can feel like wearing a unique pair of headphones that allows you to tune in to an auditory realm beyond the ordinary hearing range. These aural impressions often carry messages, guidance, or insights, potentially serving as pivotal revelations for the person receiving a reading. For instance, you might hear a whispered name or phrase laden with meaning for the querent or hear a melody that elicits deep emotions. In tarot readings, clairaudience can supply auditory clues to aid in comprehending the cards' relevance to the individual being read. You may detect a word or phrase that provides context to a card's symbolism or uncovers a hidden facet of the querent's circumstances. A common occurrence that a lot of us have had as children (or have observed in children) is that of hearing a parent or guardian calling your name and then finding out that they weren't calling you at all.

To improve your clairaudient skills for tarot readings, start by finding a quiet space. This lack of external noise allows you to tune in to the more nuanced sounds that might come through psychically. Before diving into the reading, engage in some deep breathing exercises to relax and open up your senses, making it easier for you to pick up psychic information. Once you're prepared, say a spoken request for guidance. You could direct this to your own spirit guides or to divinity. Setting this intention opens the door for clairaudient messages to enter your awareness during the reading. As you conduct the reading, pay attention to any auditory impressions. These could be words, sounds, or snippets of music that pop into your mind. Even if they don't make immediate sense, write them down for reflection later. For instance, if a song lyric keeps replaying in your mind, take it seriously; there could be a hidden message in it for you. For more long-term development, listening exercises can be invaluable. One helpful exercise is to listen to a piece of music while focusing on a single instrument in the arrangement. This trains you to isolate specific auditory cues from surrounding "noise"—a skill that becomes crucial in tarot readings. Over time, this methodical approach to listening will refine your clairaudient abilities, helping you pick up even subtle psychic sounds when you're engaged in tarot readings.

Clairalience

Clairalience, also known as clear smelling, refers to the psychic ability of perceiving scents or odors absent in physical surroundings. It's akin to having a heightened olfactory sense capable of detecting fragrances that others cannot perceive. These aromas might possess symbolic significance or a particular connection to the person being read or their situation. For instance, you might inexplicably experience the scent of a departed grandmother's perfume or encounter an odor that evokes a specific memory or emotion. While clairalience might not feature as prominently in tarot readings as other psychic faculties, it can nonetheless contribute a unique and meaningful layer to your readings. By associating cards with specific memories or emotions evoked through scents, you can offer additional context and depth to your interpretations.

To get better at recognizing psychic scents during your tarot readings, first make sure the room you're in doesn't have any strong, distracting odors. A neutral-smelling space lets your nose be more sensitive to any unusual scents that might appear. Before you even shuffle your tarot deck, spend a few minutes visualizing different smells and how they make you feel. This helps you become more aware of any psychic scents that might pop up later. As you get ready to do a reading, mentally signal that you're open to receiving messages through your sense of smell. Being intentional about this can help make clairalient experiences more likely to happen. In everyday life, practice being more aware of the smells around you. Try to notice how they make you feel or any memories they trigger. This is like building up a personal directory of smells, which you can then refer back to during tarot readings. During the reading itself, don't forget to pause now and then to see if you notice any new smells. You might not always catch a physical scent in the room, but you may still pick up something on a psychic level.

Clairgustance

Clairgustance, or clear tasting, refers to the psychic ability to discern tastes absent any physical input. It's as if you possess a uniquely sensitive palate that can identify flavors beyond the reach of normal sensory experience. These tastes may hold symbolic meanings or bear personal significance to the individual you're reading for. For instance, you might encounter a flavor reminiscent of a cherished childhood dish or a taste that connects with an imminent event or circumstance. Although clairgustance may not frequently emerge in tarot readings, it can enrich your interpretations by adding another sensory dimension. By engaging the taste buds psychically, you can deepen the insights offered by the cards and their implications for the person receiving the reading. For example, in the anecdote from page 161, I experienced the taste of citrus, a sweet and tangy flavor I associate with a balanced outcome of favorable and unfavorable results. Since our physical sense of taste and smell are closely connected in daily life, it's very common for clairgustance and clairalience to also be blended when they occur.

To fine-tune your clairgustant abilities in tarot readings, begin by neutralizing your taste palate. Steer clear of intense flavors that might skew your psychic sense of taste. Before diving into a reading, try mindful eating as a way to become more aware of various flavors. As you eat, zero in on the tastes, picking out intricate details while paying attention to the sensations they evoke. During your preparatory meditation, engage in visualization exercises focused on taste. Imagine the sensation of different flavors on your tongue, mentally tasting them to prepare for psychic taste impressions. You can also develop a personalized correlation between specific tastes and certain tarot cards based on your intuitive understanding. Over time, these taste-to-card correlations will become second nature, enriching your readings. When you're ready to start your tarot session, establish a mental readiness to receive taste-based messages. Setting this intention makes your subconscious aware that you're open to clairgustant experiences. During the actual reading, remain vigilant for any unexpected tastes that crop up in your consciousness. Take note of them even if they seem irrelevant or puzzling at the time. Later analysis might reveal that these tastes were indeed insightful cues.

Clairtangency

Clairtangency, or clear touching, refers to the psychic ability to perceive information, impressions, or insights through physical, tactile sensations. One of the common ways this occurs is through psychometry, which is physically handling an object or touching a person and gaining information about an object's history or the emotional energies linked to it. For instance, you might discern a person's emotional state by just holding their hand or discover an object's past through holding it. Psychometry is especially helpful during remote or online readings. Holding an object that belongs to the querent allows you to tap into their energy field, facilitating a more accurate and insightful lock on their personal energetic signature. Psychometry is a key skill in the repertoire of many psychics and can enhance the depth and accuracy of psychic readings. Clairtangency can also be the perception of physical stimulation caused by energy without any physical object.

Clairtangency holds a unique position in the range of psychic abilities as it serves as a bridge between psychic and intuitive information. While all psychic senses can be associated with intuitive information to some extent, clairtangency is particularly connected due to its direct, tangible interaction with the physical body, emotions, and external stimuli. Through touch we receive raw, intuitive data from our lower self, which our conscious mind can then translate into psychic sensations. The object we touch acts as a trigger, awakening our intuition and connecting us with the universal energy field. This information then rises to our conscious awareness as psychic impressions. This link between the physical world, the psychic higher self, and the intuitive lower self makes clairtangency a highly effective tool for psychic work, particularly when applied to tarot readings. In handling the cards, we're inviting our lower self to participate in the reading, providing a rich, instinctual context to the cognitive interpretation of the card's symbolism.

To deepen your clairtangency in tarot readings, start by meditating with tangible items such as crystals. Feel their texture, temperature, and energy honing your tactile intuition. You can also practice psychometry by holding personal items from friends or family members—always with their permission—and allowing intuitive information to flow through your touch. Engage with your tarot deck at a tactile level too. Slide your fingertips over the card images and be alert to the sensations and emotions that arise. This kinesthetic interaction fortifies your bond with your tarot deck and sharpens your touch-based psychic skills. Some tarot readers suggest washing your hands before a reading as a form of mental and energetic preparation, akin to a surgeon sterilizing hands before an operation. For a hands-on experiment, try a blindfold tactile test. Have a friend give you random objects while your eyes are covered and discern details about them or their owners solely through touch. Another fun exercise involves handling objects with different textures, such as silk, wool, or metal, and intuitively interpreting the symbolic meanings of these textures. If you're open to additional training, energy healing modalities like Reiki are also incredibly helpful. Such training and attunements can fine-tune your ability to sense and direct energy through your hands.

Identifying Your Psychic Strengths

Just like we all have different learning styles, we also have unique predispositions toward our psychic senses. Understanding your dominant psychic abilities is closely linked to identifying your natural learning style and your imagination. By recognizing these strengths, you can enhance your psychic capabilities and gain valuable insights into your inherent psychic leanings. By following these next four exercises and being aware of your learning style, everyday imagination, and memories, you can gain a deeper understanding of your dominant psychic abilities. Knowing what your psychic strengths are can help you know what you can rely on as your main form of psychic perception during a reading and also which areas you might need to work on. As an instructor of psychic abilities, one of my biggest pet peeves is when I hear someone say "I'm clairvoyant but don't have clairtangency" or similar statements. You have all of the clairs; it's just that some might need more work in their development. Such statements also create neuroplasticity in ways that will make it more difficult to develop those areas. So be mindful of what you say you can't do because your brain is paying attention to that.

EXERCISE 55

UNDERSTANDING YOUR PSYCHIC LEARNING STYLE

1. Take a moment to consider how you best process and understand new information. Do you prefer seeing and reading (visual), listening and speaking (auditory), or hands-on practice (kinesthetic)?
2. If you're the type who learns best through pictures or visuals, then you're probably naturally geared toward clairvoyance. Reflect on any experiences you've had with this type of psychic ability, jot down examples, and analyze their significance in your learning process.
3. If you recognized that you learn best through auditory means, you may have a natural inclination toward clairaudience, the

clair characterized by hearing voices, sounds, or music that isn't audible to others. Think about any instances when you've heard something others couldn't, and write down what you can remember.

4. If you're more of a kinesthetic learner, clairtangency could be a form of psychism that is natural for you. This is the ability to gather insights through the sense of touch. Think about times you may have had revelations while touching an object or person, and jot them down.
5. If you're someone who learns best through taste or smell, you may have a strong clairalience (smell) or clairgustance (taste) ability. Reflect on any instances where you've had such experiences. Document them and consider their relevance to your unique way of learning.

EXERCISE 56

OBSERVING YOUR SENSORY IMAGINATION

1. Start by finding a serene, quiet spot where you won't be disturbed for about ten minutes.
2. Make yourself comfortable. Close your eyes.
3. Once you're relaxed, let your thoughts roam freely. Don't try to control or analyze them, just let your imagination wander.
4. As your mind drifts, take note of any daydreams or imaginative thoughts that come up. Avoid judging or interpreting them; instead, simply observe them as they surface.
5. Focus on the senses involved in your daydreams or mental images. What do you see, hear, smell, taste, or feel? Which senses are the strongest? Which are the weakest? This will give you a clearer understanding of how your imagination operates.
6. Once your session is over, promptly write down the key points of your daydreams in your tarot journal. Include not just the characters, settings, emotions, symbols, and themes, but also note which senses were most and least active. The more detailed your record, the more helpful it will be.

∞

7. Over time, revisit your notes and look for patterns. Are certain senses more prominent in your daydreams than others? Are there recurring themes or characters? Do you daydream about the future, past, or imaginary scenarios? Observing these patterns could provide valuable insights into potential clairvoyant tendencies.

EXERCISE 57

LISTENING TO YOUR INNER EARS

1. Choose a quiet and comfortable space where you can concentrate without disturbances. Ensure your notebook and pen are ready for use.
2. Close your eyes. Take deep, slow breaths and let your body relax. Continue until your mind is calm and open.
3. Pay attention to any sounds, songs, phrases, or conversations that come to mind. Treat these as potential indications of clairaudience.
4. Simply observe the internal sounds without attempting to control or interpret them. You're an audience to these experiences.
5. As you perceive an inner sound or conversation, write it down in your notebook. Detail the source, content, and your feelings about it.
6. After documenting each experience, close your eyes and go back to the receptive state. Repeat until you've gathered enough for the day.
7. Practice this routine daily. With frequent practice, you'll become better at identifying these inner sounds and understanding their importance.
8. Reflect on your findings. Look for any trends or recurring themes. These insights will shed light on your clairaudience abilities and their potential.

EXERCISE 58

OBSERVING YOUR SENSORY MEMORY

1. Allocate some quiet time to recall significant memories from your life. As you remember these events, consciously observe how the memories come to you. Pay attention to which of your senses are most involved as you reexperience these memories. Write down any patterns or observations in your notebook.
2. As you continue to reflect on your memories, take note of whether you tend to visualize scenes from these events. Do you see images, locations, faces, or actions in a vivid, picture-like manner? If so, this could suggest a stronger inclination toward clairvoyance. Document these experiences and any images that frequently occur.
3. During your reflection, pay attention to the presence of sounds or voices in your memories. If you notice that you tend to "hear" words, music, or other sounds from your past, this might indicate a predisposition toward clairaudience. Be sure to record these experiences in detail for future reference and analysis.

EXERCISE 59

PSYCHIC PERCEPTION ALIGNMENT

This exercise aims to stimulate and balance the pineal gland, the eyes, the mastoid bones (located just behind the ears), and the throat. This process encourages energy flow, heightens our clairvoyance and clairaudience, and fosters our ability to articulate these spiritual insights. The combination of breathwork and visualization activates the higher faculties associated with these areas. The pineal gland, located deep in the center of the brain, is often referred to as the "third eye" in many spiritual traditions. This gland is associated with the production of melatonin, a hormone that helps regulate sleep patterns and circadian rhythms. In metaphysical circles, the pineal gland is also associated with inner sight and intuition. Stimulating it can help activate these faculties, giving a heightened sense of inner knowing and inner clairvoyance, helping with internal visualization.

Our physical eyes not only provide us with physical sight but are also connected to the way we perceive the world around us. This part of the exercise can help sharpen our outer clairvoyance and external visualization. The mastoid bones, located just behind the ears, are part of our auditory system. They play a role in conducting sound vibrations from the outer ear to the inner ear. By stimulating the mastoid bones, we may potentially enhance our listening skills and attune ourselves more deeply to the subtle sounds around us. This can heighten our inner and outer clairaudience, enabling us to discern spiritual messages or sounds that may otherwise go unnoticed. The throat is associated with communication and expression. By balancing the throat area, we can improve our ability to articulate our thoughts, feelings, and spiritual insights. This work can help clear blockages and improve the overall energy flow in the body.

1. Begin by focusing your attention on the pineal gland, a small, pea-sized gland located in the center of your brain. Visualize it radiating an opalescent light. As you inhale, sense this area becoming warmer and more luminous. Hold your breath for a count of ten before slowly exhaling. Repeat this three times.

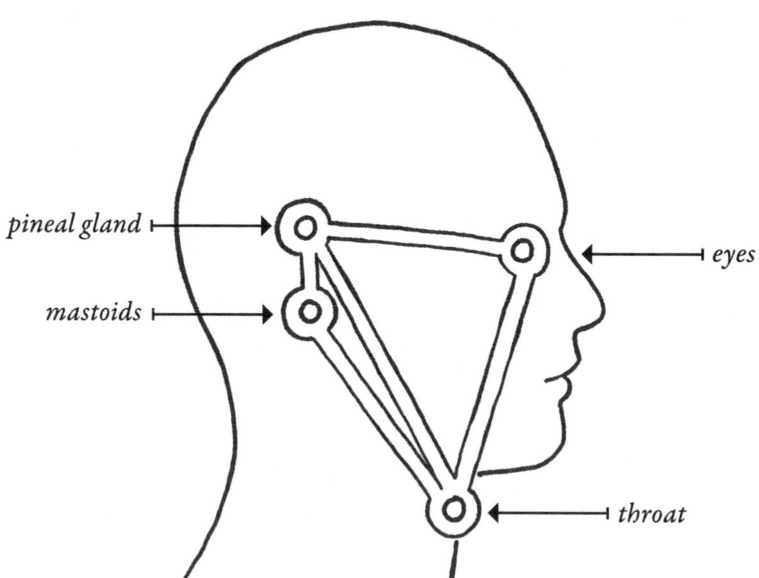

2. With your next breath, visualize the light moving outward from the pineal gland, passing through your brain, and culminating at your eyes. Your eyes serve as external gateways to your intuitive abilities.
3. Envision an opalescent pathway of light forming between the pineal gland and your eyes. Experience this pathway as warm and vibrant with energy.
4. Hold the focus of the light on your eyes for a count of ten, then slowly exhale. Perform this process three times, feeling the warmth and energy permeating your head.
5. Now guide the opalescent light from the pineal gland to the mastoid bones just behind your ears. These points are connected with our ability to perceive subtle energetic vibrations.
6. As you breathe in again, let the area around the mastoid bones fill with a crystalline brightness. Hold your breath for a count of ten, then exhale slowly. Repeat this at least three times, feeling the energy and light intensifying with each breath.
7. Next, guide the opalescent light from both your eyes and mastoids downward to your throat area, creating a pathway of light from these areas to your throat. The throat area is associated with expressing spiritual insights.
8. With your next breath, let this area fill with a crystalline brightness. Hold your breath for a count of ten, then exhale slowly. Repeat this at least three times, perceiving the energy and light intensifying with each breath.
9. To conclude the sequence, redirect your attention from your throat back to the pineal gland, completing the circuit of opalescent light connecting all areas. Feel the light's energy and intensity amplify from having activated and synchronized with the other energy points.
10. Finally, extend your awareness to your surroundings. Observe any unique or altered sensations.

EXERCISE 60

CONNECTING HIGHER SELVES DURING A READING

This exercise is a meditative practice designed to help tarot readers establish a deep, intuitive connection with the higher self of the person they're reading. In many spiritual traditions, the higher self is considered the truest, most enlightened version of oneself—a source of spiritual wisdom and insight. In tarot readings, connecting with this level of consciousness can help provide deeper, more insightful readings. It's a bridge to understanding the person's deeper needs, desires, and the spiritual or emotional roots of their situations, therefore offering more meaningful guidance.

In this exercise we use the visualization of glowing orbs to represent the higher selves of both the reader and the person being read, and an infinity sign, or lemniscate, as a symbol of the energy circuit connecting these higher selves. The lemniscate is most notably seen in the tarot as being above the Magician's head and the figure in the Strength card's head. The purpose of this exercise is to open a clear channel for communication, allowing the reader to gain clearer psychic information during the tarot reading that transcends the ego of the middle self of both yourself and the person you're reading.

1. Close your eyes and take a deep breath. Visualize a glowing orb of energy above your head. This orb represents your higher self, your source of wisdom and intuition. See it glowing brightly, full of life and potential.
2. Now, in the same manner, visualize another glowing orb above the head of the person you're reading. This orb represents their higher self, their soul's essence, and their purest form of wisdom and intuition.
3. Once you've visualized both orbs clearly, imagine an infinity sign, a lemniscate, outlining and connecting the two orbs. Each orb resides within one of the infinity sign's loops.
4. Envision this sign as an energy circuit. Energy from your higher self flows through one loop of the infinity sign, crosses the center, and flows into the higher self of the person you're reading before it returns to you through the other loop of the infinity sign.

5. As you envision this energy flowing between you and the higher self of the person you're reading, you may want to use a mantra or affirmation to strengthen and empower the connection. This can be something like, "I am connected with the wisdom of the higher self of the person I'm reading."
6. Once the connection is established and empowered, keep your mind open to receive messages from the higher self of the person you're reading. These might come in the form of images, emotions, or simply intuitive feelings.
7. Now you are ready to start your tarot reading. As you shuffle, draw, and interpret the cards, maintain the visualization of the energy circuit and stay open to the messages from the higher self of the person you're reading.
8. Once the reading is complete, gently let the image of the energy circuit fade, thanking the higher self of the person you've read for the insights and guidance.

EXERCISE 61

ENERGETIC RECALIBRATION

Engaging in tarot readings often results in an energetic intertwining with others. This connection, while enriching and fostering empathy, can lead to an unintended energy exchange. We might absorb some of the other person's energy, and vice versa. While this blending can deepen spiritual connections, it's crucial to preserve our unique energetic identity. Unplanned energy carryovers can disrupt our energy balance, possibly leading to fatigue or emotional turbulence. To prevent this, it's essential to ensure everyone retains their distinct energy, averting potential energy drainage or inadvertent acquisition of the other's traits after a reading.

A strategic technique combining spiritual cleansing and energy retrieval can effectively ensure each energy fragment is returned to its rightful owner, reinstating a balanced energetic ecosystem. This practice not only allows us to regain our own energy but also helps others to do the same. It acts as an energy sorting system, ensuring each absorbed energy particle is returned to its source. As a result, it cultivates an atmosphere of balance, healing, and completeness, optimizing our functioning within our energy field and respecting others' energetic boundaries.

1. Focus your attention on the space a few feet above your head. Visualize a celestial silver orb about the size of your head gently floating in this space.
2. Consider this orb a blank canvas. With an imagined marker of obsidian ink, inscribe your name upon its surface.
3. Watch as your signature imprints onto the orb, sparking a transformation within it. The orb starts to pulsate, radiating a translucent silver glow, acting like an energy magnet.
4. The glowing sphere now begins to retrieve the energy you may have unconsciously shed during your spiritual journey or healing work. It collects your vital force from individuals you've interacted with as well as environments you've been in. Watch as it begins to gather the fragmented pieces of yourself lost or displaced across time, space, or parallel realities.
5. Simultaneously envision an identical sphere above the head of the person for whom you're performing a reading. Etch

their name onto this orb, allowing it to function in the same way as yours, drawing back their lost or scattered energy and consolidating their life force.

6. Take a deep, invigorating breath as you observe the transformation of the orbs. Their silver radiance shifts to a warm, golden glow, signifying the successful gathering of energies.
7. Visualize the golden light from these orbs showering down upon you and the other person. As if under a gentle rain of energy, the recovered fragments of your and their life force are returned to your bodies and auras.
8. Acknowledge your newly restored wholeness by affirming "I am whole" and encourage the other person to do the same. Allow yourself a moment to truly immerse in this sensation of completeness.
9. Any remaining energy that doesn't belong to either you or the other person should be grounded back into the earth. Visualize this excess energy descending and reconnecting with the nurturing core of our planet.

Psychic Testing and Development with Tarot Cards

Zener cards, created by psychologist Karl Zener, were designed to explore and test psychic abilities. A typical deck has twenty-five cards grouped into five sets, each with its own symbol like a circle, square, wavy lines, cross, or star. The symbols are the only thing on the card, making it a fair test for the guesser. In a usual setup, one person, the sender, shows the card back, not revealing the front's symbol, to the other person, who is the receiver. The receiver then takes a guess at what the symbol could be. This goes on for several rounds, and the sender keeps track of the guesses. After that, they run the numbers to see if the receiver's guesses beat the odds of random guessing. If they do, it could mean the receiver has some psychic talent. While Zener cards are a go-to for this kind of thing, you're not stuck with them. Tarot decks can be used in a similar way, and they offer a lot more visual detail, opening up new possibilities for psychic exercises.

EXERCISE 62

TAROT PRECOGNITION TEST

1. Open your eyes and shuffle your tarot deck while setting the intention to tune in to the energy of the cards without looking.
2. Lay out the shuffled deck face down on a table or surface in front of you. Observe the cards and see if any particular card stands out or catches your attention.
3. Position your nondominant hand about an inch or two above the cards. Slowly move your hand back and forth over the cards, allowing yourself to sense any differences in energy or vibrations emanating from each card.
4. When you feel drawn to a specific card, pause and direct your attention to that card. Keep your hand above the card and try to sense its energy. Pay attention to any feelings, sensations, or impressions that come to you.
5. Once you have a sense of the card's energy and identity, make a mental note or say out loud your guess for which card it is.
6. Turn the card over to see its identity. Don't be disheartened if your guess is incorrect; this exercise is about practice and honing your psychic ability. Try to stay optimistic knowing that with practice the chance of getting them right will increase.
7. Continue the exercise with other cards in the deck. Focus on sensing the energy and identifying the cards without looking.
8. After completing the exercise, take some time to reflect on your experience. Write in your journal about the sensations, feelings, or impressions you received during the exercise. Note any patterns or insights that emerged.

EXERCISE 63

TELEPATHIC TAROT TEST

1. To begin this exercise, find a partner who also has a tarot deck. Both of you should perform the preliminary exercises. Sit facing each other to establish a strong connection.
2. Decide who will be the sender and who will be the receiver for the first round. The sender will mentally transmit an image of a tarot card, and the receiver will psychically attempt to identify the card based on the impressions received.
3. The sender should shuffle their tarot deck and randomly select a card. Study the card carefully, focusing on its imagery, colors, and symbols. Once a clear mental image is formed, close your eyes and concentrate on sending this image telepathically to the receiver.
4. The receiver should close their eyes and focus on their third eye area (located between and slightly above the eyebrows). Be open and receptive to any images, feelings, or impressions that come to you, attempting to "see" the card being sent by the sender. It's important to clarify here that you're not linking with the card itself to see the card they have; rather, you're trying to receive the information directly from the sender.
5. After a few minutes, the receiver should describe any images or impressions they received. The sender then reveals the chosen card to compare and discuss the results.
6. Now switch roles, with the other person becoming the sender and the original sender becoming the receiver. Repeat the process to allow both participants to experience both sending and receiving.
7. Continue practicing and become more comfortable with the exercise. Try to increase the complexity of the images you send, incorporating multiple cards or focusing on more detailed aspects of the cards' imagery.

8. After each round, take time to discuss your experience with your partner. Share any challenges faced, as well as any successes or breakthroughs. Journal about the exercise, noting any patterns, insights, or areas for improvement.

Remote Viewing

Remote viewing is the practice of using clairvoyance to gather information about a distant or unseen target, location, or event through the mind's eye. The viewer attempts to perceive and describe details beyond their immediate perception or geographical location. The process involves a designated viewer who enters a relaxed and meditative state, directing their consciousness toward the target to access information. The target can be a physical location, object, person, or even a future or past event. Information may be received in the form of images, impressions, feelings, or symbolic representations of the target. Remote viewing has been extensively explored and studied in parapsychological research, particularly during the 1970s and 1980s. Various governments and organizations even took it seriously and investigated its potential applications in military and intelligence settings.

EXERCISE 64

REMOTE VIEWING WITH TAROT

1. Begin by grounding and centering yourself. Find a quiet place where you can relax, away from distractions. Focus on your breath and calm your mind, guiding yourself into a relaxed alpha state.
2. When you're grounded and relaxed, open your eyes and shuffle your tarot deck. As you do this, set the intention that you're going to tune in to the energy of a card for remote viewing its imagery and details.
3. Draw a card from the deck, but do not look at the image on the card. Hold the card face down and carry it to another room. Place it on a surface without looking at its face.

4. Return to your original location and close your eyes. Take a few more deep breaths, focusing on your third eye area, which is located between and slightly above your eyebrows.
5. Visualize yourself mentally "traveling" to the location of the face-down card in the other room. Once you feel like you have mentally arrived at the card's location, allow your intuition to guide you.
6. Without physically looking at the card, attempt to perceive the imagery, colors, symbols, and details of the card. Be open to any impressions, sensations, or visualizations that come to you.
7. After a few minutes, open your eyes and write down any images or impressions you received during the remote viewing exercise in your notebook or journal. Be as detailed as possible.
8. Now, go to the other room and turn over the card. Compare the actual tarot card with the impressions and images you recorded. Take note of any similarities, differences, or interesting insights.
9. Repeat this exercise with different cards and even different locations if possible. As you become more proficient, increase the complexity of your remote viewing exercises.
10. After completing the exercise, spend some time reflecting on your experience. Review the impressions and images you recorded and look for any patterns or insights.

Remote Viewing's Application in Tarot

Remote viewing can play an instrumental role in psychic tarot reading, particularly when the tarot reader needs to focus on or target specific aspects that aren't readily accessible or apparent. There are various scenarios where this focused approach can provide valuable insights and enhance the overall reading experience. For instance, if the tarot reading involves understanding a situation or context occurring at a distance, whether physical or temporal (in the past or future), remote viewing can offer unique insights. This becomes especially useful when the individual being read for isn't located in the same place as the tarot reader or when the query pertains to events or circumstances that have happened in the past or are yet to occur. There may also be instances where the person being read for is grappling with a complex issue or a hidden aspect of their life that they cannot articulate or are entirely unaware of. In such cases, remote viewing can help the tarot reader target these concealed elements, offering deeper insights and potentially revealing information that can guide the reading.

In the search for lost objects or missing persons, psychics often resort to remote viewing. By focusing their psychic abilities and intent on this specific target, they can "see" or "feel" the location of the object or person, thereby providing valuable insights or clues. To gain a deeper understanding of a person's situation or problem, a tarot reader may need to establish a deeper connection with the person. Remote viewing can help in this process by enabling the reader to target and explore specific events in the person's life or their emotional and energetic states. This deeper connection often leads to more insightful and meaningful guidance and advice. For tarot readers who also engage in energy healing or spiritual practices, remote viewing can be a powerful tool. They can use it to target and perceive the individual's aura or energy field, allowing them to identify any energy blockages or disturbances and provide the appropriate healing or cleansing.

Remote Viewing with Tarot

WHAT THIS CAN LOOK LIKE

A few years back, a woman who lived far from me reached out. She was in a distressing situation, and though we couldn't meet physically, we set up a remote tarot reading via video call. The woman had lost a cherished brooch, an intricately designed piece passed down in her family for generations. She was particularly distraught because she had planned to give it to her daughter on her upcoming wedding day. She hoped the tarot could provide clues to finding it. As the reading started, I shuffled the cards with a clear focus: *Where is the brooch?* I drew a card and placed it on the table. It was the Hermit. Generally, this card relates to introspection and searching, often in solitude. Given the nature of our query, it suggested that the brooch might be close by, perhaps concealed in an often-ignored spot.

Feeling that a deeper connection was needed to guide this woman, I decided to employ my remote viewing skills. I started by grounding myself, feeling my presence rooted deeply in my surroundings. With a calm and focused mind, I shifted my attention to my third eye. Visualizing myself astrally arriving in her home, I intended to connect with the energy of the brooch. As I navigated through her space with my mind's eye, a particular image grew strong: an area with a wooden floor and a small rug. It seemed insignificant, but its energy resonated with the message of the Hermit. I trusted my instincts and relayed this information to the woman, suggesting that the brooch might be tucked away near or under this rug. Full of hope and anticipation, she placed the call on hold to explore this area in her living room. A few nerve-wracking moments passed before I heard an exuberant voice from the other end. She had found the brooch! It was in a drawer of a seldom-used coffee table placed exactly on the rug I mentioned. It wasn't on the rug itself, but this was definitely a pretty dang spot-on hit.

EXERCISE 65

GROUP TAROT TELEPATHY DEVELOPMENT

This group telepathy development is a method designed to cultivate and explore telepathic abilities within a group environment. This exercise not only fosters a sense of unity but also helps participants tap into their latent psychic talents. It allows you to assess the group's collective telepathic accuracy and provides insight into how different people work psychically. It's especially interesting to note how different people might pick up different aspects of the same card, reflecting the diversity and complexity of psychic perception.

1. Start the exercise by selecting a single card from the tarot deck. Do not show this card to the group. Instead, spend some time studying its imagery, symbolism, and the overall energy it resonates with.
2. After you've familiarized yourself with the card, ask everyone in the group to close their eyes gently. Ask them to tune in to their intuition and clear their minds of any distractions.
3. Encourage the group members to open their minds and focus on the card you're holding. Ask them to use their intuition to perceive the details, colors, and symbols of the card.
4. Allow a few minutes for the participants to concentrate and receive any impressions or insights about the card. Make sure the environment is calm and quiet during this time to allow everyone to focus.
5. After the designated time, ask everyone to open their eyes. Request that they write down their thoughts, feelings, and any details they sensed about the card.
6. Collect everyone's written impressions or, alternatively, have people go around in a circle and share their impressions verbally. This step helps with validating each participant's experience and can provide valuable feedback about their intuitive abilities.
7. Once everyone has shared their impressions, reveal the actual card you selected at the beginning of the exercise. Compare the actual card's imagery and symbolism with the group's collective impressions.

EXERCISE 66

YOUR MENTAL TAROT DECK

You can mentally pull a card for any situation you encounter in daily life. Whether meeting someone new, listening to what someone is saying, facing a decision, or any scenario you can think of, this mental card drawing can offer guidance. Just ensure you approach this practice with clarity and openness, aiming to genuinely tap into your psychic ability rather than being influenced by your own biases or preconceptions. Over time, as your visualization skills strengthen, you may even find that you can perform this exercise without closing your eyes. The mental card you pull may initially seem unrelated to the situation at hand, but with time and reflection, its relevance often becomes apparent. This skill can greatly enhance your everyday life, not only strengthening your intuitive muscles but also deepening your connection to the tarot.

1. Visualize a deck of tarot cards on your mind's screen. You may notice a calming energy radiating from the imagined cards.
2. In your mind, shuffle this deck and draw a card from it. Observe the card you drew.
3. Notice any feelings, sensations, or impressions that arise as you visualize this card. Try not to judge or question the card that appears; accept it as it is, and trust its message.
4. Spend a few moments pondering how this card relates to the situation you drew it for. How might it guide or inform you? It might not make complete sense immediately, but take note of what you drew as its significance might become clearer later on.
5. Once you have spent adequate time with the card, express gratitude for its guidance and return it to the deck in your visualization.
6. When you feel ready, gently open your eyes, bring yourself back to normal waking consciousness, and reground yourself.

Your Mental Tarot Deck

WHAT THIS CAN LOOK LIKE

A few years back, I found myself at a career crossroads. I'd received an offer for a job that looked incredible on paper. However, something deep down made me hesitate. While the prospects and benefits were enticing, I couldn't shake off an inexplicable feeling of unease. I knew I needed some guidance, so I decided to use the technique of mentally pulling a tarot card to gain clarity. I found a quiet place and took a few moments to ground myself. As I reached the alpha brainwave state, I visualized a deck of tarot cards on the screen of my mind. I mentally shuffled the deck, asking for guidance about accepting this new job offer, then drew a card. In my mind, I saw the imagery of the Eight of Cups. This card often symbolizes moving on, letting go, and seeking a higher purpose, even if it means leaving behind something that may appear valuable. It suggested that the shiny new job offer might not be what my soul truly needed.

The image of the card and its message resonated deeply with me. It echoed my initial unease about the job offer and provided the clarity I was seeking. I decided to trust my intuition, reinforced by the message from the Eight of Cups, and declined the job offer. Some of my friends and family were surprised by my decision. But only a few months later, news surfaced that the company I had almost joined was going through severe internal issues and financial trouble. If I had accepted the offer, I would have been screwed. Looking back, the decision to mentally pull a tarot card guided me at a critical juncture in my life. The seemingly obscure message of the Eight of Cups ended up being an incredibly accurate forewarning, and this experience reaffirmed my belief in the power of intuition and the insight that tarot, even when visualized mentally, can provide in our everyday life.

Another example of how this technique can be put into practice happened during a time when a new woman entered my social circle. A mutual friend brought her into the circle, and instantly she radiated social energy, eager to create tight-knit connections with everyone. Although her charm was appealing, I found myself feeling a little uneasy around her without quite knowing why. So, trusting my intuition, I decided to use my mental tarot drawing technique to get a better understanding of her true intentions. I began the process by finding a quiet space and bringing myself into a state of calm. Once in the alpha brainwave state, I visualized a deck of tarot cards, mentally shuffling it and focusing on the question: *What were this woman's true intentions?* Drawing a card from the deck in my mind, I saw the image of the Seven of Swords. Known to symbolize deception or hidden motives, the card immediately resonated with my initial unease. It suggested that beneath her charming exterior, there might be manipulation or selfish motives at play.

The message from the Seven of Swords warned me to exercise caution and hold her at arm's length. I chose to proceed carefully, observing her actions and interactions over the next few weeks. Over time, her initial charm started to wane, exposing a pattern of manipulative behavior and actions aimed at serving her own interests. It became clear she was exploiting her friendships in the group for her own advantage. In the end, the mental tarot card draw had provided an accurate warning about her true motives. I was able to protect myself and my friends from potential harm by trusting the intuitive guidance provided by this technique.

9
∞

Tarot and Mediumship

Despite my career as a tarot reader and psychic, I was skeptical about mediumship. It didn't quite align with my belief in reincarnation.[19] But that skepticism faded in my early thirties, thanks to my friend Danielle Dionne, an astonishingly gifted medium. One evening at her home, I persuaded her to give me a reading. She knew little about my history from before I had moved to New England, and certainly nothing about Susan, who I wrote about in the beginning of chapter 8. First up was my grandfather, a complex figure in my life. If you've read my book *Mastering Magick*, you know we didn't exactly get along. Danielle not only described him to a T but also conveyed his plea for my forgiveness. Surprisingly, I granted it. Holding on to that animosity served no purpose. But what convinced me of Danielle's abilities was what happened next. She began to describe a woman roughly our age with a goth vibe, dark makeup, and a sharp, somewhat acerbic wit. "That's Susan," I said. Danielle revealed that Susan and I had ended our friendship on strained terms but that Susan was visiting me from the other side regularly, mostly in dreams, and that I probably knew that already. Susan wanted to express her love and pride for the path I was on. She even foresaw "big things" in my future.

The final detail sealed my belief in mediumship for good. Danielle said Susan had a message for her mother and asked if I was in contact with her. I confirmed that Susan's mom and I had grown close since her passing. Danielle then said, "This might sound odd, but she keeps showing me scissors

19 For my understanding of how mediumship, reincarnation, and ancestral practices can all be simultaneously true, check out chapter 6 of *Psychic Witch.*

and telling her mom to put them away." I was floored. Susan had hanged herself in her mother's house. Susan's mother was the one who found her. Her mom had frantically searched for scissors to cut her down while on the phone with emergency services. Traumatized, she began to hoard scissors, stashing them everywhere, from her car to her purse. She had only confided this to me, and I had told no one. The message was beyond a doubt from Susan, offering both closure and proof that our connection to loved ones extends beyond this physical world.

Mediumship Is a Bridge

Mediumship is most commonly thought of as a practice that helps connect with spirits of those who have passed on from this life. This is true, but mediumship enables communication with a broad range of spirits, not just those who have passed away. This includes interactions with spirit guides, nature spirits, and other nonphysical entities. That means that all of the interactions you've had with your tarot spirit guide were instances of mediumship. Spirit communication can bring comfort, guidance, and closure, and tarot cards can be a fantastic tool for enhancing communication during mediumship sessions.

Serving as a bridge between the spirit world and the querent in a mediumship session, the medium receives messages, impressions, and advice from spirits, sharing this information with the querent. Tarot cards can enrich this communication, offering a vibrant and symbolic language that nurtures a connection with the spirit world, gathering messages and impressions from spirits. Mediumship can be a deeply personal and transformative experience, allowing the medium to explore their spiritual path and strengthen their bond with the spirit world. It's also a powerful way to gain guidance and insights from spirits on various topics, such as personal growth, relationships, career, or spirituality.

Because the tarot deck features a collection of archetypal images, symbols, and themes representing different aspects of human experiences and the spiritual sphere, the medium can interpret these images and symbols to receive messages and impressions from spirits, sharing this information with the querent in a meaningful and insightful manner. During a mediumship session, the medium may use tarot cards in a variety of ways. For instance, they might utilize specific tarot spreads designed for mediumship work, focusing on messages from the spirit, the spirit's personality and attributes, or the spirit's relationship with the querent. The medium may also use tarot cards to confirm information they receive from the spirit or to provide additional insights and guidance to the querent.

Engaging in mediumship via tarot requires careful preparation and intention setting. To begin, identify the spirit or entity you wish to connect with, and clarify the information you hope to glean from this interaction. Concentrate your thoughts and energies, honing in on your specific objective and desired outcome. The selection of your tarot deck is a personal choice, and it should resonate deeply with you. Choose a deck that not only appeals aesthetically but also feels energetically aligned with your intentions. This resonance will aid in cultivating a deeper connection to the spiritual energies you wish to channel. However, preparing your personal energy and your tarot deck are just the first steps in the process.

Prior to opening any channels of communication with the spiritual realm, you must ensure your deck is purified and charged. This could involve cleansing the deck with incense, placing it under the moonlight, or using crystals. This purification process is essential to remove any residual negative or heavy energies that could disrupt or distort your communication with the spirit world. Your personal protection should not be overlooked during these practices. Prior to initiating any form of spirit communication, remember to conduct protection exercises. This could involve visualizing protective light around you, calling upon protective entities, or creating a protective boundary. These measures will safeguard your energy and space, preventing any unwelcome or harmful energies from infiltrating your reading. When engaging with spiritual energies, respect and caution are of utmost importance. I suggest always approaching mediumship with a clear mind, pure intentions, and a protected space.

EXERCISE 67

BLOOMING BREATH FOR MEDIUMSHIP

The following breathing exercise aims to guide you toward a state of consciousness that is more conducive to mediumship. At the heart of this practice lies the symbolism of the Fool card from the Rider-Waite-Smith Tarot, which embodies an invitation for you to approach life with an open heart and an open mind. The Fool encourages you to embark on your journey with pure intentions, free from preconceived notions or expectations, and embrace the lessons that unfold along the way. Embracing this mindset is particularly helpful for those seeking to enhance their mediumship abilities, as it fosters a connection with higher-vibrational spiritual energies and enables the reception of messages without judgment or interference. By evoking the essence of the Fool card and envisioning a white rose in different stages of blooming, this exercise encourages you to cultivate receptivity, authenticity, and a sense of openness, all of which are essential for successful mediumship.

1. Through your nose, inhale a long and steady breath to the count of six. On the crown of your head, visualize a white rose—similar to the one held by the figure in the Fool card from the Rider-Waite-Smith Tarot—in a state of blooming, transitioning from a bud to its full, radiant beauty. Imagine that time is slowing down during this process.

2. Hold the breath inside your filled lungs for the count of six while visualizing the white rose in its full bloom, open and resplendent.
3. Through your mouth, exhale a long and steady breath to the count of six. Envision the white rose in a state of closing, transitioning from its peak back to a closed bud. Imagine that time is slowing down during this process.
4. Hold the breath outside of your empty lungs for the count of six while visualizing the white rose in its closed bud state.
5. Repeat the entire process until you feel a complete shift in your own energy and the energy of the room. This is going to feel different for everyone, so trust your own perception and intuition for when to stop. Be sure to continue to imagine time slowing down as you perform this exercise.
6. When you feel that this state of consciousness has been achieved correctly, imagine the white rose in full bloom staying open on the crown of your head.

EXERCISE 68

CONNECTING TO FREQUENCIES OF LIGHT

This visualization exercise serves to elevate our state of consciousness and enhance our mediumship abilities. Building upon the previous practice, this technique draws inspiration from the Fool card in the Rider-Waite-Smith Tarot, incorporating the radiant energy of the white sun and the symbolic purity of the white rose. By directing the white sun's light onto the white rose placed on our crown, we facilitate a heightened vibrational frequency and an openness to Spirit, in whatever way we personally relate to the highest divinity. This practice opens us up to greater receptivity, enabling us to connect with spiritual insights and messages from the higher realms. Through this exercise, we establish a strong bond with the spiritual energies that encompass us, elevating our vibration and taking a significant stride forward in our mediumship development.

1. Sit comfortably in a state of calm and openness, having completed the previous exercise.

2. Visualize the white sun from the Fool card in the Rider-Waite-Smith Tarot shining down on you. This sun represents your personal concept of divinity.
3. Direct the white sun's light onto the white rose placed on your crown, visualizing the rose absorbing the light and glowing even brighter.
4. Feel the light of the white sun permeating every cell of your body, raising your vibrational frequency.
5. Allow the energy to cleanse and align your energy centers, promoting clarity and heightened awareness.
6. Sense a connection forming between you and the spiritual realm, making you a clear channel for messages and insights.
7. Embrace the warm and uplifting energy as you align with the frequencies of light and spirit.
8. Bask in this state of elevated being, feeling the harmony between the white sun, the white rose, and your own energetic frequency.
9. When ready, gently bring yourself back to the present moment, carrying the heightened awareness and spiritual connection with you.

The Sensitivity of Mediumship Readings and Discernment

Years back, despite being at the peak of my psychic career, I carried an air of skepticism and hesitance toward mediumship. The idea of connecting with departed loved ones was a delicate matter for me. I was conscious of the deep sensitivities involved, and the fear of making an error and potentially causing distress or offense was a weighty one, far surpassing the concerns tied to tarot or psychic readings that don't involve mediumship. However, an event in Salem one October forever changed my perspective. It was a time when the veil between our world and the spiritual realm was believed to be at its thinnest, and the insistence of a particular spirit was impossible to ignore. During a reading, the spirit's presence was so pronounced, it compelled me to relay its presence to the querent. I cautiously broached the subject, expressing that I sensed an additional presence accompanying them. Upon receiving their approval, I began to confirm the identity of the spirit, who then delivered messages that turned out to be deeply healing and comforting for the individual receiving the reading. This experience was a turning point for me. It emphasized the critical role mediumship can play in providing solace and closure. I started to cultivate my mediumship abilities further, learning to trust in them more.

During a mediumship session, I have one key rule with the sitter. Until I have completely verified the spirit's identity, the sitter can only confirm or deny my insights with a simple yes or no and not give me any information or details about the spirit. It's only after we're both confident in the spirit's identity that they are then allowed to respond more elaborately to the information being relayed. This protocol not only reassures the querent of the authenticity of the contact by ensuring that they aren't leading you, but also alleviates any apprehension I may have about misinterpretation. There are instances where the sitter is unsure of the spirit's identity, either because they're not recognizing the cues or due to the spirit disguising itself. There are also occasions where I may not accurately perceive the spirit. In such cases, if the sitter cannot confirm the spirit's identity, I mentally dismiss the spirit, extend an apology to the sitter, and explain that spirits don't always communicate clearly. We then continue with a psychic tarot reading that excludes mediumship. Despite initial reservations, embracing and refining my mediumship abilities has not only empowered me to deliver more impactful readings but has also facilitated healing for those seeking to connect with their loved ones in the spirit world.

EXERCISE 69

SEEING THE AURA

In basic terms, an aura is the energetic shield that encapsulates an individual. This energy shield is far from homogeneous; instead, it consists of various layers that bleed into each other. Think of a rainbow. When we look at a rainbow in the sky, we can clearly discern separate bands of color, but if we look closely, these bands blend together; it can be difficult to tell where one begins and the other ends. Using clairvoyance, we're able to discern the varying layers of the aura along with the diverse colors, shapes, and forms nestled within it. This exercise can come in extremely helpful within mediumship, which we'll see in a bit.

1. Soften your eyes into an unfocused gaze. Your vision should be relaxed and not concentrated on any particular object. A great way to develop this gaze is to use a window. Alternate between looking through the window at a faraway point to looking at the window itself and your reflection in it, if possible. Then relax your gaze so that you aren't looking at or through the window, but rather just taking everything in, near and far, without straining.
2. Try to perceive with the entirety of your visual field, taking in not only what is directly in front of you but also the peripheral sights.
3. Position your hand in front of you, preferably against a dimly lit, single-color surface. A wall or floor could serve as an ideal backdrop. While black or white surfaces usually work best, any color will suffice.
4. With your hand as the focal point, cast your gaze beyond the physical. Envision your hand as a window, allowing you to perceive the aura surrounding it.
5. Over time and with regular practice, you will begin to discern the etheric body of the aura. This typically manifests as a faint translucent white or gray haze that closely mirrors the contours of your hand.
6. To perceive beyond the etheric layer of the aura, extend your focus further, enlarging the area of attention around your hand while maintaining a relaxed and receptive gaze.

7. Once you are able to perceive an aura, embark on the process of color visualization. Ask yourself: "If this aura had a color, what would it be?" Trust your initial instinct, even if the color isn't immediately apparent.
8. Use your visualization techniques to fill in the color. For instance, if the color blue came to mind, visualize the aura being suffused with that hue.
9. The process of projecting potential colors and receiving them in your mind's eye initiates a dialogue between your subconscious, conscious mind, and the universe, enhancing your ability to perceive these auras.
10. For those with a strong internal clairvoyance, it might be easier to close your eyes, re-create the image, and envision the aura's color.
11. To harmonize your internal and external clairvoyance, alternate between visualizing the aura internally and externally. This can be done by opening and closing your eyes periodically to compare the imagined and perceived aura.
12. Gradually increase the speed at which you alternate between internal and external visualization, eventually leading to a state of rapid blinking. This practice facilitates the outward projection of your inner vision.
13. If the color you're projecting onto the aura changes unexpectedly, embrace it. This change is likely a refinement of your perception by your higher self. Note that sparks, shadows, or sudden flashes of color are normal during this process, and we'll explore that soon.

Aura Colors

The following list provides broad interpretations of what various aura colors might represent. However, these interpretations are neither absolute nor definitive; they are suggestions from subjective experience. The meaning of aura colors can vary greatly from person to person and may be influenced by numerous factors such as personal experiences, cultural context, and individual perception. Just like learning a new language, understanding the colors of the aura is a process that involves patience, observation, and a degree of intuition. Therefore, while this list can serve as a helpful guide and starting point, the true understanding of what each color signifies within an aura will largely depend on your personal insight and experiences. Your interpretations of these colors will evolve and become more nuanced as you continue to explore and learn from each aura you encounter. Your personal understanding of the aura's subtle language and the interpretations you arrive at will be as unique and individual as the auras you're reading.

BLACK: Functions as a shield and may suggest a person is defending themselves or hiding secrets. It can indicate physical imbalances and aura field cracks or leaks under specific situations, or negativity or negative forces at work.

BLUE: Illustrates tranquility, placidity, faithfulness, honesty, solemnity, lively imagination, and acute intuition. Its deeper hues may allude to isolation, the quest for spirituality, and good discernment. Its murkier tones can signal obstructed understanding, gloom, apprehension, absent-mindedness, and hypersensitivity.

BROWN: Depicts earthiness, new growth, commitment, organization, and the drive to achieve. When seen on the face or head, it might suggest a need for better judgment.

GOLD: Symbolizes dynamic spiritual vigor, devotion, powerful enthusiasm, deep inspiration, and revitalizing energy. Its murkier tones point toward an ongoing spiritual awakening and the process of transformation.

GRAY: Often the initial aura color detected. If seen in extensive darker hues, it may indicate miasma (energetic uncleanliness) or someone who is hiding huge secrets, or it may be indicating physical issues if it's just in one area of the aura matching the body.

GREEN: Indicates finesse, burgeoning compassion, advancement, comfort, peace, reliability, and openness. Its darker or muddier tones can point to indecision, penny-pinching, jealousy, over-attachment, self-questioning, and distrust.

ORANGE: Embodies the attributes of coziness, creative spirit, emotional intelligence, courage, happiness, extroversion, and the emergence of fresh insights. Its duller hues may indicate egotism, ostentation, stress, or self-obsession.

PINK: Represents sympathy, love, cleanliness, pleasure, comfort, and a deep sense of togetherness. Depending on its shade, it can also imply naivety and the dawn of new affection and outlooks.

RED: Emphasizes robust dynamism, raw originality, intensity, and life-giving energy. It encompasses emotions like enthusiasm, fury, romance, and rapid alterations. If overly prevalent or murky, it may indicate hyperactivity, swelling, disequilibrium, anxiety, ferocity, or hastiness.

SILVER: Silver can indicate high perceptiveness, psychic ability, vivid imagination, an inclination to mediumship, innovative creativity, and insightfulness.

VIOLET AND PURPLE: Connote tenderness, metamorphosis, self-determination, intuition, psychic ability, and mysticism. Their murkier shades can suggest a need to overcome obstacles, intense sexual daydreams, dictatorial tendencies, need for compassion, and feelings of misapprehension.

WHITE: Regularly spotted prior to other hues, it signifies honesty, purity, and the arousal of increased creativity.

YELLOW: Yellow imparts positivity, intellectual engagement, new knowledge prospects, wisdom, and cognitive excellence. Its deeper or muddier shades might point to overanalysis, stringent criticism, and sentiments of underappreciation.

Ways to Identify the Spirit

I learned this technique from Danielle Dionne. If you're curious about exploring mediumship in more depth, her book *Magickal Mediumship* is a must-read, and she shares her version of this approach there (especially see chapter 7). Danielle bases her teachings on classic Spiritualist techniques, focusing on the relationship between the spirit and the person receiving the reading, known as the "sitter." The method emphasizes observing the sitter's aura and locating certain signals, often appearing as sparks, to identify spirits related to the sitter. These sparks can also indicate how the spirit is related to the sitter, generationally speaking. My own observations align somewhat with Danielle's but have their own unique characteristics. As you delve into this technique, you'll likely find that your experiences will also vary, adding your own nuances to this method.

For instance, if you notice sparks from the shoulder to ear region of the sitter, it typically suggests the spirit is from the sitter's own generation—think siblings, spouses, or close friends. These are individuals who have been through life's ups and downs with the sitter. Sparks appearing above the ear suggest spirits from an older generation, like parents or other elder family members. These spirits often come through with advice, wisdom, or perhaps unresolved matters. If the sparks manifest below the waist—or in the chest area if the sitter is seated—this usually points to a spirit from a younger generation, such as a child or grandchild. Usually below the sitter's knees is where pets and animal companions make their appearance. Spirits like these often communicate to offer comfort or love. The aura serves dual roles: it holds our spiritual energy and acts as a channel for spiritual communication. As such, applying this technique improves the quality of the messages and brings about healing, understanding, and a closer relationship with the spirit world. The way each person experiences this can differ; not all will see sparks in the aura, as people's spiritual perceptions are highly individualized. Some may notice other signs that guide them to a particular area of the aura or simply feel an intuitive pull toward a specific zone.

1	higher self, spirit guides, ancestors
2	grandparents, great-grandparents
3	parents
4	uncles and aunts
5	partners and spouses
6	siblings and cousins
7	friends
8	children
9	nephews and nieces
10	grandchildren
11	pets

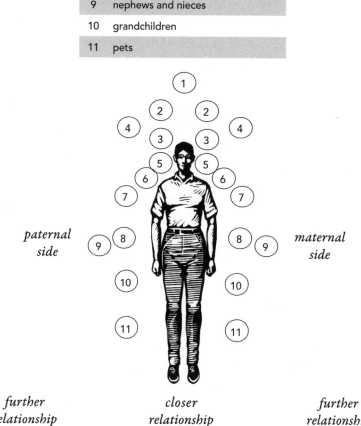

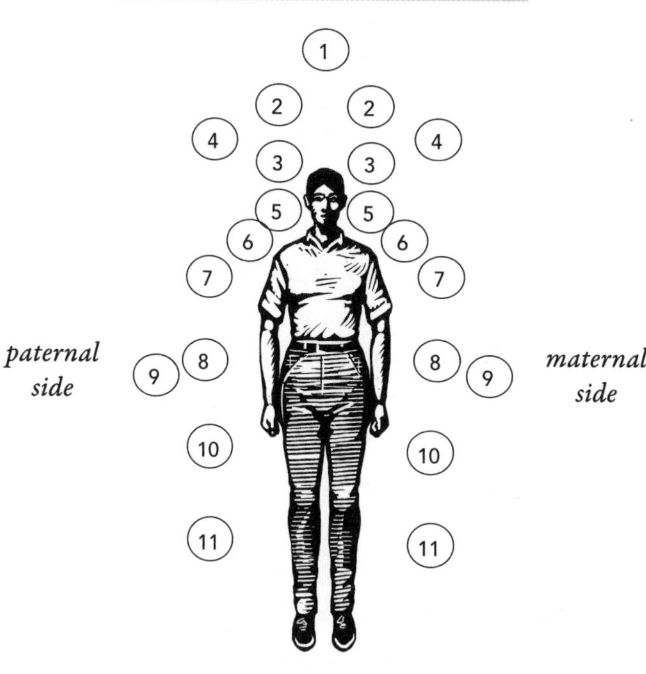

further relationship

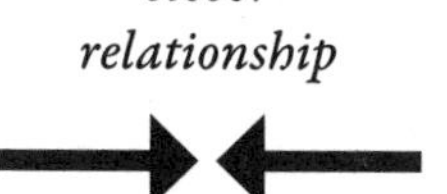

further relationship

Understanding the relationship between the spirit and the sitter goes beyond generational connections. The proximity of sparks or focal points in the aura gauges the closeness of the bond when the spirit was alive. If these indicators are closer to the sitter, it suggests more of an intimate connection with the spirit. This could involve immediate family members, close friends, partners, or mentors with whom the sitter shared a deep emotional or physical bond. If the sparks or focal points are farther away from the sitter within the aura, it implies more of a distant relationship with the spirit. These could be acquaintances, distant relatives, or people the sitter interacted with less frequently. Though the messages from these spirits may not have the same personal impact as those whom the sitter had a deeper relationship with, they can still offer meaningful insights and affirmations of the continuity of life beyond the physical realm.

Gender in Mediumship

When it comes to gender identification during spirit communication, Danielle suggests a nuanced approach. Instead of relying strictly on traditional male and female divisions, she encourages the use of terms like "masculine energy" or "feminine energy" or "non-binary energy." These expressions reflect how the spirit identified or presented themselves during their earthly life. You might find that a spirit's gender expression may not always align with their physical gender, and their sexual orientation may not necessarily surface during gender exploration. As a medium, be patient and open-minded, allowing the spirit to express their gender identity in their own way. If the information is unclear, seeking direct clarification from the spirit is recommended. Incorporating evidence of gender expression in spirit communications can enhance mediumship skills, and practicing with a development group or friends can help fine-tune these abilities. Danielle's teachings emphasize personalizing the approach to mediumship and respecting each spirit's individuality. Every spirit is unique, and acknowledging and respecting their individuality is vital in communications with them.[20]

20 If you're looking for great resources on tarot and queerness, I highly recommend the books *Queering the Tarot* by Cassandra Snow and *Radical Tarot* by Charlie Claire Burgess.

EXERCISE 70

VERIFYING HOW A SPIRIT PASSED

Creating a communication system with your tarot spirit guide can be a deeply personal and rewarding process. In my case, I use the symbolism of roses, but you can use any symbols that resonate with you. Feel free to use my rose system as a starting point or create a system entirely your own. While I'm sure there's a time when this system may not have worked, I can't remember it, as it's almost always accurate. Here's an overview of how to use a tarot spirit guide and a symbolic system to verify a spirit's identity.

1. First, you'll need to decide on a symbol system. For me, different colors of roses work best, each color representing a different cause of death. Your system can be entirely unique; it should feel intuitive to you.
2. Next, it's time to get into a meditative state and connect with your tarot spirit guide. This requires relaxation, entering into alpha, intention, and visualizing a clear connection with your guide.
3. Once the connection is established, start communicating with your guide. If you're trying to identify a spirit, ask your guide to confirm how the spirit passed using your symbol system.
4. Then comes the interpretation of the symbol. For instance, in my system, a white rose would represent a peaceful or natural death, a black rose would suggest death from illness or medical complications, a red rose would indicate an unnatural or violent death, and a blue rose would point to suicide or overdose.
5. You'll then need to share this interpretation with the person you're reading for to see if the information matches what they know about their departed loved one.
6. Depending on the feedback you receive, you might have to refine your interpretation or ask your guide for further clarification on how they passed. For example, I will often ask my spirit guide to bring a subtle understanding of how they physically felt when passing and highlight relevant areas of their body that were connected to their passing.

∞

Verifying How a Spirit Passed

WHAT THIS CAN LOOK LIKE

Once, I sat across from a woman who had come for a mediumship reading. Her eyes carried that unique blend of curiosity, hope, and the subtle weight of loss often seen in those grieving a loved one. As I tuned in to the energies surrounding us, I felt the distinct presence of a female spirit linked to her. The location of the spark in her aura led me to believe this was a sisterly connection. When I relayed this to her, she confirmed that she had indeed lost her sister. Seeking further confirmation, I called upon my tarot spirit guide, my barn owl. As our connection deepened, I could visualize the owl in my mind's eye, and I mentally asked it to show me how the loved one had passed. As the session progressed, the barn owl, always a trustworthy ally, flew around the woman in my mind's eye, encircling her as if surveying, understanding, communicating with the spirit attached to her. Then my owl came back to me with a rose clutched in its talons: a blue one. I delicately asked the woman, "Your sister . . . did she pass away from an overdose?" The immediate welling of tears in her eyes confirmed my insight. The blue rose, symbolizing a life taken by one's own hand or an overdose in my symbolic system, had once again accurately communicated the cause of passing. I then asked the spirit to come forward and see what messages they had for the sitter. Don't worry; the rest of the reading and messages from her sister were incredibly healing for her.

EXERCISE 71

PERFORMING A TAROT MEDIUMSHIP SESSION

Tarot mediumship combines the practices of tarot reading and mediumship, offering a distinct way to explore spiritual connections. The exercise is tailored to help you communicate with spirits through the tarot cards, guided by your trusted tarot spirit guide. Throughout this exercise we actively invite communication from the spirit world, staying receptive to any messages or guidance they might share. However, it's crucial to vet any spirit carefully, employing a mix of intuitive insight and logical analysis. If something feels off or makes you uneasy, remember you can always ask your tarot spirit guide to remove the spirit from the reading. You can then revert to a conventional tarot reading, placing faith in your guide's protective wisdom. Sometimes the person being read may recognize a spirit but choose not to communicate with them. This personal boundary should be honored at all times.

1. After doing your foundational practices, perform the blooming breath (exercise 67) and connect with the frequencies of light (exercise 68).
2. Call upon your tarot spirit guide, allies, and other helpers for protection and guidance during this journey. Envision a bright, protective light surrounding you, reinforcing your spiritual defenses.
3. Connect your higher self with the sitter's higher self.
4. Begin by observing their aura. If the aura comes into focus, pay attention to any sparks within it and home in on it.
5. Tell the person you're reading what you're picking up, including the gender of the spirit and what the relationship to them might be. If they can confirm that they understand who that might be (without telling you), then proceed.
6. Mentally ask your tarot spirit guide to show you how the person passed away (such as the rose method). Relay this information to your sitter. If they confirm that, then proceed.
7. Deliver a mental invitation to the spirit to see if it's willing to communicate with you. Keep an open mind and prepare to receive any impressions, messages, or guidance.
8. Envision the spirit stepping forward and take note of their appearance as well as their personality.
9. Shuffle your tarot deck and draw the cards. You can either draw one card or a full spread; it's up to you as the medium and tarot reader. Be open to the impressions and messages that the tarot cards present to you. Mentally ask the spirit to tell you something about each card or the cards in general.

10. Use open-ended questions that allow for more detailed and informative responses from the spirits. This approach helps avoid unintentionally leading the spirit or influencing their responses.

The Relationship Between the Mediumship Session and the Tarot Reading

In my years as a tarot reader, I've often noticed a significant connection between a tarot reading and the appearance of a departed loved one's spirit. When someone consults the cards and a spirit of a deceased family member or friend shows up, a correlation frequently emerges. While this may not be a universal experience, it has been a recurring theme in my own work, adding an extra layer of depth and wisdom to the reading. For example, it's quite common for the spirit to have encountered a life situation similar to the current issue or question that the person consulting the tarot is grappling with. This kind of synchronicity can offer unique advice or perspectives, drawing on the spirit's own life experiences.

Often I've found that the spirit's characteristics, whether strengths or weaknesses, become pertinent during the tarot reading. The spirit might represent qualities the person seeking guidance should embrace or perhaps traits to be cautious of, all aligned with the messages from the tarot cards. The spirit's life lessons and characteristics can clarify the direction hinted by the tarot, while the reading might reveal specific details of the spirit's message or influence. Thus, the tarot reading and communication with spirits can mirror and amplify one another, giving the individual more thorough insight during their session.

The Relationship Between the Mediumship Session and the Tarot Reading

WHAT THIS CAN LOOK LIKE

I distinctly recall providing a tarot reading for a middle-aged woman who sought advice about a lifelong aspiration she had yet to act upon. As I shuffled and laid out the cards, the Fool and the Nine of Cups emerged, hinting at the

beginnings of a journey and the potential fulfillment of desires and dreams. Yet, coupled with the Four of Cups—a card that often signifies missed opportunities and contemplation—it was clear that she held a dream close to her heart but had yet to take the leap of faith. As the session progressed, a distinct presence made itself known: a feminine energy that strongly resonated with a motherly figure. As I opened myself to the mediumship aspect of the session, a clear vision emerged: a tranquil island destination and a cruise ship sailing under a brilliant sun. Relaying this vision to the woman, I explained how it seemed her mother's spirit was communicating these specific scenes. She responded with a mix of astonishment and warm remembrance. Her mother, she said, had always dreamed of a family vacation, a cruise to the Bahamas, but it was a dream left unrealized before her passing. Suddenly, the narrative in the cards and the mother's spirit's message began to make sense. The spirit was using her own unfulfilled dream, the much-anticipated cruise, to echo the message in the tarot reading. She was urging her daughter not to let her dreams stagnate, to embrace the Fool's adventurous spirit, and seek the emotional satisfaction indicated by the Nine of Cups.

Another session that illustrates the interrelationship between tarot and mediumship involved a young gay man who sought guidance through a tarot reading. As I laid out the cards, they told a poignant story. The Eight of Swords and the Devil card surfaced, signifying a feeling of entrapment and manipulation. The Four of Cups indicated dissatisfaction, a yearning for more, while the Five of Pentacles spoke of a fear of isolation and dread of being alone if he decided to leave his current relationship. It was clear he was enduring an emotionally abusive relationship, but fear held him captive.

As we transitioned into the mediumship portion of the session, a strong, independent energy made itself known: his grandmother's spirit. She was a formidable figure, unafraid to assert herself. I kept receiving a recurrent vision of her forcefully removing a wedding band and throwing it away. When shared, this vision elicited surprise and then understanding from the young man. He revealed that his grandmother had been in a brief unhappy marriage before meeting his grandfather. When her first husband slapped her just a month into their marriage, she had immediately packed her bags and left him, paving the way for her to meet and marry his grandfather, with whom she shared a loving, mutually respectful relationship.

The connection between the tarot reading and the message from his grandmother was remarkable. She was urging him to draw upon her courage and resilience to maintain firm personal boundaries of what wasn't acceptable in a relationship and leave him immediately, refusing to settle for less. The most heartening revelation came toward the end of the session. His grandmother communicated a powerful message: she had known about his sexuality for a long time and loved him unconditionally, just the way he was. The young man had always been cautious about revealing his sexuality to his devoutly religious grandmother, fearing he might lose her love. The realization that his grandmother loved him regardless and was also guiding him in his romantic relationships brought much-needed healing that he wasn't even aware that he needed before getting the reading.

EXERCISE 72

CLOSING DOWN YOUR MEDIUMSHIP SESSION

Closing down properly after your mediumship reading is essential for releasing lingering energies, protecting your own energy field, and establishing healthy boundaries between the spirit world and the physical world. This practice enables you to transition back to your everyday life with clarity and balance. By following these steps, you can confidently and smoothly conclude your session and return to your ordinary reality. Remember to take care of yourself after the session, engage in grounding activities, and practice self-care to maintain your energetic well-being.

1. Express your gratitude to the spirit of the deceased for their communication and guidance.
2. Mentally release any attachment to the spirit or information received during the reading, allowing them to return to their own space and energy.
3. Thank the tarot spirit guide, allies, and helpers for their protection and guidance throughout the session.
4. Express gratitude to the higher self of both yourself and the sitter for facilitating the connection and communication.
5. Visualize a gradual closure of the connection between your higher self and the sitter's higher self, allowing the energy to gently return to its normal state.
6. Perform energetic recalibration (exercise 61).
7. Take a few deep breaths and visualize a bright, cleansing light surrounding you and the sitter, clearing any residual energies.
8. Thank the sitter for their openness and participation in the session.
9. Envision the white rose on your crown closing.
10. Reground and center yourself.
11. Return any cards back to the tarot deck and put it away, symbolizing the end of the reading.
12. Take a moment to reflect on the experience and any insights gained during the reading.
13. Offer a final expression of gratitude to the divine, however you perceive it, for the spiritual connection and the opportunity to serve as a medium.

∞

VII
THE CHARIOT.

10

∞

Diving Deeper into Psychic Tarot Theory

Exploring advanced tarot concepts helps us explore the cards' deeper mysteries. This journey deepens our grasp of how tarot's symbols relate to psychic truths and plunges us into a world of timeless wisdom and hidden meanings. These concepts touch on everything from fate to shared subconscious ideas and powerful collective energies. Rooted in ancient times, they shed light on the deeper purposes of tarot and psychism, marrying historic insights with metaphysical theory. In this perspective, tarot cards are more than tools for prediction; they act as connectors, linking our conscious thoughts to the numinous shared currents of the mind and the mysteries of life and existence. Studying these older ideas helps us understand tarot's symbolism and its connection to the subconscious. In this way, tarot taps into universal patterns and reveals unseen facets of our mind. Grasping these deeper concepts not only prepares us for the concluding exercises in this book but also tackles those hard to answer questions about how and why tarot works.

Free Will vs. Predetermined Fate

A common debate in divination revolves around the concepts of free will and fate. Are our lives dictated by destiny or do we have the power to shape our future? Tarot philosophy accommodates both these perspectives. Tarot cards are instruments that help us tap into our own intuition and inner wisdom. When we ask tarot a question, we aren't looking for fixed predictions. Instead, we seek guidance and insights to make better decisions. Tarot recognizes the power of free will and understands that our choices significantly influence our life path. The future isn't fixed but reflects the energy and circumstances at the time of the reading. Tarot can reveal potential outcomes of our choices, but the final decision is always ours. This acknowledgment of free will is empowering because it places us as active participants in our lives, capable of shaping our destiny. While tarot provides guidance and insight, we hold the final say.

The prospect of seeing the future is enticing. Even though tarot can't provide specific details like winning lottery numbers—and believe me, I've tried—it can provide a sense of what's ahead. By interpreting current energies and circumstances, tarot becomes a valuable tool for identifying potential challenges and obstacles. Tarot reads the current energy and provides a forecast based on the most likely outcome, or it shows where it can go. This insight allows us to make well-informed decisions and take proactive steps toward the best possible outcome. As Rachel True explains,

> Tarot is exceptional at laying out possible future outcomes based on present energies. However, nothing is set in stone; your future is always shifting based on your choices. We are always becoming.[21]

In essence, tarot functions like a personal early warning system, a sort of psychic road map keeping us alert to the unforeseen.

Tarot should serve as a tool that empowers us to make informed decisions that align with our values and goals. Think of it as a GPS system: it suggests the best routes to our destination, but we decide which path to take and how to handle any detours. Tarot should offer good advice, not dictate our actions or control our life. Instead, it should help us make better decisions by providing clearer perspectives. With tarot's guidance, we can make choices that align with our goals and navigate life's ups and downs to achieve the best possible outcomes. However, tarot shouldn't replace our personal power and independence. The idea of a rigid, unchangeable future, while simple, undermines the purpose of using tarot. If everything were predetermined, why use divination at all? We'd just be observers in life, waiting for fate to

21 True, *True Heart Intuitive Tarot*, xi.

take its course. But we know that we have the power to shape our future. We believe in the power of intention and manifestation—the ability to mold our reality through focused energy and willpower. Theresa Reed nails it when she writes, "The cards tell a story . . . but you write the ending."[22] This idea emphasizes that the future isn't a fixed point but a constantly changing canvas colored by our desires and choices.

EXERCISE 73

MAPPING YOUR PATH TO YOUR IDEAL CHOICE SPREAD

1. Identify a particular situation or decision that you are facing.
2. Shuffle your tarot deck while focusing your thoughts on this situation or decision.
3. Draw two tarot cards from your deck. Lay them face up on a table. Each card represents a different potential outcome that would be desirable for the situation.
4. Analyze the symbolism of the first card. Consider how this path aligns with your personal values, long-term goals, and immediate needs.
5. Repeat this analysis for the second card. Reflect on how each path could potentially influence your life.
6. Once you've interpreted each card and reflected on each potential outcome, decide which one you would most like to work toward. This decision should be based on how well each path aligns with your values and goals.
7. Set your intention on creating a path to this chosen outcome. Shuffle your tarot deck once again, focusing on the outcome you desire.
8. Draw three more tarot cards. These cards will provide insights into the steps you can take to achieve your goal.

22 Reed, *Tarot: No Questions Asked*, 14.

9. Interpret the first of these three cards (labeled "3" in the diagram). Consider it as an action step or an attitude to adopt in the journey toward your goal.
10. Repeat the interpretation for the second and third cards, thinking about each card as another step toward your goal.
11. After reflecting on these steps, write them down in a journal or somewhere you can refer back to. Make sure to note any thoughts, feelings, or insights that came up during this exercise. Moving forward, use these insights as a guide in your decision-making process. They will help illuminate your path toward the outcome you desire.

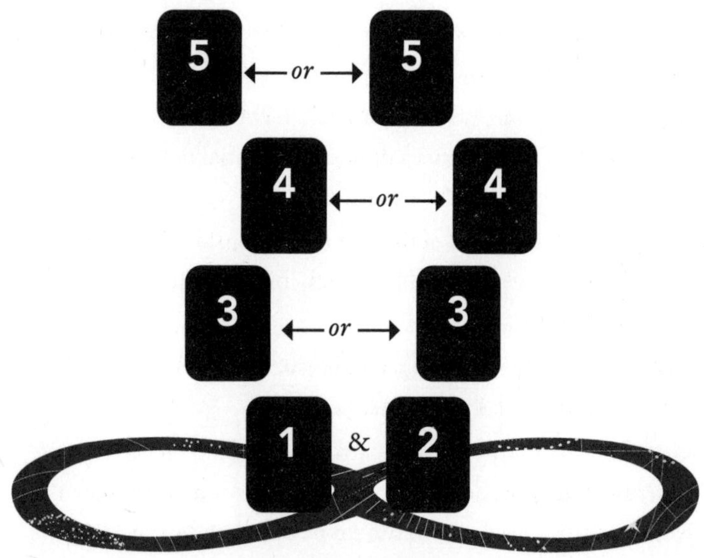

Mapping Your Path to Your Ideal Choice

WHAT THIS CAN LOOK LIKE

My friend had been contemplating purchasing a new home for his growing family for some time. He was torn between two different options: a cozy home close to his work or a quaint cottage in the countryside. Seeing his indecision, I offered a reading to help him gain some insights. As he focused on his house-buying dilemma, I shuffled the cards carefully. I drew two cards from the deck and placed them face up on the table. I explained to him that

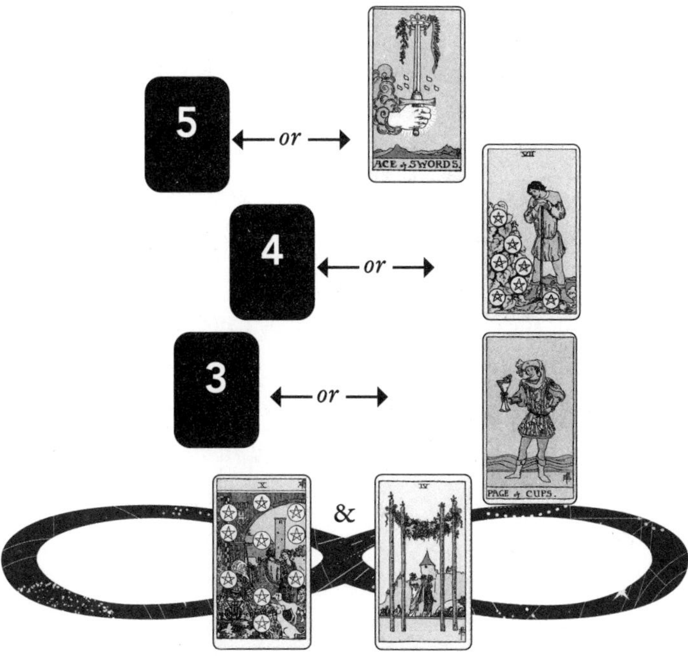

each card represented a potential outcome for each of the houses he was considering. The first card was the Ten of Pentacles, a card often associated with family and generational wealth. I suggested to him that this could represent the cozy home close to his work, providing him with more time with his family due to less commuting. The second card was the Four of Wands, a card often associated with harmony, tranquility, and joy. I told him that this card could be associated with the peacefulness and happiness of the quaint cottage in the countryside.

After analyzing each card, he felt drawn toward the tranquil life the countryside house might offer, as suggested by the Four of Wands. I then reshuffled the deck while focusing on his desired outcome. I drew three more cards to offer insights into the steps he could take toward this goal. The Page of Cups was drawn first. I suggested that this card was advising him to follow his intuition and listen to his heart. The next card was the Seven of Pentacles. I interpreted this as a call for patience and long-term planning. The last card was the Ace of Swords, which I explained was a reminder to take the time to gather all necessary information before making a final decision. Feeling more settled, he wrote down his insights and the steps he had to take. He used this guidance to help him navigate his house-buying process and ended up happily buying the house and moving based on the reading.

Neoplatonism and the Chaldean Oracles

The ancient concept of the anima mundi, or world soul, embodies the belief that the world or the universe is animated by its own unique soul that binds and connects all life forms within it. The Fool's Journey in the tarot can be seen as a spiritual path toward the unity of the World card, symbolic of the anima mundi. This idea, deeply entrenched in ancient philosophies, has meandered through time, adapting and evolving. Its foundations can be pinpointed to the teachings of Plato. Though Plato never explicitly labeled it as such, traces of the anima mundi are evident in his dialogue *Timaeus*, wherein he speaks of the world soul as the essence that the divine craftsman, or Demiurge, uses to bring life to the cosmos. This line of thought was further enriched by the Stoics, who posited that a divine, rational principle called the Logos permeates the universe, vitalizing and ordering everything within. The Neoplatonists of the Hellenistic period, particularly luminaries like Plotinus, further refined Plato's initial insights. Plotinus's *Enneads* paints the world soul as a celestial bridge connecting the divine with the material.

Similarly, the Chaldean Oracles, a mystical document of that age, portrayed the world soul as a conduit for divine energies transitioning from higher realms to the physical world and vice versa. While the origin of these oracles is shrouded in mystery, often linked to the mythical Julian the Theurgist, their impact is palpable. These writings shed light on the complex interweaving of the cosmos and human spirit and provide guidelines for sacred, spiritual rituals. Iamblichus, a leading figure in Neoplatonism and an avid devotee of the Chaldean Oracles, was convinced that they held divine mysteries unlocked through theurgical practices. Theurgy, which translates to "god work," is a mystical technique that employs ritual magick to unite with the divine. Iamblichus's reverence for the Chaldean Oracles further underlines their seminal role in shaping Neoplatonic philosophy. Fast forward to the Renaissance, where this concept experienced a revival. Intellectuals such as Marsilio Ficino, Giovanni Pico della Mirandola, and Giordano Bruno reinvigorated the concept of anima mundi, drawing from classical and Hermetic doctrines. Later, during the Romantic era, visionaries like Goethe and Coleridge turned to the idea of the world soul to articulate their sense of nature's interconnectedness and vitality.

The Collective Unconscious and The Anima Mundi

Carl Jung, the renowned Swiss psychologist of the early 1900s, introduced the groundbreaking concept of the collective unconscious. Beyond the access of everyday consciousness, this realm is shared among all humans and is infused with universal symbols, patterns, and narratives known as archetypes. These archetypes subtly shape our thoughts, feelings, and actions, laying the groundwork for our instincts and intuition. The inner fabric of Jung's theory also finds striking parallels in various spiritual traditions that speak of the "inner planes"—nonphysical realms teeming with symbolic or archetypal beings, reflecting the universal themes found in the collective unconscious. Occultist Gareth Knight, trained in the esoteric school founded by Dion Fortune, writes that

> we may perhaps feel, at this point, that we are drifting toward a central field which may be the same thing under different terminology and from a different viewpoint. The depth psychologist sees it as "the collective unconscious," the occultist sees it as "the inner planes."[23]

Beyond merely being a psychological construct, Jung's vision delved into the spiritual dimensions of existence. He recognized the anima mundi as a celestial tether binding all life forms and preserving nature's harmony, mirroring his conceptualization of the collective unconscious. This idea is eloquently captured in his words: "The idea of the anima mundi coincides

23 Knight, *Experience of the Inner Worlds*, 126.

with that of the collective unconscious whose centre is the self."[24] This harmonization of the anima mundi and the collective unconscious is helpful for decoding tarot theory. It helps give us a much more expansive framework for understanding the inner planes and why the cards are so psychically potent with their ability to tap into the fabric of reality itself as well as the psyches of the self and others.

The Collective Unconscious and Archetypes

The concept of archetypes—which are symbols, patterns, or characters that are universally recognized—finds its roots deeply embedded in ancient philosophy, most notably in Platonism. Plato posited abstract, nonmaterial forms such as Justice or Beauty as holding a deeper reality than their expressions in the physical realm. He saw these forms as eternal blueprints, molding every perceptible thing around us. The term *archetype* itself—derived from the Greek words *arche* and *typos*, which translate to "first/primary" and "pattern/impression" respectively—reiterates Plato's foundational ideas. This conceptual framework saw an evolution during the late Hellenic and early medieval periods. Neoplatonists, iterating Plato's ideology, put forth that these archetypal forms radiated from a singular unified source: the anima mundi.

To drive home this concept, consider a realm where the ultimate, flawless concept of a cup exists. Here in the real world, we have endless variations of that perfect idea: from disposable paper cups to elaborately designed handcrafted chalices, like what is depicted on the Ace of Cups. But no matter their form, they all hearken back to that single ideal version of a cup. What makes a cup truly a cup? Fundamentally, it holds liquid for drinking and is easy to grasp. If it has a handle, it might lean into the mug category. If it's too large or impractical, then it ventures into bowl territory. The incredible range of cups we interact with every day can all be traced back to one ideal Cup form, which highlights the notion that even the most ordinary objects are connected to a higher, perfect, idealized concept.

24 Jung, *Dreams*, 118.

Enter Carl Jung, who placed archetypes at the heart of his theory of the collective unconscious. According to Jung, these ageless symbols, encompassing motifs like the Hero, the Mother, and the Shadow, recurrently appear in dreams, arts, and religious motifs. Transcending a purely psychological lens, Jung believed these archetypes were intrinsic to the very fabric of the universe, even referring to them as "spirits" in later discourses. Jung was aware that our experiences with archetypes are subjective. They can't be verified through scientific methods because they go beyond our physical senses and exist entirely in our minds. He argued that our internal worlds and the larger cosmos reflect each other, with the collective unconscious acting as the bridge between the two through our subconscious. So, in a sense, everything is in our minds, but we need to change our perspectives of what the mind is and its relationship and impact upon reality.

Just as Plato posited an ideal form for objects like cups in our example, or more abstract ideas like justice or beauty, archetypes are easier to understand when we look at roles that people take on, and this was the particular area of exploration that Jung was interested in. For example, the archetype of the Teacher serves as an idealized concept that encapsulates the essence of guidance, instruction, and inspiration. This concept transcends the specifics of classroom educators to include spiritual guides, mentors, and even parents. Regardless of the form they take, these figures share core qualities such as fostering curiosity, encouraging critical thinking, and nurturing personal growth. This archetype can also be seen in a Jungian light as a "wise old person" or guiding force that illuminates the path to self-discovery and greater understanding. In this way, the various teachers we encounter are individual expressions of a broader universal concept. They're archetypal.

Individuation and Alchemy

Jung's concept of individuation was deeply inspired by the alchemical stages in alchemy, which he saw as a metaphor for the psychological transformation individuals undergo on their quest for self-discovery and self-realization. By recognizing and integrating the symbolism of these alchemical stages, Jung provided a framework for understanding the journey toward becoming a whole and integrated individual. His fascination with alchemy extended to European, Middle Eastern, and Taoist traditions, allowing him to draw from their ancient wisdom and psychological insights, which continue to be valuable tools in modern psychology and personal development. Jung's exploration of alchemy also enabled him to decipher the hidden messages of the unconscious, leading to the development of his transformative concept of individuation, which remains influential today in psychotherapy and self-awareness practices.

He perceived the alchemical processes as symbolic representations of the psychological transformations that an individual undergoes on this path. Jung did not interpret these alchemical stages in a literal sense. Instead, he recognized their allegorical nature and drew from their ancient wisdom and psychological insights, which remain pivotal in modern psychology and personal development. As conceptualized by Jung, individuation allows individuals to evolve from dividuals—fragmented versions of themselves—to become integrated and whole individuals. By consciously embracing and integrating these archetypes, one can transcend their unconscious sway and undergo personal transformation.

For Jung, the alchemical stage of calcination parallels the onset of individuation, where individuals confront the shadow, the ignored or rejected facets of their persona. Much like the decomposition of a substance to ash, this confrontation requires facing one's vulnerabilities, fears, and negative tendencies, leading to the dismantling of ego defenses. Dissolution, the subsequent alchemical stage, represents the deeper exploration into one's unconscious mind. It signifies the relinquishing of long-held beliefs, resulting in the further dissolution of the ego and a union with the expansive collective unconscious. As one progresses, the stage of separation emphasizes distinguishing the genuine self from the persona, the facade presented to the world. This discernment allows individuals to shed attributes not aligned with their core self. As the alchemical journey continues, the conjunction phase reflects the harmonization of opposing aspects of their psyche. Fermentation denotes a pivotal point in individuation, symbolizing personal rebirth, deeper insights, invigorated creativity, and a strong connection with the unconscious. Following this transformation, the distillation phase mirrors the honing of consciousness, leading to elevated awareness levels and movement toward the essence of the self. In the finale of the alchemical process, coagulation results in the creation of the philosopher's stone, emblematic of completion and enlightenment. In individuation, this stage symbolizes the comprehensive realization and acceptance of the self, marking psychological and spiritual wholeness.

Individuation and the Monomyth

The concept of individuation has greatly influenced cultural and psychological narratives about the journey of the self. This journey, a personal odyssey of self-realization and psychic integration, finds parallels in Joseph Campbell's monomyth, more commonly known as the Hero's Journey. Outlined in his seminal work *The Hero with a Thousand Faces*, the Hero's Journey details the universal stages of a mythological adventurer. At its core, this journey reflects the process of individuation. Campbell was familiar with Jung's work and openly acknowledged the impact of Jungian concepts on his understanding of myth.

The Hero's Journey can be seen as a narrative version of the individuation process, emphasizing universal patterns across different cultures and mythologies. In the early stages of the Hero's Journey, the call to adventure corresponds with the initial phases of individuation, where individuals grapple with feelings of unease or dissatisfaction in their lives. As the hero undergoes initiation and trials, this parallels the challenging confrontation with Jung's notion of the shadow. During this period, by facing and surmounting challenges, the hero works to meld their unconscious elements into their conscious self. Finally, the atonement and return phase of the Hero's Journey echoes the culmination of the individuation process, where reconciliation and integration occur, leading to a holistic realization of the self.

The Fool's Journey

This framework subsequently influenced many interpretations of narrative structures, including the Fool's Journey. This concept, introduced by Eden Gray in *A Complete Guide to the Tarot*, depicting the evolution of an individual as they traverse through life's challenges and experiences as the Fool of the tarot through interacting with the archetypes of the major arcana. Gray's work in the 1970s made tarot more accessible to the general public. By emphasizing the narrative structure in the major arcana, Gray indirectly highlighted the parallels with Campbell's Hero's Journey, suggesting that both paths, though different in their imagery and symbols, chart a course through universally resonant experiences of growth, challenge, death, rebirth, and eventual mastery or enlightenment. This interconnectedness underscores the idea that there's a shared narrative pattern in human consciousness—one that stories, myths, symbols, and archetypes seem to echo across cultures and ages.

EXERCISE 74

PERSONAL ALCHEMY SPREAD

Here is a tarot spread exercise for individuation using the seven stages of the alchemical process, which can be incredibly insightful for spiritual development and personal growth.

1. **Calcination:** Shuffle your tarot deck while focusing on the aspects of your ego and attachments that may be holding you back. Draw a card. This card represents these aspects that you need to acknowledge and let go.
2. **Dissolution:** Shuffle the deck again, this time focusing on your unconscious emotions. Draw a card. This card represents the hidden emotions you need to bring to the surface, acknowledge, and then release.
3. **Separation:** As you shuffle the deck once more, think about separating the valuable parts of yourself from those which no longer serve you. Draw a card. This card represents the aspects

of yourself that you need to focus on and integrate into your life.

4. **Conjunction:** Shuffle and draw another card. This card represents the integration of your useful qualities into a harmonious whole. Reflect on how the card's meaning can be applied to your journey toward self-realization.
5. **Fermentation:** Shuffle your deck and draw a card. This card will represent the personal or spiritual insights that will come to you in this stage. This card should be given ample time for reflection and understanding.
6. **Distillation:** After contemplating on the previous stage, shuffle and draw another card. This card will guide you toward refining your understanding of self, helping you distill the essence of who you are.
7. **Coagulation:** Shuffle your deck for the last time and draw a card. This card symbolizes how you can manifest your true, integrated self in the world. Reflect on how you can align your lifestyle with this true self. Celebrate this newfound understanding.

Personal Alchemy Tarot

WHAT THIS CAN LOOK LIKE

In a time of transition in my life, I decided to reach out to my tarot deck to guide me through the process of individuation, drawing on the symbolism of the alchemical process. Here is what that reading looked like, based on my notes in my tarot journal. Interestingly, each card seemed to have resonated with each step in the alchemical process itself. For the first stage, calcination, I shuffled my deck, focusing on my ego and the attachments that might be holding me back. I drew the Four of Cups; the man's refusal of the cup offered by a divine hand resonated with me. It suggested that I was entangled in a cycle of dissatisfaction, my vision clouded by past disappointments. This realization was my first step.

Moving to dissolution, I shuffled my deck again, allowing my thoughts to delve into my unconscious emotions. The card I pulled was the Moon. Its depiction of a wild, untamed path reminded me that I had fears and insecurities lurking beneath the surface. It was clear to me that acknowledging these feelings was a crucial part of my journey.

In the separation stage, I pulled the Empress after reshuffling my deck. I took this as a sign that my nurturing and creative abilities were valuable parts of myself that I needed to focus on and further integrate.

The conjunction phase brought me to the Two of Cups. The card signified unity, partnership, and connection, suggesting that integrating my qualities included fostering my relationships as conduits for my creative expressions.

As I shuffled my deck and thought about the fermentation stage, I pulled the Hermit. I understood this as a cue that my spiritual growth would require periods of solitude and self-reflection.

Entering the distillation phase, I drew the Ace of Swords. The card spoke to me of mental clarity and breakthroughs, hinting that refining my self-understanding would bring about a new level of clarity about who I was and my purpose.

For coagulation, I pulled the World. This card is a symbol of fulfillment, completion, and achievement, and I felt it was telling me that my journey of individuation was leading me to a place where someday I will be ready to fully express my true self and true will in the world.

Tarot and Archetypes

The tarot operates as a collection of universal symbols and archetypes that resonate with our shared inner and outer experiences. These symbols mirror Plato's concept of Ideal Forms, manifesting as recognizable figures or roles like the Hero or the Fool. Beyond archetypal roles, the tarot also encapsulates fundamental human themes such as love and change. By engaging with these symbols, we unlock deep self-awareness and obtain valuable perspectives. The major arcana cards, for instance, deal with the essential life-altering events and principles that affect us all, while the minor arcana cards delve into the everyday, detailing our personal attributes and situations. Thus, the tarot acts as an accessible conduit for deeper self-awareness and a bridge to the unseen dimensions of our psyche. As acclaimed tarot expert Rachel Pollack put it,

"The Tarot gives us the archetypal in a form that we can use, for healing as well as self-discovery."[25]

The archetypal symbols in tarot cards also offer a direct line to the divine through the symbolic. Carl Llewellyn Weschcke, former publisher at Llewellyn and former Grandmaster of the Aurum Solis, illuminated this aspect of tarot. He writes that

> the Tarot is a system, not a "thing," and as such the Tarot stands alone and independent to fulfill its purpose of providing an inner experience of contacting the divine powers and incorporating them into your own psyche, fostering your psychic development and empowerment. You will then be able to use these powers in solving personal life problems by taking action on the invisible planes . . . Seeing the Tarot as a genuine symbolic summary of the divine powers at work throughout the cosmos, we enter into new relations and responsibilities as conscious co-creators, knowing that every thought and action has consequences beyond our personal sphere. Even our divination becomes more than interpretation, opening an interactive channel to influence the outcome of the reading.[26]

Weschcke's insights highlight that using tarot is an interactive process, a cooperative endeavor with spiritual energies. Rather than merely peeking into our current circumstances or potential futures, each reading becomes a dynamic dialogue with divine forces. This interaction has the power to modify the very energy patterns that influence our lives. In this sense, tarot is more than a mechanism for gaining clarity; it's a means to connect and collaborate with spiritual entities capable of impacting the reading—and, by extension, the future—in real time.

Synchronicity

Synchronicity was first introduced by Jung as a term to describe coincidences that, while not causally linked, hold deep symbolic significance for those who experience them. As a concept, this was meant to provide an explanation for coincidences that lack a traditional cause/effect explanation—those

25 Pollack, *Rachel Pollack's Tarot Wisdom,* 45.

26 From the foreword written by Carl Llewellyn Weschcke in de Biasi, *The Divine Arcana of the Aurum Solis*, xvi–xvii.

occurrences that suggest the universe itself is providing us with subtle clues, weaving our internal worlds with the external. Jung's interest in synchronicity was ignited not only by the meaningful coincidences experienced by his patients but his own.

One striking example from Jung's practice involved a patient recounting a dream in which she was presented with a golden scarab beetle. As she shared this dream, just such a scarab entered the room—an occurrence that to Jung epitomized synchronicity. For Jung, such coincidences were activated when an archetype within one's unconscious mind was stimulated, manifesting itself in reality. This connection between personal experiences and the collective unconscious is where synchronicity emerges. Often catching individuals off-guard, intensifying the impact and inspiring a sense of awe and wonder, these synchronicities often appear as though orchestrated by some unseen hand for a higher purpose.

Synchronicity and Divination

The ancient Chinese divination method of I Ching further informed Jung's viewpoint. The *I Ching*, or *Book of Changes*, is an ancient Chinese text used for divination and wisdom. By casting a set of coins or sticks, one can derive one of sixty-four hexagrams, each with its unique interpretation. For Jung, the I Ching wasn't just a matter of random chance; it was evidence of synchronicity in action. He believed that the resulting hexagram was a direct reflection of the querent's current psychological state and the nature of their inquiry. The way the coins or sticks fall was influenced by the deep psychic state of the person casting them. He believed that the I Ching serves as a bridge enabling communication between the conscious mind and the unconscious realm, bringing forth insights otherwise hidden.

The tarot, like the I Ching, is also a form of divination. Each card has a wealth of symbolism and meaning. When a person shuffles and draws the cards, the resulting spread is believed, in a Jungian sense, to be a manifestation of the querent's psyche and its interaction with the external world. Just as with the I Ching, the tarot cards drawn are not merely a result of random chance. It's a synchronous event that mirrors the individual's inner state, concerns, and potential trajectories. In other words, through reading tarot, we consciously invoke synchronicity. As Madame Pamita writes in her book *Magical Tarot*,

> The tarot is a little more direct than just bumping around out in the world and paying attention to the little things that match up to give us messages. We intentionally sit down and ask a specific question and then shuffle the deck to intuitively order those symbolic and synchronous cards that will give us the answer.[27]

How This Ties Into Psychic Tarot

The relationship between the collective unconscious, psychic ability, and tarot is rooted in deep interconnectedness. Psychic insights, often drawing from the vast shared reservoir of the collective unconscious, gain depth and clarity with the tarot. With its symbolic depth, tarot amplifies these insights, acting not just as a tool but as a catalyst, opening doors to deeper psychic revelations. When drawing a card, its symbolism sharpens our intuitive focus, guiding us to specific messages or vibrations from the broader collective unconscious of the inner planes. This interaction, complemented by the energies of the individual seeking guidance, creates an atmosphere ripe for psychic perception. When a tarot reading results in a card aligning perfectly with an individual's situation, that's synchronicity in action. Far from being passive, tarot cards actively shape and guide our psychic flow. Their symbols, tied to universal archetypes, resonate with our intuitive and psychic abilities, uniting our personal stories with larger universal themes.

EXERCISE 75

SYNCHRONICITY AND TAROT INTERPRETATION

1. Close your eyes, take a few deep breaths, and bring to mind a synchronicity you've experienced recently. This could be something seemingly random that you keep seeing over and

27 Pamita, *Magical Tarot*, 3.

over everywhere. Once you have this in mind, write it down in your journal.

2. Still focusing on your synchronicity, hold it in your mind as you shuffle your tarot deck. This will help set your intention for the tarot draw. The aim is to draw a card that could provide further insights or clarity about your synchronicity.
3. When you feel ready, draw a card from the tarot deck. Place the card in front of you. If you read with reversals, make sure to pay attention to whether the card is upright or not as this will influence its meaning.
4. Take a moment to observe the imagery, colors, and symbols on the card. Jot down your initial reactions, feelings, and thoughts about the card in your journal. Don't worry about the traditional card meanings at this point; just focus on what you personally observe and feel from the card.
5. Feel free to call on your tarot spirit guide to see if you can get more insight into the card.
6. Reflect on the meaning of the card and how it might relate to your synchronicity. What additional insights does the card offer? How does it resonate with your synchronicity? Write your insights in your journal.
7. Finally, take some time to reflect on the entire exercise. How do you feel? What new insights have emerged? Is there a new perspective on the synchronicity you experienced? Write any final thoughts or feelings in your journal.

Thoughtforms and Egregores

We previously explored thoughtforms earlier in this book, but let's explore it more in depth to gain a better understanding of tarot theory. A thoughtform is a mental concept deeply rooted in Theosophy and certain esoteric traditions. This mental or emotional construct stems from an individual's thoughts, feelings, or beliefs. At their simplest, thoughtforms are fleeting emotions or ideas we experience daily, like the fleeting anger when someone cuts us off in traffic or the surge of joy when seeing a loved one. These passing thoughts emit energy but typically dissolve quickly. More potent emotions or thoughts that are sustained and focused can give rise to stronger, longer-lasting thoughtforms. For instance, an ambition nurtured over years can amass energy and intent, forming a more potent thoughtform. This principle underpins certain manifestation and visualization practices. But these constructs don't just remain in the mind; when concentrated, they can manifest in the inner planes, embodying the strength and essence of the originating thought or emotion.

Though a thoughtform originates from an individual's psyche, it can, when sufficiently empowered, function independently. It might then influence the person's surroundings or even their own emotional and mental states. This connection between the creator and the thoughtform can become cyclical: the thoughtform, if regularly energized, can amplify the originating emotion in the creator. The nature, duration, and strength of a thoughtform largely hinge on the intensity and persistence of the initial emotion or thought. Without continual nurturing they might fade, but with consistent energy they can endure for longer spans. In certain traditions, exceptionally potent thoughtforms are viewed similarly to spirits, interacting like nonphysical entities. Many magickal practitioners deliberately craft these thoughtforms for specific tasks.

Egregores

Egregores elevate the idea of thoughtforms to a group level. This term signifies a collective energy that emerges when multiple individuals harbor shared beliefs or intentions. This combined force surpasses the individual inputs and can function independently. Comparing the two, if individual thoughtforms are seen as cells of psychic energy, an egregore is the body formed from these cells. An egregore emerges when multiple thoughtforms, driven by the common goals and feelings of a group, merge. Unlike thoughtforms that typically arise from an individual, egregores are fundamentally tied to collectives and are strengthened with more people fueling it with their focus and energy. Once formed, an egregore can influence its group members and, when powerful enough, even impact real-world events in line with the group's intentions. Just like with individual thoughtforms, the relationship between an egregore and its group members is symbiotic.

Egregores permeate several group dynamics due to their inherent nature, thriving on shared intention and focus. Companies, for example, have their unique cultures where collective energies embody the company's ethos and can affect everything from employee morale to brand perception. Sports teams, political groups, religious congregations, social clubs, and even online communities also possess their distinct egregores formed from shared emotions, beliefs, or interests. The reciprocal relationship between an egregore and its members plays a pivotal role. If the group's concentration falters or disagreements surface, the egregore can weaken or change. Acknowledging these entities' existence and impact can yield deep insights into the unseen forces directing collective pursuits.

HRU: The Angel of Tarot

The angel of the tarot, often referred to as HRU in occult traditions like the Golden Dawn, is perceived as a unifying, guiding spiritual entity or force that oversees the tarot, tarot readings, and its practitioners. The main idea is that when you shuffle a tarot deck or lay out a spread, you're not just dealing with merely cards; you're also tapping into a greater spiritual entity or force that governs and channels the tarot's wisdom. This concept can be somewhat abstract, akin to trying to understand dimensions perfectly beyond the ones we perceive in everyday life. Similarly, HRU exists in a metaphysical space that doesn't necessarily conform to linear or rational understanding. It's a presence that may offer guidance or influence but does so in ways that can appear mysterious, inconsistent, or paradoxical to our limited perceptions.

HRU isn't confined to a singular interpretation. Different occult traditions and individual practitioners might have their unique understandings and methods for working with this spiritual force. According to Jean-Louis de Biasi, Hermetic philosopher and current Grandmaster of the Ordo

Aurum Solis, the angel of the tarot is the result of all the people who have ever used the tarot over time creating an egregore that now has a life of its own.[28] Occultists like Arthur Waite, Pamela Colman Smith, and Aleister Crowley, who have played significant roles in shaping modern tarot, deeply embraced the idea of the angel of the tarot. As members of the Hermetic Order of the Golden Dawn, they viewed HRU as a guiding spirit with the capacity to unveil deep wisdom and concealed truths through tarot readings. According to the tarot manuscripts of the Golden Dawn, HRU is referred to as "the Great Angel overseeing the workings of the Secret Wisdom."

Crowley saw a correspondence between HRU and Heru-Ra-Ha and believed them to be the same entity. Heru-Ra-Ha is a composite deity within Thelema, bringing together two different aspects of the Egyptian god Horus. Both HRU and Heru-Ra-Ha are considered overarching intelligences or divine forces governing the unfolding of events or insights through the tarot itself. The linking of HRU with Heru-Ra-Ha allowed Crowley to align his Thelemic worldview directly into the Thoth Tarot deck, making the deck not just a tool for divination but also a key to Thelemic cosmology and philosophy. In traditional tarot decks, such as the Rider-Waite-Smith, the Judgement card typically portrays an angel blowing a trumpet, often interpreted as a harbinger of resurrection or final judgment. Crowley replaced this with the Aeon card in his Thoth Tarot deck, which is a shift that aligns more closely with Thelemic doctrines and Egyptian mythology.

In the Aeon card of the Thoth Tarot, you'll notice that the angel is replaced with both aspects of Heru-Ra-Ha instead. Horus the Child, or Hoor-paar-kraat, is seen in the foreground, signifying the passive form of Spirit, while Ra-Hoor-Khuit is in the background, symbolizing the active form of Spirit. Instead of the traditional angel with a trumpet calling souls to judgment at the end times, here the dual aspects of Heru-Ra-Ha serve as a representation of the new aeon of Horus, an era defined by individualism, direct personal gnosis, and the application of will, as per Thelemic tenets.

28 de Biasi, *The Divine Arcana of the Aurum Solis,* 61–62.

This shifts the focus from an ending of an aeon toward that of a dawning of another.

In Crowley's belief, the illustrations of his Thoth Tarot represented the "Book of the Law," with HRU serving as the influential angel presiding over the tarot. Kenneth Grant, Crowley's personal secretary and an initiate of the Ordo Templi Orientis, saw HRU as the divine muse inspiring the imagery of the Thoth Tarot. On the topic of HRU, Aleister Crowley writes,

> To divine concerning a matter is little more than to calculate probabilities. We obtain the use of minds who have access to knowledge beyond ours, but not to omniscience. HRU, the great angel set over the Tarot, is beyond us as we are beyond the ant; but for all we know, the knowledge of HRU is excelled by some mightier mind in the same proportion. Nor have we any warrant for accusing HRU of ignorance or error if we read the Tarot to our own delusion. He may have known, he may have spoken truly; the fault may lie with our own insight.[29]

This quote echoes the idea that any insight provided by HRU during our tarot readings is never wrong. However, our interpretations of what HRU is conveying through the cards can be incorrect due to our limited understanding or perspective. It also emphasizes that while tarot is predictive, the prediction is the path of most likely probability of what is going to happen if things keep unfolding as they are. This provides room for one's own free will in the face of fate and places the responsibility of how we interpret the cards on us and not on the angel of the tarot.

As we can see, the concept of HRU offers multiple interpretations, each with its unique nuances and benefits. When viewed as an egregore, or a collective consciousness shaped by the beliefs and practices of tarot practitioners throughout history, a tarot reading takes on a participatory quality. You're not merely flipping cards; you're connecting to a pool of wisdom and intentions that extends across time and space, adding weight and shared meaning to the reading. Seen as an angelic force, HRU lends a divine, protective aura to the tarot experience. The cards become channels for cosmic truths and guidance, transcending their status as mere symbols.

29 Crowley, Desti, and Waddell, *Magick: Liber Aba: Book 4*, 263.

Seeing HRU as an overarching Jungian archetype of the tarot as a whole invites personal insights through tapping into the collective individual archetypes the tarot presents within its cards. If HRU is seen as a deity, the tarot reading turns into an act of worship or spiritual communion, making the reading a sacred interaction that involves the seeker, the deity, and the cards.

These interpretations can coexist, offering a multifaceted understanding that enriches each tarot reading. Such a reading becomes a complex interaction with higher intelligences, be they collective thought, angelic entities, archetypal images, divine forces, or a combination of these ideas. Thus, belief in HRU elevates tarot reading from a basic divinatory practice to a multilayered spiritual engagement. This deepens the reading's nuances, enabling it to address not just immediate issues but also existential queries. Tarot reading becomes an ongoing dialogue between the reader, the cards, and the entity or concept that HRU represents. A conscious invocation of and connection to HRU further intensifies this connection to the tarot, which can greatly elevate your readings.

EXERCISE 76

MEETING HRU

Close your eyes, take a deep breath, and enter the realm of your inner tarot temple. As you step inside, notice the familiar surroundings, the soft glow of candlelight, and the comforting scent of incense. This is your sacred space—your sanctuary for introspection and self-discovery.

As you wander around, exploring the nooks and corners of your temple, you suddenly notice something different: a previously unnoticed staircase tucked away in a hidden corner. The steps beckon you, inviting you to embark on a new journey. Curiosity piques your interest, and you decide to climb the staircase. With each step you feel a sense of anticipation and wonder, as if you are ascending to a higher realm of consciousness. As you reach the top, you find yourself in an awe-inspiring chamber, a temple like no other you have seen before. The room is aglow with radiant light, emanating from a magnificent stained glass window depicting HRU, the angel of the tarot. Vibrant colors dance across the walls, illuminating patterns that seem to come alive with every breath you take.

At the center of the temple stands a statue of HRU, a numinous being with a gentle smile and eyes that radiate wisdom and understanding. You feel a deep sense of connection and reverence as you approach the angelic presence. The energy in the room envelops you, filling you with a deep sense of peace and serenity. As you stand before HRU, you notice the most awe-inspiring aspect of this angelic presence: magnificent, divine wings that stretch out with the grace of a falcon in flight. The vibrant feathers are a mosaic of colors, glistening with celestial light, reflecting the essence of the cosmos. These wings, with their transcendent beauty, seem to connect heaven and earth, bridging the realms of the divine and the mortal.

In the presence of HRU's falcon wings, you feel a deep connection to the realm of spirit and the infinite possibilities that lie beyond the material world. They symbolize the ability to soar above the mundane, see life from a higher perspective, and tap into the boundless wisdom of the universe. As you gaze upon these majestic wings, feeling the power and ancient wisdom they hold, a sense of wonder washes over you. They seem to hold the secrets of the universe, carrying the energy of countless cosmic cycles. It's as if they are the embodiment of flight, freedom, and transcendence, guiding souls toward higher realms of consciousness.

These beautiful wings seem to whisper ancient knowledge, telling tales of past civilizations, forgotten mysteries, and the eternal dance of creation and transformation. You feel enveloped in their embrace, as if they are offering protection and guidance on your spiritual journey. In this moment of communion, HRU begins to reveal insights and revelations, not through words but through images and feelings. You see flashes of symbolism and archetypal representations that resonate deep within your soul. It's as if the entire tarot deck is coming alive, its energies and messages flowing into your being. These insights leave you in awe as you recognize the significance of this encounter. HRU has bestowed upon you a divine gift, opening your eyes to the interconnectedness of all things and the wisdom of the universe.

With a heart full of gratitude and reverence, you bid farewell to HRU, knowing that this sacred temple will always be available to you whenever you seek guidance and inspiration. You begin your descent down the staircase, back to your inner tarot temple, carrying the wisdom of HRU within your heart. When you open your eyes, take a moment to reflect on the journey you have just taken. Cherish the connection with HRU and the insights gained as you continue your life's path guided by the angelic presence of the tarot's divine guardian with beautiful falcon wings.

EXERCISE 77

THE EVOCATION PRAYER TO HRU

Initiates of the Hermetic Golden Dawn are taught a prayer to call upon HRU before a tarot reading by invoking IAO to bring forth HRU. The acronym IAO is an intoned formula that has its roots in occultism and represents the deities Isis, Apophis, and Osiris. This powerful combination of divine forces symbolizes the divine eternal cycle of life, death, and rebirth. By invoking the energy of IAO, one can tap into this universal power of the cyclic stages of life and gain a deeper understanding of the mysteries of existence. Here is the traditional Hermetic Order of the Golden Dawn prayer of evocation to HRU:

> I invoke thee, IAO, that thou wilt send HRU, the great Angel that is set over the operations of this secret Wisdom, to lay his hand invisibly upon these consecrated cards of art, that thereby we may obtain true knowledge of hidden things to the glory of thine ineffable Name. Amen.[30]

In this prayer, we humbly reach out to the divine IAO, invoking the powerful HRU, the esteemed egregore angel, the guardian of esoteric knowledge. With reverence we seek HRU's assistance in infusing these sacred tarot cards with enhanced insight, granting us a deeper understanding of the hidden truths that lie behind the veil. Our earnest aspiration is to illuminate the divine Name, to unveil the mysteries that lie in the heart of these cards. With sincere devotion, we trust in the divine power we invoke, seeking to gain understanding and knowledge that will illuminate our path and guide us on our spiritual journey. As we offer this prayer, we envision HRU's majestic falcon wings encircling the sacred space in which we read the tarot. Enveloping ourselves, the cards, and anyone else present, these celestial wings create a magickal circle, a sacred space of protection and communion. With faith in the divine forces we invoke, we say "amen," affirming our complete trust and surrender to the wisdom and guidance that HRU brings forth. If you're uncomfortable with amen, you can say something else such as "Amun" (the name of the Egyptian creator deity) or "So mote it be!" May this sacred connection strengthen our spiritual insights and lead us closer to the divine truth.

30 Louis, *Tarot Beyond the Basics*, 104.

EXERCISE 78

HRU'S LIBRARY OF THOTH'S TAROT MYSTERIES

In this exercise, you will enter your internal tarot temple and ascend to HRU's chamber, where ancient wisdom awaits. As you open the door to a vast and infinite library, you will discover the encoded knowledge of the tarot's deepest secrets.

1. Enter your internal tarot temple and go up the staircase to the chamber of HRU, the angel of the tarot.
2. As you enter you are bathed in a warm golden light. The energy fills the air as you stand in awe.
3. Amidst the chamber, a door catches your attention that is decorated with engravings of the four angelic hands of the ace suits in the tarot. In the center is an image of Thoth, the Egyptian ibis-headed god. In old lore about the tarot, it was believed that the tarot was the lost book of Thoth himself.

4. Trust your intuition as you open the door, revealing a vast and infinite library holding the tarot's deepest mysteries.

5. Explore the library, which is filled with ancient scrolls, dusty tomes, and mystical artifacts. Sense the wisdom and ancient knowledge resonating from every corner.
6. Approach the central table and find a glowing emerald book resting on a velvet pillow. This book contains the encoded knowledge of the tarot's deep mysteries. To access the information, place your hands gently on the emerald cover and connect with HRU's guiding energy.
7. As you open the emerald book, a surge of divine energy flows through you. The pages come alive, filled with images, symbols, and insights that resonate with your soul. Allow yourself to absorb the knowledge and wisdom within.
8. Take your time to explore the teachings encoded within the emerald book, knowing HRU is guiding you to the knowledge you need most. Trust that this sacred space is tailored to your spiritual journey.
9. Express gratitude to HRU for their guidance and teachings you have received. Close the emerald book, knowing you can access this sacred library whenever you need to delve deeper into tarot's mysteries.
10. Begin your descent down the secret passage stairway, carrying the energy and wisdom of HRU within you. Return to your temple, knowing that HRU's guidance will always be with you on your tarot exploration.
11. When you are ready, open your eyes, bringing the insights and inspiration from HRU's secret library into the waking world. Embrace the wisdom you have received and know that you can always return to this sacred space to deepen your connection with the mysteries of the tarot.

The Unfolding Mysteries of the Tarot

In my personal experience, the knowledge obtained from HRU's library during the meditation may not always be immediately apparent or fully processed. It's as if the insight gathered from that sacred space lingers in the depths of my subconscious, waiting for the right moment to emerge and make its presence known. On several occasions, I've been amazed by how later that night, in the realm of dreams, I stumble upon intriguing perspectives about the hidden symbolism within the tarot. These dreamscapes offer a surreal yet deep encounter with the mysteries encoded within the cards. Within those dreams I find myself exploring the tarot's imagery and symbolism in ways that go beyond my conscious understanding. It's as if my subconscious mind operates as a channel for the angel of the tarot, exposing complex relationships and deep meanings that bypass conscious comprehension. Upon waking I'm left with vivid fragments of the dream, each containing valuable insights about tarot's deeper layers. These dream revelations are like hidden gems waiting to be unearthed and examined in the light of day.

What astonishes me even more is that, as I delve into the symbolism discovered in my dreams, I later come across tangible evidence that verifies the validity of those insights. It's as if the universe itself conspires to confirm the wisdom received from HRU's library through synchronicity. Scraps of the dream knowledge reveal themselves in unexpected ways, like chance encounters with rare tarot-related information or sudden realizations about the cards during my daily activities. These synchronicities serve as validation that the guidance received is genuine and worth exploring further. This unfolding journey of discovery is both humbling and awe-inspiring. It reminds me that the mysteries of the tarot are vast, and there's always more to learn and uncover. The information from HRU's library isn't meant to be understood all at once; it's a process of gradual assimilation and integration. I really value the way meditation, dreams, and everyday life seem to blend together, strengthening my connection to HRU. This presence keeps guiding me as I dig deeper into the hidden meanings in the tarot cards. I stay open to unexpected moments that give me a peek into bigger spiritual questions. I have faith that HRU's insights will keep adding layers of understanding to my tarot readings and personal growth. I hope you experience the same in your own journey.

VIII
STRENGTH.

∞

Conclusion

In her insightful book *The Artist's Way*, Julia Cameron strikes a chord with her statement that

> art is not about thinking something up. It is about the opposite—getting something down. The directions are important here.[31]

This notion echoes strongly with the practice of psychic tarot reading. Like an artist bringing an abstract vision into reality, a tarot reader lets the cards unfold their stories, not inventing tales but revealing narratives. Each card in a tarot spread paints part of this narrative like brushstrokes on a canvas. In the hands of a skilled psychic reader, these cards reflect our deepest thoughts and link us to shared human experiences. The reader's talent lies in merging their psychic intuition with the cards' symbolic "colors," unveiling insights about personal and interpersonal dynamics.

Tarot readings delve beneath the surface, making the invisible visible and giving form to hidden thoughts and feelings. Tarot serves as a bridge between the seen and unseen, illuminating aspects of psychic and intuitive information waiting to be brought forth. Like paint dabs on an artist's palette, each card adds a distinct hue to the tarot reading's overall picture. The psychic art of tarot reveals our inner selves and life's external mysteries. Tarot readings clarify complex emotions and experiences, enhancing our understanding of our place in the world. Engaging in these practices enriches our perception. They offer a more lucid understanding of our identity, the nature of our connections with others, and our place in the larger narrative of the world, enhancing our comprehension of life's ever-evolving story.

31 Cameron, *The Artist's Way: 30th Anniversary Edition*, 117.

The psychic aspect of the tarot reading aligns more with artistry than a rigid science. Through it we cultivate a unique bond with the collective unconscious, guided not by rigid rules but by the vibrant colors of our psychic imagination. This imagination acts as our paintbrush, bringing to life the narratives hidden within the tarot. Our imaginative power leads us beyond mundane realities, allowing us to leap over the bounds of conventional logic, much like artists who capture something more provocative from their inner worlds to convey through their medium. In the art of psychic tarot, imagination isn't just useful; it's essential. In a similar vein to the unique perspective a painter brings to their view of the world, it's the lens through which we gain psychic insights. The true beauty of tarot, much like that of a masterpiece, lies in its ability to forge connections and convey authenticity. Just as an artist may fear a misplaced brushstroke, we too may feel trepidation at the thought of misinterpreting the cards. However, in the psychic art of tarot, these so-called mistakes are valuable teachers. They mirror the Fool's journey, who steps into the unknown with open arms, ready to learn from his experiences—mistakes included.

The more we engage with tarot, the more instinctively it comes to us. It's a lot like art in that sense—deeply personal and unique to each individual. While we may start with traditional methods that create a strong foundation, every tarot reader, much like an artist, eventually develops their own distinctive style. What works for one person may not for another, and that's the real charm of tarot: its ability to be personalized and adaptable. Think of your internal tarot temple as your own personal art studio. In this space you hone your intuition and spiritual insights; it's a place of active involvement and exploration. Your tarot spirit guide is akin to your muse, shedding light on your journey and infusing your readings with inspiration. As this relationship strengthens, your readings become richer and more nuanced. Your interpretations start to echo with greater clarity, mirroring the deep connection that forms between you as the reader and the querent, much like the relationship between an artist and their audience.

I trust that these exercises have prepared you for an exciting adventure in intuitive discovery and psychic expression. With every shuffle and spread of your tarot deck, may you delve deeper into the beauty of this art that enriches other people's lives. As we conclude, picture yourself as the tarot's Fool, standing at the edge of a wondrous journey. Take that step with the courage and optimism of an artist approaching a blank canvas, armed with a vivid imagination and the strong conviction that the Spirit of Tarot, much like a wise art mentor, will lead you toward your greatest potential as long as your intentions are sincere and passionate.

IX
THE HERMIT.

Appendix A

Psychic Affirmations and the Tarot

THE FOOL: "I am open to new experiences and perspectives, awakening my psychic insights."

THE MAGICIAN: "I have all the tools and abilities within me to unlock my psychic potential."

THE HIGH PRIESTESS: "I trust my intuition and the wisdom it brings; it guides me toward deeper understanding."

THE EMPRESS: "I nurture my psychic gifts and watch them flourish and grow."

THE EMPEROR: "I am in command of my psychic abilities, controlling them with wisdom and strength."

THE HIEROPHANT: "I am guided by universal wisdom and am connected to the spiritual realm."

THE LOVERS: "I allow love to guide my psychic journey, bringing clarity and unity to my mind, body, and spirit."

THE CHARIOT: "I am moving forward with determination and confidence in developing my psychic abilities."

STRENGTH: "I am strong and resilient, and my psychic strength grows with each passing day."

THE HERMIT: "In solitude, I find the light of my psychic knowledge illuminating the path forward."

WHEEL OF FORTUNE: "I trust in the flow of the universe, knowing it enhances my psychic abilities."

JUSTICE: "I seek truth and balance, strengthening my psychic insight."

THE HANGED MAN: "By gaining new perspectives, I expand my psychic consciousness."

DEATH: "I let go of old limitations, making room for enhanced psychic awareness."

TEMPERANCE: "I harmonize my mind, body, and spirit to tap into my psychic wisdom."

THE DEVIL: "I am breaking free from all self-imposed barriers, enhancing my psychic abilities."

THE TOWER: "Though change may be chaotic, it clears the path for my psychic awakening."

THE STAR: "I trust in the guidance of the universe, enhancing my psychic awareness."

THE MOON: "I am connected with my subconscious, unveiling hidden psychic insights."

THE SUN: "I am surrounded by positive energy, awakening my psychic abilities."

JUDGEMENT: "I am awakening to higher levels of consciousness and psychic understanding."

THE WORLD: "I am fully connected to the universal wisdom, realizing my psychic potential."

ACE OF PENTACLES: "My psychic journey is just beginning, and the universe supports my every step."

TWO OF PENTACLES: "I maintain balance between my physical and spiritual self, enhancing my psychic abilities."

THREE OF PENTACLES: "As I collaborate with others, my psychic insights grow and deepen."

FOUR OF PENTACLES: "I am secure in my psychic abilities, grounding them in daily life."

FIVE OF PENTACLES: "Even in times of difficulty, I find the strength to deepen my psychic abilities."

SIX OF PENTACLES: "As I generously share my psychic insights, I receive further wisdom from the universe."

SEVEN OF PENTACLES: "I patiently cultivate my psychic abilities, knowing that they will grow with time and care."

EIGHT OF PENTACLES: "With consistent practice, I hone my psychic abilities and deepen my spiritual insight."

NINE OF PENTACLES: "I enjoy the fruits of my psychic growth, appreciating the wisdom it brings into my life."

TEN OF PENTACLES: "I am rich in psychic wisdom, bringing harmony and insight into my life."

PAGE OF PENTACLES: "Curiosity and openness guide my psychic development."

KNIGHT OF PENTACLES: "I remain steadfast and dedicated in my pursuit of psychic knowledge."

QUEEN OF PENTACLES: "I am nurturing and kind, using my psychic abilities for the greater good."

KING OF PENTACLES: "I am grounded in my psychic abilities, using them with wisdom and discernment."

ACE OF SWORDS: "My mind is clear and focused, perfect for developing my psychic abilities."

TWO OF SWORDS: "I find peace amidst confusion, allowing my psychic intuition to guide me."

THREE OF SWORDS: "I can heal from any pain, using these experiences to deepen my psychic understanding."

FOUR OF SWORDS: "In times of rest and solitude, my psychic abilities flourish."

FIVE OF SWORDS: "I learn from conflict and discord, using these experiences to hone my psychic wisdom."

SIX OF SWORDS: "I trust in my journey, knowing that each move I make enhances my psychic abilities."

SEVEN OF SWORDS: "I trust in my own wisdom and intuition, guiding me toward stronger psychic insights."

EIGHT OF SWORDS: "I free myself from limiting beliefs, opening up to limitless psychic potential."

NINE OF SWORDS: "I release fear and anxiety, knowing they only cloud my psychic vision."

TEN OF SWORDS: "I learn from endings, using these moments to bring about psychic rebirth."

PAGE OF SWORDS: "My curiosity fuels my journey, guiding me toward deeper psychic knowledge."

KNIGHT OF SWORDS: "My courage and ambition drive my psychic development."

QUEEN OF SWORDS: "I use my discernment and wisdom to guide my psychic journey."

KING OF SWORDS: "I am master of my thoughts, using my clarity of mind to enhance my psychic abilities."

ACE OF WANDS: "I am filled with potential and ready to ignite my psychic abilities."

TWO OF WANDS: "I am open to new paths and possibilities, expanding my psychic vision."

THREE OF WANDS: "I have the power to shape my future, guided by my psychic insights."

FOUR OF WANDS: "I celebrate my progress and achievements on my psychic journey."

FIVE OF WANDS: "I learn from challenges and conflicts, using them to refine my psychic abilities."

SIX OF WANDS: "I confidently share my psychic insights, using them to uplift others."

SEVEN OF WANDS: "I stand strong in my beliefs, fueling my psychic strength and resilience."

EIGHT OF WANDS: "I move swiftly with clarity and purpose on my psychic journey."

NINE OF WANDS: "I am resilient and determined to continue nurturing my psychic abilities despite any obstacles."

TEN OF WANDS: "I release unnecessary burdens, making room for psychic growth."

PAGE OF WANDS: "I embrace a sense of wonder and curiosity, enhancing my psychic exploration."

KNIGHT OF WANDS: "My passion and determination guide my journey, strengthening my psychic abilities."

QUEEN OF WANDS: "I am a beacon of warmth, courage, and psychic wisdom."

KING OF WANDS: "I lead with my intuition, using my psychic gifts to inspire and enlighten."

ACE OF CUPS: "I am open to the abundance of psychic intuition flowing within and around me."

TWO OF CUPS: "Through connections with others, I deepen my psychic understanding and empathy."

THREE OF CUPS: "In the joy of shared experiences, my psychic abilities are heightened."

FOUR OF CUPS: "I seek wisdom and meaning beyond the visible, enhancing my psychic perception."

FIVE OF CUPS: "I release past disappointments to make space for growing psychic awareness."

SIX OF CUPS: "By honoring my past and my inner child, I open the door to psychic insights."

SEVEN OF CUPS: "I discern between illusion and truth, sharpening my psychic vision."

EIGHT OF CUPS: "I have the courage to leave behind what no longer serves my psychic development."

NINE OF CUPS: "I trust that my wishes and psychic aspirations are being fulfilled."

TEN OF CUPS: "I am aligned with inner and outer harmony, boosting my psychic abilities."

PAGE OF CUPS: "With an open heart and curious mind, I am receptive to psychic messages."

KNIGHT OF CUPS: "I follow my heart and intuition fearlessly, enhancing my psychic abilities."

QUEEN OF CUPS: "I trust my intuition and nurture my psychic abilities with love and compassion."

KING OF CUPS: "I am balanced and in control of my emotions, guiding my psychic abilities with wisdom."

Appendix B

Emergency Resources

Sometimes issues surface during tarot readings that are way out of your league, and people are sometimes more willing to tell a tarot reader stuff they wouldn't tell anyone else. Being a tarot reader isn't a free pass to play therapist, lawyer, or doctor. You also don't want to be that reader who ends up in legal trouble because of overstepping boundaries.

Keep a list of hotlines or websites handy so if the conversation takes a serious turn, you can point people in the right direction. In many cases you may be saving a life by doing so.

I've compiled some resources for you on these topics here:

www.Auryn.net/emergency

X
WHEEL of FORTUNE.

Bibliography

Adam, Elliot. *Fearless Tarot: How to Give a Positive Reading in Any Situation*. Llewellyn, 2020.

———. *Tarot in Love: Consulting the Cards in Matters of the Heart*. Llewellyn, 2023.

Antenucci, Nancy. *Tarot Rituals: Ceremonies, Ideas, and Experiences for the Tarot Lover*. Llewellyn, 2022.

Antenucci, Nancy, and Melanie Howard. *Psychic Tarot: Using Your Natural Psychic Abilities to Read the Cards*. Llewellyn, 2011.

Arrien, Angeles. *The Tarot Handbook: Practical Applications of Ancient Visual Symbols*. Penguin, 1997.

Auryn, Mat. *Mastering Magick: A Course in Spellcasting for the Psychic Witch*. Llewellyn, 2022.

———. *Psychic Witch: A Metaphysical Guide to Meditation, Magick, and Manifestation*. Llewellyn, 2020.

Braden, Nina Lee. *Tarot for Self Discovery*. Llewellyn, 2002.

Brennan, Barbara Ann. *Light Emerging: The Journey of Personal Healing*. Random House, 2011.

Bunning, Joan. *The Big Book of Tarot: How to Interpret the Cards and Work with Tarot Spreads for Personal Growth*. Weiser, 2019.

Burgess, Charlie Claire. *Radical Tarot: Queer the Cards, Liberate Your Practice, and Create the Future*. Hay House, 2023.

Cameron, Julia. *The Artist's Way*, 30th anniversary ed. Penguin, 2016.

Campbell, Joseph. *The Hero with a Thousand Faces*. New World Library, 2008.

Chang, T. Susan. *Tarot Correspondences: Ancient Secrets for Everyday Readers*. Llewellyn, 2018.

Chang, T. Susan, and M. M. Meleen. *Tarot Deciphered: Decoding Esoteric Symbolism in Modern Tarot*. Llewellyn, 2021.

Cicero, Chic, and Sandra Tabatha Cicero. *Tarot Talismans: Invoking the Angels of the Tarot*. Llewellyn, 2006.

Cicero, Chic, Lon Milo DuQuette, and Israel Regardie. *The Complete Golden Dawn System of Magic*. Falcon, 2020.

Cicero, Chic, Sandra Tabatha Cicero, and Pat Zalewski. *The Golden Dawn Enochian Skrying Tarot: Your Complete System for Divination, Skrying, and Ritual Magick*. Llewellyn, 2004.

Colish, Marcia L. *The Stoic Tradition from Antiquity to the Early Middle Ages*. Germany: Brill, 1990.

Coyle, T. Thorn. *Evolutionary Witchcraft*. Penguin, 2005.

Crowley, Aleister. *Book of Thoth*. Weiser, 1969.

Crowley, Aleister, Mary Desti, and Leila Waddell. *Magick: Liber ABA,* book 4. Weiser, 1997.

Curtiss, F. Homer, Harriette Augusta Curtiss, Manly P. Hall, A. E. Thierens, Papus, S. L. MacGregor Mathers, Arthur Edward Waite, Eliphaz Levi, P. D. Ouspensky, and P. R. S. Foli. *The Tarot: A Collection of Secret Wisdom from Tarot's Mystical Origins*. Foreword by Juliet Sharman-Burke. St. Martin's, 2021.

de Biasi, Jean-Louis. *The Divine Arcana of the Aurum Solis: Using Tarot Talismans for Ritual and Initiation*. Llewellyn, 2011.

Dionne, Danielle. *Magickal Mediumship: Partnering with the Ancestors for Healing and Spiritual Development*. Llewellyn, 2020.

Dominguez, Jr., Ivo. *Keys to Perception: A Practical Guide to Psychic Development*. Weiser, 2017.

———. *Spirit Speak: Knowing and Understanding Spirit Guides, Ancestors, Ghosts, Angels, and the Divine*. New Page, 2008.

Drury, Nevill. *The Watkins Dictionary of Magic: Over 3,000 Entries on the World of Magical Formulas, Secret Symbols, and the Occult.* Watkins Media, 2011.

DuQuette, Lon Milo. *Understanding Aleister Crowley's Thoth Tarot: New Edition.* Weiser, 2017.

Elford, Jaymi. *Tarot Inspired Life: Use the Cards to Enhance Your Life.* Llewellyn, 2019.

Ende, Michael. *The Neverending Story.* Penguin Young Readers Group, 1993.

Fortune, Dion. *The Cosmic Doctrine.* Weiser, 2000.

———. *The Mystical Qabalah.* Weiser, 2022.

———. *Spiritualism in the Light of Occult Science.* Rider, 1931.

Gad, Irene. *Tarot and Individuation: A Jungian Study of Correspondences with Cabala, Alchemy, and the Chakras.* Nicolas-Hays, 2004.

Gilbert, Elizabeth. *Big Magic: Creative Living Beyond Fear.* Penguin, 2016.

Graham, Sasha. *Llewellyn's Complete Book of the Rider-Waite-Smith Tarot: A Journey Through the History, Meaning, and Use of the World's Most Famous Deck.* Llewellyn, 2018.

———. *The Magic of Tarot: Your Guide to Intuitive Readings, Rituals, and Spells.* Llewellyn, 2021.

Gray, Eden. *The Complete Guide to the Tarot: Determine Your Destiny! Predict Your Own Future!* Random House, 1982.

Greer, Mary K. *Archetypal Tarot: What Your Birth Card Reveals about Your Personality, Your Path, and Your Potential.* Weiser, 2021.

———. *Mary K. Greer's 21 Ways to Read a Tarot Card.* Llewellyn, 2011.

———. *Tarot for Your Self: A Workbook for the Inward Journey,* 35th anniversary ed. Weiser, 2019.

Greer, Mary K., and Tom Little. *Understanding the Tarot Court.* Llewellyn, 2004.

Halvorson, Ailynn. *The Tarot Apothecary: Shifting Personal Energies Using Tarot, Aromatherapy, and Simple Everyday Rituals.* Llewellyn, 2022.

Hanson, Rick. *Hardwiring Happiness: The New Brain Science of Contentment, Calm, and Confidence.* Harmony/Rodale, 2016.

Hauser, Christine. 2023. "A Pennsylvania Shop Offered Tarot Readings. Then the Police Came," *The New York Times,* October 15, 2023. https://www.nytimes.com/2023/10/14/us/pennsylvania-witchcraft-tarot-law-police.html.

Hendrickson, Nancy. *Ancestral Tarot: Uncover Your Past and Chart Your Future.* Weiser, 2021.

Hesselroth, Denise. *Intentional Tarot: Using the Cards with Purpose.* Llewellyn, 2020.

Hunter, Devin. *The Witch's Book of Power.* Llewellyn, 2016.

Huson, Paul. *Dame Fortune's Wheel Tarot: A Pictorial Key.* Witches Almanac Limited, 2017.

———. *The Devil's Picturebook: The Compleat Guide to Tarot Cards: Their Origins and Their Usage.* iUniverse, 2003.

———. *Mystical Origins of the Tarot: From Ancient Roots to Modern Usage.* Inner Traditions/Bear, 2004.

Jones, Diana Wynne. *Howl's Moving Castle.* HarperCollins, 2001.

Jung, C. G. *Jung on Active Imagination.* Princeton UP, 2015.

———. *Letters of C. G. Jung: Volume 2, 1951–1961.* Taylor and Francis, 2015.

———. *Man and His Symbols.* Random House, 2012.

Jung, C. G., and Gerhard Adler. *Collected Works of C. G. Jung, Volume 9 (Part 1): Archetypes and the Collective Unconscious.* Princeton UP, 2014.

———. *Dreams* (from volumes 4, 8, 12, and 16 of *The Collected Works of C. G. Jung*). Princeton UP, 2010.

———. *On the Nature of the Psyche* (from *Collected Works,* vol. 8). Princeton UP, 1969.

———. *Psychology and Alchemy* (from *Collected Works*, vol. 12). Princeton UP, 1980.

———. *Synchronicity: An Acausal Connecting Principle* (from *Collected Works,* vol. 8). Princeton UP, 2012.

Knight, Gareth. *Experience of the Inner Worlds*. Skylight Press, 2010.

Kraig, Donald Michael. *Modern Magick: Twelve Lessons in the High Magickal Arts*. Llewellyn, 2010.

———. *Tarot and Magic.* Llewellyn, 2002.

Leadbeater, C. W. *Man, Visible and Invisible: Examples of Different Types of Man as Seen by Means of Trained Clairvoyance.* Theosophical Publishing, 1927.

Lewis, C. S. *The Magician's Nephew*. HarperCollins, 2014.

Louis, Anthony. *Llewellyn's Complete Book of Tarot: A Comprehensive Guide*. Llewellyn, 2016.

Nichols, Sallie. *Tarot and the Archetypal Journey: The Jungian Path from Darkness to Light*. Weiser, 2019.

Nugteren, Albertina. *Religion, Ritual and Ritualistic Objects*. Spain: MDPI Books, 2019.

Pamita, Madame. *Madame Pamita's Magical Tarot: Using the Cards to Make Your Dreams Come True*. Weiser, 2018.

Plato. *Timaeus and Critias*. Penguin, 2008.

Penczak, Christopher. *The Inner Temple of Witchcraft: Magick, Meditation and Psychic Development*, 20th anniversary ed. Llewellyn, 2021.

Plotinus. *The Enneads*. Penguin, 2005.

Pollack, Rachel. *The Complete Illustrated Guide to Tarot*. Barnes and Noble, 1999.

———. *Rachel Pollack's Tarot Wisdom: Spiritual Teachings and Deeper Meanings*. Llewellyn, 2014.

———. *Seventy-Eight Degrees of Wisdom: A Tarot Journey to Self-Awareness*. Weiser, 2020.

———. *A Walk Through the Forest of Souls: A Tarot Journey to Spiritual Awakening*. Weiser, 2023.

Reed, Theresa. *The Cards You're Dealt: How to Deal When Life Gets Real*. Weiser, 2023.

———. *Tarot: No Questions Asked: Mastering the Art of Intuitive Reading*. Weiser, 2020.

———. *Twist Your Fate: Manifest Success with Astrology and Tarot*. Weiser, 2022.

Reed, Theresa, and Shaheen Miro. *Tarot for Troubled Times: Confront Your Shadow, Heal Your Self, Transform the World*. Weiser, 2019.

Robinson, Dawn. *Pamela Colman Smith, Tarot Artist: The Pious Pixie*. Fonthill Media, 2020.

Shaw, Gregory. *Theurgy and the Soul: The Neoplatonism of Iamblichus*. Pennsylvania State UP, 1995.

Snow, Cassandra. *Queering the Tarot*. Weiser, 2019.

True, Rachel. *True Heart Intuitive Tarot, Guidebook and Deck*. HarperCollins, 2020.

Waite, A. E. *The Pictorial Key to the Tarot: An Illustrated Guide*. Random House UK, 2021.

Weber, Courtney. *Tarot for One: The Art of Reading for Yourself*. Weiser Books, 2016.

Welch, Michelle. *Spirits Unveiled: A Fresh Perspective on Angels, Guides, Ghosts & More*. Llewellyn, 2022.

Wen, Benebell. *Holistic Tarot: An Integrative Approach to Using Tarot for Personal Growth*. North Atlantic Books, 2015.

Index

To Write to the Author

If you wish to contact the author or would like more information about this book, please write to the author in care of Llewellyn Worldwide and we will forward your request. Both the author and the publisher appreciate hearing from you and learning of your enjoyment of this book and how it has helped you. Llewellyn Worldwide cannot guarantee that every letter written to the author can be answered, but all will be forwarded. Please write to:

Mat Auryn
Llewellyn Worldwide
2143 Wooddale Drive
Woodbury, MN 55125-2989

Please enclose a self-addressed stamped envelope for reply or $1.00 to cover costs. If outside the USA, enclose an international postal reply coupon.

Many of Llewellyn's authors have websites with additional information and resources. For more information, please visit our website:

WWW.LLEWELLYN.COM

XI
JUSTICE.